lonely planet

BEST BIKE RIDES JAPAN

BEST DAY TRIPS ON TWO WHEELS

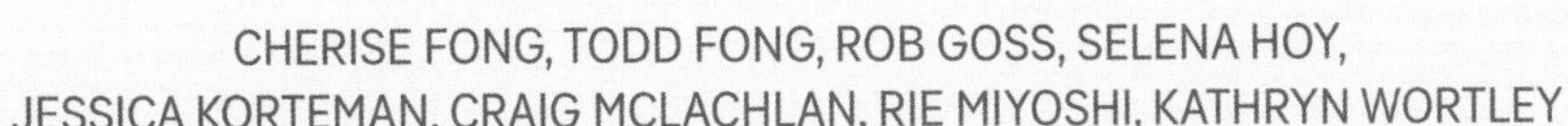
CHERISE FONG, TODD FONG, ROB GOSS, SELENA HOY,
JESSICA KORTEMAN, CRAIG MCLACHLAN, RIE MIYOSHI, KATHRYN WORTLEY

Contents

PLAN YOUR TRIP

Welcome to Japan ... 4
My Perfect Bike Ride ... 6
Our Picks ... 8
When to Go ... 16
Get Prepared for Japan ... 18

BY REGION

Shimanami Kaidō ... 24
Tobishima Kaidō ... 30

AROUND TOKYO ... 35

Chōshi Geopark ... 38
Fuji Kawaguchiko ... 44
Tsukuba Kasumigaura Ring Ring Road ... 48
Izu Peninsula: Numazu to Shuzen-ji Onsen ... 52
Also Try ... 56

CENTRAL HONSHŪ (CHŪBU) ... 59

Sado ... 62
Toyama Bay ... 66
Karuizawa ... 72
Lake Hamana ... 76
Also Try ... 80

KANSAI ... 83

Wakayama & the Kinokawa ... 86
Kyoto Without the Crowds ... 90
Lake Biwa ... 96
Ise ... 100
Also Try ... 104

HIROSHIMA & WESTERN HONSHŪ ... 107

Matsue, Shinji-ko & Izumo ... 110
Tottori's Yumigahama ... 114
Hiroshima Peace Ride ... 118
Also Try ... 122

NORTHERN HONSHŪ (TŌHOKU) ... 125

Hirosaki ... 128
Matsushima Circuit ... 132
Tōno ... 138
Sakata Art Ride ... 142
Also Try ... 146

HOKKAIDŌ ... 149

Sapporo Explorer ... 152
Niseko Yōtei-zan Loop ... 158
Biking Around Tōya-ko ... 162
Biei's Patchwork Road ... 166
Abashiri on Two Wheels ... 170
Also Try ... 174

SHIKOKU ... 177

Shimanto-gawa Trail ... 180
Yumeshima Kaidō ... 184
Shōdoshima ... 190
Tokushima & Around ... 194
Also Try ... 198

KYŪSHŪ & OKINAWA ... 201

Yuka Family Road ... 204
Nichinan Coast ... 208
Ibusuki Poké Trail ... 212
Maple Yabakei Road ... 218
Iejima ... 222
Also Try ... 226

TOOLKIT

Arriving ... 228
Getting Around ... 229
Accommodation ... 230
Bikes ... 231
Health & Safe Travel ... 232
Responsible Travel ... 233
Nuts & Bolts ... 234

RUSSIA
CHINA
NORTH KOREA
SOUTH KOREA
JAPAN
Sakhalin
Sea of Okhotsk
SEA OF JAPAN (EAST SEA)
NORTH PACIFIC OCEAN
East China Sea
HOKKAIDŌ p149
CENTRAL HONSHŪ (CHŪBU) p59
NORTHERN HONSHŪ (TŌHOKU) p125
HIROSHIMA & WESTERN HONSHŪ p107
AROUND TOKYO p35
KANSAI p83
SHIKOKU p177
KYŪSHŪ & OKINAWA p201
Wakkanai
Asahikawa
Kitami
Sapporo
Hokkaidō
Kushiro
Tomakomai
Hakodate
Aomori
Hirosaki
Hachinohe
Akita
Morioka
Sakata
Sendai
Niigata
Fukushima
Nagaoka
Noto Peninsula
Iwaki
Toyama
Nagano
Utsunomiya
Kanazawa
Mito
Fukui
Honshū
Matsue
Maizuru
Biwa Ko
Gifu
TOKYO
Okayama
Kyoto
Nagoya
Osaka
Hamamatsu
Hiroshima
Kitakyūshū
Nara
Matsuyama
Tokushima
Shikoku
Fukuoka
Oita
Kochi
Izu-Shoto
Nagasaki
Kyūshū
Miyazaki
Kagoshima
Ōsumi
Nampo-Shoto
Okinawa
Naha
0 200 km
0 100 miles

Welcome to Japan

Japan's public transport system is rightfully praised, with its intricate networks of trains and subways stretching to many corners of the country. Perhaps you've even ridden the famed shinkansen (bullet train), and admired the view as the scenery whizzed past.

Stepping off the train and mounting a much simpler machine is the ideal way to nose into those parts of Japan that aren't serviced by the rail system: narrow lanes lined with ceramic-tile-roofed houses, country shrines and emerald rice paddies are perfect for exploring on two wheels.

In recent years, the cycling infrastructure in Japan has become even stronger: car-free paths crisscross the nation's forests and along rivers, and bicycle-rental stations have sprung up liberally, many offering e-bikes to tackle the country's prodigiously hilly terrain.

So, here's to a bit of wind in your hair, the exhilaration of a downhill swoop, and the feeling of really having earned that end-of-the-day hotpot and flask of sake.

Awa-odori Matsuri festival, Tokushima (p196)

YASUYOSHI CHIBA/AFP VIA GETTY IMAGES

新のんき

My Perfect Bike Ride

Rob Goss

TŌNO

P138

I've lost count of how many times I've visited Tōno over the years, cycling around when the rice paddies have been a lush green in early summer or yellowing just before the autumn harvest. The countryside and its peace and quiet are one reason I keep coming back, but so are the rural traditions – whether that's preserved farmhouses that offer glimpses into the past or the colourful folklore, with its tales of mischievous sprites and mysterious creatures.

Selena Hoy

FUJI KAWAGUCHIKO

P44

Looping around lake Kawaguchi-ko is perfectly my speed. It's flat, almost car-free, and the scenery is iconic, with Mt Fuji reflecting in the lake like a mirror and the pampas grass swishing all around. I've brought several family members along to do the ride, and even kids can join in. And of course, my favourite part is refuelling – there are lots of cute bakeries and cafes to stop at and have a coffee.

Craig McLachlan

BIKING AROUND TŌYA-KO

P162

I love the ride around Tōya-ko in Hokkaidō. What a fun time pedalling around an almost perfectly circular caldera lake, with a treasure hunt along the way – 58 artworks of the Tōya Gurutto Sculpture Park scattered around the lake. The views are always changing too, with stunning 1898m Yōtei-zan, the Mt Fuji lookalike of Hokkaidō, away to the north, and active volcanoes Usu-zan and Shōwa Shinzan to the south. Soak in Tōya-ko Onsen after the ride for a perfect day.

Jessica Korteman

SHIMANAMI KAIDŌ

P24

No matter how many times I return to the Shimanami Kaidō, I can't help but be impressed by the concept alone. Crossing an entire sea by bicycle? It sounds implausible, yet from one bridge-connected island to another, a one-of-a-kind cycling trail across the archipelagos of the Inland Sea becomes reality. Now with the adjacent 'sea roads' of Yumeshima and Tobishima adding even more to explore, this is always a multiday stop for me.

Todd Fong

LAKE HAMANA

P76

I love riding along the shore of Lake Hamana, from where it meets the sea at Bentenjima to the colourful Pal Pal amusement park, it's a flat ride with a refreshing breeze. Two of Hamamatsu's beautiful flower gardens, Hamanako Garden Park and Hamamatsu Flower Park, are along the route and are fantastic detours to enjoy seasonal displays of flowers from spring until autumn.

Cherise Fong

TSUKUBA KASUMIGAURA RING RING ROAD

P48

The less-travelled north shore of Kasumigaura is wonderfully remote, where I can ride for several kilometres without crossing another cyclist, just soaking up the tranquil lakeside atmosphere between farmlands and wetlands, with the occasional splash of a jumping fish. Cycling on the smooth, seamless path around the gentle contours of the lake lulls me into a rolling meditation. I continue on to Lake Kitaura, then stop under the giant red *torii* gate to watch the sunset on the horizon.

AAPHAKON YUSOMSRI/GETTY IMAGES

Kawaguchi-ko and Mt Fuji (p44)

Rie Miyoshi

NISEKO YŌTEI-ZAN LOOP TRAIL

P158

Niseko in Hokkaidō is more famous for its snow season, but it is so refreshing in summer. It's cooler than other parts of Japan, making it an excellent cycling spot. The development of mountain-biking trails and forest adventure parks makes it an exciting green-season destination. Travellers can also experience authentic Japan with fresh local food – from land and sea – and natural hot springs. On top of that, iconic Yōtei-zan makes this cycling route impressive.

Kathryn Wortley

NICHINAN COAST

P208

The Devil's Washboard is a reminder of nature's immense power and wondrous beauty. The waves that crash and foam on the undulating basalt rocks reveal deep ridges carved out over centuries, and leave behind crystal-clear blue water in the ocean pools. As the morning sun reflects off the sea, this part of the Nichinan Coast, with its lines of palm trees, could not look more spectacular, from either direction.

Our Picks

BEST SCENIC RIDES

If you're looking for sweeping vistas and plenty of photo opportunities, look no further. Japan loves a good view – just ask the country's prolific *ukiyo-e* artists who immortalised many of them in woodblock prints. You can see the country's dramatic coastline, vivid ocean and bucolic farmland on these rides. Matsushima is considered to be one of the iconic 'Three Views of Japan'.

TOP TIP

Most locals will be more than happy to snap a picture if you ask.

Toyama Bay

Ride along one of UNESCO's Most Beautiful Bays in the World.

P66

Izu Peninsula: Numazu to Shuzen-ji Onsen

Mt Fuji is a constant companion while cycling the Izu Peninsula.

P52

Biei's Patchwork Road

Undulating roads weave through a floral rainbow.

P166

HIROSHI H/SHUTTERSTOCK

TOP TIP

Riding through rice paddies with a chorus of frog-song is sublime!

Biei (p166), Hokkaidō

Nichinan Coast

Travel through Nichinan-Kaigan Quasi-National Park for dramatic cliffs and ocean spray.

P208

Matsushima Circuit

The coastal views here inspired artists and poets.

P132

Matsushima Bay (p132)

TOP TIP

Helmets are mandatory in Japan, though enforcement is inconsistent.

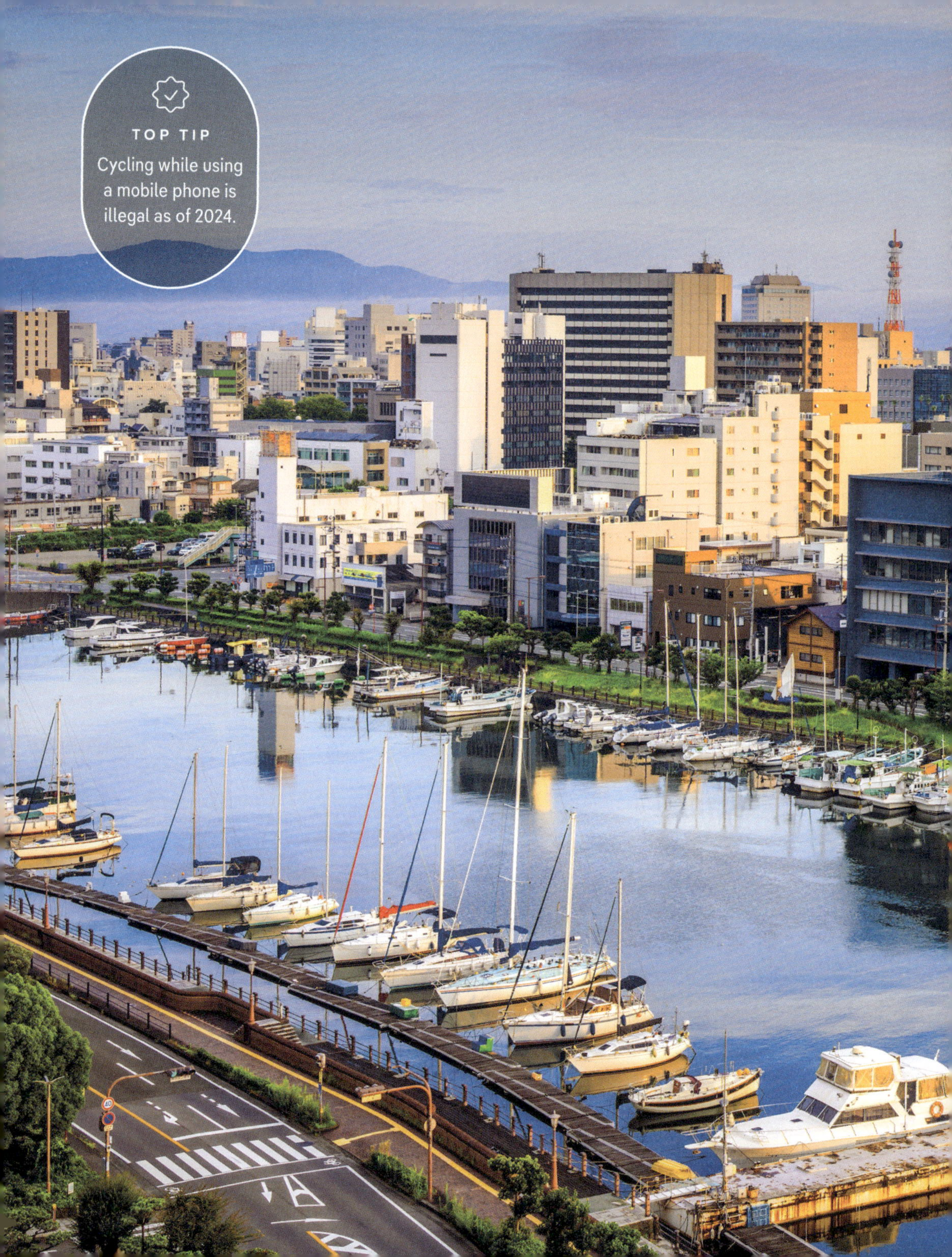

TOP TIP

Cycling while using a mobile phone is illegal as of 2024.

Our Picks

BEST URBAN RIDES

Japan is one of the top cycling nations in the world, with about 15% of daily outings taken on a bike. Many Japanese cities are well suited to cycling; frequently, going by bike might even be faster than by public transport, with more interesting scenery. These city rides give a window into each town's rhythm while avoiding a lot of the mass-tourism traffic.

TOP TIP

There may be a parking charge for your bicycle in busy areas. Check signs nearby for more information.

Kyoto Without the Crowds

Get away from the throngs and roll through the streets like a local.

P90

Hiroshima Peace Ride

Hiroshima's quest for peace is illuminated on this thought-provoking journey.

P118

TOP TIP

Drive and ride on the left. Take care to look both ways, especially if you're used to being on the other side.

DISTINCTIVE SHOTS/SHUTTERSTOCK

Sapporo Explorer

Get a feel for this modern, park-filled city with stops for bird's-eye views.

P152

Hirosaki

Castles, orchards, museums and gardens, all right in town.

P128

Tokushima & Around

Dance, textile art and puppet theatre are a few highlights in this southern city.

P194

Tokushima CIty (p194)

Our Picks

BEST FAMILY RIDES

Japan has plenty to offer for kids and adults alike, and these easy to moderate rides include lots of fun stops. Parks abound, you'll find interesting folklore about tricky mythical creatures, and nobody does cute better than Japan: you'll meet cartoon anthropomorphic mascots in nearly every town. And of course, there are lots of snacks along the way – for motivation, sustenance and rewards.

TOP TIP

The Mamachari, shortened from 'mother's chariot', comes with a basket and can be fitted with one or even two child seats.

1

Ibusuki Poké Trail

A fun and easy ride with the chance to spot Pokémon manhole covers along the route.

P212

Lake Hamana

Flower gardens and a retro amusement park make a fun family day out.

P76

Niseko Yōtei-zan Loop Trail

Stops include an adventure park, a dairy farm (with ice cream) and an ostrich farm.

P158

TKYSZK/SHUTTERSTOCK

Niseko Ostrich Farm (p159)

Tōno

History combines with fun and cute folklore on this rural ride.

P138

Fuji Kawaguchiko

A loop around lake Kawaguchi-ko with pleasure boats and Mt Fuji looming in the near distance.

P44

Lake Hamana Garden Park (p76)

TOP TIP

Stay hydrated with some of Japan's favourite sports drinks, which are even sold frozen in the summer. Pocari Sweat, anyone?

Our Picks

BEST ISLAND RIDES

It's not hard to find an island ride in a country of over 14,000 islands, though only about 400 are inhabited. Some of these islands are accessible by bridges, but you'll need to hop on a ferry to reach others. The sea is central to Japan's sense of identity, and you can get a taste of the ocean and fisherfolk culture on these rides.

TOP TIP

Cycling on footpaths is usually allowed if there isn't a dedicated bike lane, but cede to pedestrians and walk your bike if it's crowded.

Iejima

The so-called 'peanut island' played an important part in the Battle of Okinawa near the end of WWII.

P222

Shimanami Kaidō

This island-hopping ride is a national cycling route for a reason.

P24

Tobishima Kaidō

Seven bridges connect seven islands as stepping stones between Honshū and Shikoku.

P30

TOP TIP

Many rental bikes come with a simple wheel-lock mechanism. Get the staff to show you how to use it, and don't lose the key!

FLORIAN AUGUSTIN/SHUTTERSTOCK

Shimanami Kaidō (p24)

Sado

Look for wildlife, and experience traditional theatre and music on the island of Sado.

P62

Yumeshima Kaidō

Hop across four tiny islands on the Inland Sea.

P184

Our Picks

BEST ART RIDES

Art and fresh air: what could be a better way to feed the soul? Japan is a haven for art lovers, and you'll find well-funded high-quality museums in the most unexpected rural places. The Inland Sea islands, which include Shōdoshima, are an example of this, and elsewhere the country is bursting with tiny ateliers, niche museums and sculpture parks – perfect for exploration on two wheels.

TOP TIP

If you rent an e-bike, make sure your battery has a good charge, as if it runs down, bikes can be heavy to ride without power.

Sakata Art Ride

Tour art and photography museums, and see traditional architecture.

P142

Biking Around Tōya-ko

There are 58 sculptures on the loop around this gleaming caldera lake – can you spot them all?

P162

TOP TIP

Call or book ahead when possible, as some rental shops have limited stock.

LYDIAREI/SHUTTERSTOCK

Mikasa Hotel (p74), Karuizawa

Ise

Learn about the art, rituals and crafts associated with Ise-jingū, one of Japan's most important spiritual sites.

P100

Shōdoshima

Olives, soy sauce and open-air sculpture characterise this 'small bean' island.

P190

Karuizawa

Find art museums, lots of exclusive galleries, and retro-modern European-style architecture in this mountain town.

P72

When to Go

Spring and autumn are the best seasons for cycling in Japan; save summertime for the north and winter for the south.

I LIVE HERE

CYCLING IN JAPAN'S POWDER SNOW CAPITAL

Satoshi Nagai, Executive Assistant at the Luxe Nomad and organiser of Niseko Classic bike races. *@theluxenomad*

Niseko, globally known for its powder snow, is heaven for cyclists: hill climbs, descents, long flats. Road, gravel, mountain bike. Whatever your preference, Niseko has got you covered. My personal favourite is the Niseko Annupuri loop, which is a great combination of climbs and descents. The 10km-long descent from Niseko Annupuri's peak is especially stunning on summer mornings, when you can (if you're lucky) see a panorama of the sea of clouds. The route is also fascinating in autumn when the leaves turn colour.

If you ask people in Japan, most will choose either spring or autumn as their favourite season. Both are temperate, punctuated by the vaunted cherry blossoms in spring and the blazing foliage in autumn. The mild weather and natural conditions are perfectly suited to cycling. Summers can be brutally, sometimes dangerously hot, especially in low-lying areas, although you can still catch a breeze in Hokkaidō and in mountainous regions. Snow takes over in Hokkaidō and Tōhoku from at least November until March, while the *tsuyu* (rainy season) hits the islands in June and July, bypassing Hokkaidō.

Snowbound

Hokkaidō and northern Honshū are covered in snow through the winter. In southern Honshū, Shikoku and Kyūshū, winter tends to be sunny and dry with only occasional snow, but it can be bitterly cold and unpleasant for all but the hardiest bike nerds, and rental facilities may be shut.

Plum Rains

June and July (May for Okinawa) are dominated by *tsuyu*, poetically translated as 'plum rains'. These torrential downpours can go on for days or weeks on end, though they largely skip over Hokkaidō, making the northernmost island a good choice for summer cycling.

Weather Watch (Tokyo)

JANUARY	FEBRUARY	MARCH	APRIL	MAY	JUNE
Average daytime max: **9°C**	Average daytime max: **10°C**	Average daytime max: **14°C**	Average daytime max: **18°C**	Average daytime max: **23°C**	Average daytime max: **25°C**
Days of rainfall: **3**	Days of rainfall: **5**	Days of rainfall: **7**	Days of rainfall: **8**	Days of rainfall: **8**	Days of rainfall: **9**

TAKASHI IMAGES/SHUTTERSTOCK

Aomori Nebuta festival float

Island-Hop

Okinawa has a subtropical climate, meaning that even in winter, the temperature averages about 15°C. In direct opposition to Hokkaidō, cycling is comfortable in autumn, winter and spring, and a lot of the prefecture's smaller islands are well suited to bicycle exploration, like Ride 35: Iejima (p222).

ACCOMMODATION

Hotels fill up fast around holidays and festivals, so be sure to book ahead if your trip will coincide with Golden Week (end of April/early May), school holidays (end of March) or Obon (mid-August). If you're travelling with your own bike, check in advance that your lodging allows it; a partial list can be found at cyclistwelcome.jp/en.

MAJOR FESTIVALS

The already lively Tokyo neighbourhood of Asakusa positively vibrates during the **Sanja Matsuri**, where 100 portable shrines are hoisted by thousands of scantily clad, sometimes tattooed and inebriated, bearers. **May**

Japan's biggest LGBTIQ+ Pride festival, **Tokyo Rainbow Pride**, is held yearly in Yoyogi Park, drawing over 200,000 people to a weekend of musical performances, stalls and a huge parade through Shibuya. **June**

At Kyoto's **Gion Matsuri**, extravagant, gilded floats pay homage to sea god Susano-o in this thousand-year-old Shintō festival, one of Japan's top three celebrations. **July**

Fanciful floats are lit from within like enormous paper lanterns for **Aomori Nebuta**, taking the shape of dragons, warriors and goddesses. They're accompanied by raucous music and dancing across several cities in Aomori over the course of a few weeks. **August**

JULY
Average daytime max: **29°C**
Days of rainfall: **10**

AUGUST
Average daytime max: **31°C**
Days of rainfall: **8**

SEPTEMBER
Average daytime max: **27°C**
Days of rainfall: **9**

OCTOBER
Average daytime max: **22°C**
Days of rainfall: **8**

NOVEMBER
Average daytime max: **17°C**
Days of rainfall: **6**

DECEMBER
Average daytime max: **12°C**
Days of rainfall: **4**

Get Prepared for Japan

Useful things to load in your bag, your ears and your brain

WATCH

Old Enough *(Netflix; 2022)* Small children run errands, followed by a camera crew.

Kiki's Delivery Service *(Hayao Miyazaki, 1989)* A witch and her cat run a delivery service in a seaside town.

Dreams *(Akira Kurosawa, 1990)* Eight linked short films based on the director's dreams.

Love Village *(Netflix, 2023)* Eight people renovate a country house and look for love.

Shoplifters *(Hirokazu Kore-eda, 2018)* A Tokyo family scrapes by, aided by shoplifting.

Clothing

Come prepared to ride in style. You should be able to pick up last-minute items in larger cities, but for some of our more rural rides you'll need to plan ahead.

Helmet Required in Japan; most bike rental shops have them.

Sun protection Pack sunglasses, a hat, sunblock and UV layers.

Light daypack On easier rides, you may be able to use a Mamachari (a typical city bicycle with a front basket), but for most rides you'll need to carry essentials.

Layered clothing Consider including a windbreaker and a neck-warmer to ward off chill.

Sensible shoes Suitable for pedalling and side quests.

Rainwear A light rain jacket and trousers will be invaluable in a sudden downpour.

Gloves Especially for longer rides.

Hydration Make sure you bring plenty of liquids.

Snacks Convenience stores have several fun options for a mid-ride energy boost.

First-aid kit A mini kit with basic antiseptic, bandages and gauze can come in handy for minor road rash.

Mobile phone and spare battery Call for help, use the maps.

Handlebar phone mount This handy little device attaches your phone to the handlebars for easy map reference.

CLOCKWISE FROM TOP LEFT: JESSICA2/SHUTTERSTOCK, WEST_PHOTO/SHUTTERSTOCK, AFRICA STUDIO/SHUTTERSTOCK, LANDSCAPEMANIA/SHUTTERSTOCK

Cycling the Shimanami Kaidō (p24)

LISTEN

12 *(Ryuichi Sakamoto, 2023)* Piano electronica on one of the prodigious composer's last albums.

Deep Dive *(japantimes.co.jp/deep-dive)* Editors from *The Japan Times* go in-depth about current events in Japan on this weekly podcast.

Sunshower *(Taeko Onuki, 1977)* Breezy, groovy city pop from the genre's queen, and a great day-trip soundtrack.

Easy Japanese *(NHK World Japan)* Simple Japanese lessons are broadcast but also available on demand.

Words

Cycling

Bicycle Jitensha

Cycling Saikuringu

Road bike Rōdo baiku

Mountain bike Maunten baiku

Town bike with a front basket Mamachari

E-bike Dendō ashisuto jitensha

Helmet Herumetto

Can we get there by bicycle? Soko ni jiten-sha de ikemasu ka?

I'd like to hire a bicycle. Jitensha o karitai no desu ga.

Greetings

Hello! Konnichiwa!

Good morning Ohayō gozaimasu

Good evening Konbanwa

Good luck/You can do it! Ganbatte!

Be careful Ki o tsukete

Danger! Abunai!

What a beautiful day. Subarashī hi desu ne.

Bon voyage! Yoi tabi o!

See you later Mata ne

Goodbye Sayōnara

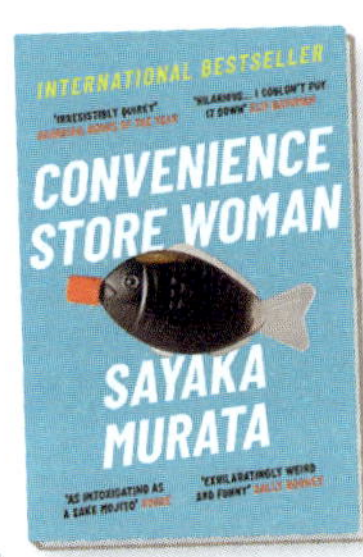

READ

Convenience Store Woman *(Sayaka Murata, 2018)* A view of society from inside a 24hr neon-lit fishbowl.

Breasts and Eggs *(Mieko Kawakami, 2019)* Three women navigate their relationships, their bodies and society.

Awesome Nightfall: The Life, Times, and Poetry of Saigyo *(Saigyō, William R Lefleur, 2012)* Bashō's 12th-century predecessor; warrior, monk and poet.

The Woman in the Dunes *(Kōbō Abe, 1964)* A man goes becomes trapped in a sandpit with a woman.

Directions

Road Dõro/michi

Slope Saka

Uphill Noborizaka

Downhill Kudarizaka

Right Migi

Left Hidari

Straight Massugu

Near Chikai

Far Tõi

Easy Kantan

Difficult Muzukashii

Where is...? …wa doko desu ka?

Does this road go to...?
Kono michi wa …e ikimasu ka?

How far until ...?
…made wa dono gurai desu ka?

What is this place called?
Koko wa nan to iu tokoro desu ka?

Parking Chūshajō

Can you show me (on the map)?
(Chizu de) oshiete kuremasen ka?

Weather

How's the weather today? Kyō no tenki wa ikaga desu ka?

How's the weather tomorrow?
Ashita no tenki wa ikaga desu ka?

Nice weather! Ii otenki desu ne!

Sunny Hare

Rain Ame

Cold Samui

Hot Atsui

Services

Convenience store Konbini

Hotel Hoteru

Campsite Kyanpujō

Restaurant Resutoran

Hospital Byōin

ATM Ētīemu

Food Tabemono

Drink Nomimono

Water Mizu

Sleep Neru

Rest Yasumu

Where's a (supermarket)?
(Sūpā) wa doko desu ka?

Can you recommend a restaurant?
Doko ka ī restoran o shitte imasu ka?

What time does it open?
Nanji ni akimasu ka?

How much is...?
…wa ikura desu ka?

I'd like to make a reservation.
Yoyaku o onegaishimasu.

Emergencies

Help! Tasukete!

Stop! Tomare!

There's been an accident.
Jiko desu.

Please call an ambulance.
Kyūkyūsha o yonde kudasai.

I'm lost.
Michi ni mayoimashta.

FREEDOM-MANJ/SHUTTERSTOCK

Sake barrels, Ise-jingū shrine (p100)

商標
登録商標
田光
純米醸造
合名会社 早川酒造
TABIKA
登録
八千代
高級清酒
小川本家
三重の寒梅
日本酒
夢窓
登録商標
寒紅梅
名聲薫四海
芳醇無比
株式会社 寒紅梅酒造
伊賀上野
登録商標
福和蔵
屋八兵衛
創業文化二年
登録商標
瀧自慢
瑞色冠天下
優芳清酒
瀧自慢酒造
登録 金鳳 商標
神樹千歳芳
鉾杉
ホコスギ
芳醇無比
河武醸造
登録
伊勢
聖徳満四海
高橋酒造
登録商標
田光
純米醸造
TABIKA
登録商標
参宮
瑞気満一天
清酒
澤佐酒造
天
清酒
早川酒造
るみ子の酒
鈴鹿蔵元
作
ZAKU
若戎
縁起祝酒
登録商標
福和蔵
おかげさま

BIKE RIDES

Contents

Shimanami Kaidō 24

Tobishima Kaidō 30

AROUND TOKYO 35

CENTRAL HONSHŪ (CHŪBU) 59

KANSAI 83

HIROSHIMA & WESTERN HONSHŪ 107

NORTHERN HONSHŪ (TŌHOKU) 125

HOKKAIDŌ 149

SHIKOKU 177

KYŪSHŪ & OKINAWA 201

01

Shimanami Kaidō

DURATION	DIFFICULTY	DISTANCE	START/END
8hrs	Intermediate	58km	Onomichi/ Imabari

TERRAIN	Paved; bicycle paths and road cycling

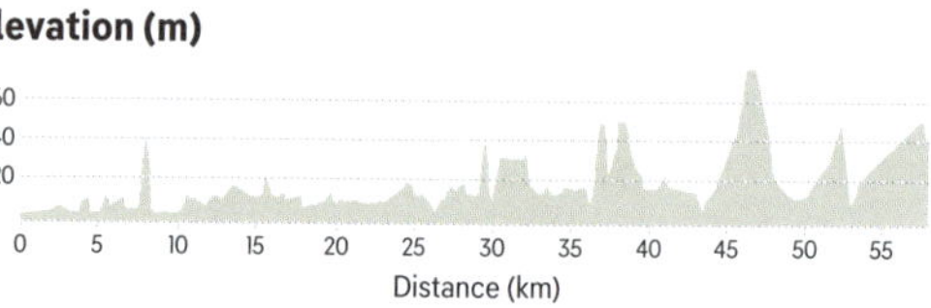

One of Japan's most renowned cycling destinations, the Shimanami Kaidō (しまなみ海道) attracts visitors from all over the world to make this epic sea crossing. The 58km route over six bridge-connected islands in the Inland Sea stitches together gorgeous seascapes from Hiroshima on mainland Honshū all the way to Ehime on the island of Shikoku. Beyond the views, Ehime is a maritime centre and citrus capital providing tangy treats and cultural sights. While the ride can be done in a day, spending a night (or two) befits the cycle's relaxed vibe.

Bike Hire

Rent a bike from the Giant Store at Onomichi U2 or JR Imabari Station *(bicyclerental.jp/en; closed Tuesday)* or from one of 10 public rental locations along the route *(visitshimanami.com/bike-rental)*.

Starting Point

The Shimanami Kaidō can be completed in either direction, starting from Onomichi on the Hiroshima side or from Imabari on the Ehime side. Ferries go to other select starting points.

01 The retro port town of Onomichi (尾道) in Hiroshima, Honshū's gateway to the Shimanami Kaidō, is a fine place for a casual day and night pre- or post-ride. Meander the nostalgic shopping arcades and narrow hillside paths with its notable population of slumbrous cats. For structure to your wanderings, follow the 'Temple Walk' or 'Literary Path' and get a visual of the bike journey beyond on Senkō-ji-yama (144m), with lovely views to the islands from its hilltop temple and observatory.

While considered the Hiroshima starting point of the Shimanami Kaidō, the Shin-Onomichi and Onomichi

ERAMIYA/SHUTTERSTOCK

Shirataki-yama

bridges that connect Honshū with the first island of Mukai-shima are not pedestrian- or bicycle-friendly; you'll need to take a ferry over the 300m channel instead.

02 On Mukai-shima (向島) you'll really get acquainted with the Shimanami Kaidō and its guiding 'blue line'. After disembarking the ferry, the line will split, offering two different routes. Don't think too hard on it; they will merge again in around 200m. Once you hit the main road, Mukai-shima's recommended 9km route goes west across the northern section of the island, past shops and residential areas to the coast.

Follow the waterline and roadside citrus stalls south, stopping for photos at the bright red Mukai-shima Bridge. If you're taking things slow, detour across the bridge to explore neighbouring Iwashi-jima and its *torii* gate by the water at Itsukushima Shrine. To continue on the blue line, proceed past the red bridge towards the Tachibana Coast and your first major incline up to the 1339m-long Inno-shima Bridge.

03 You'll arrive on Inno-shima (因島) by the Innoshima Island Amenity Park precinct with a playground, lighthouse and campsite. On warm days, the Amenity Pool (summer only) and Shimanami Beach are favourites for a splash. Stop into Hassaku-ya (October to mid-August) to try their *hassaku daifuku* – delicious *mochi* rice cakes filled with white bean paste and juicy *hassaku*, a citrus fruit endemic to Inno-shima.

The blue line will take you on a 9km western route, but it's worth venturing off it to visit Shirataki-yama, a breathtaking 227m-high peak lined with 700 sculptures of Buddha's disciples. You'll have to work hard for it; it's a steep 2.5km ascent up the 'Shirataki Flower Line' and a further 10-minute climb on foot from the '8th station' parking area. It's believed Kannon-dō Temple atop the mountain was

Take a Break

Located at a midpoint along the Inno-shima cycle, HAKKŌ PARK (HAKKŌパーク) is a roadside station and fermentation facility operated by food company Manda Hakkō. In addition to a cafe and shop, there are expansive gardens and a seaside foot bath. A playground, koi pond, splash pool, goat-petting area and nursing room make it a particularly family-friendly stop. Free guided tours by reservation explain the fermentation process *(mandahakkopark.com)*. The park is typically closed on Wednesdays.

founded as a lookout by pirate turned naval forces, the Murakami Suigun. Luckily, it's all downhill to rejoin the blue line as you head towards the 790m Ikuchi Bridge, stopping at HAKKŌ Park en route.

Before crossing, consider cycling another 3km to either Suigun-jō (Innoshima Navy Castle) for more pirate history or Ōyama Shrine for the on-site Jitensha-jinja, Japan's only dedicated bicycle shrine, to pray to the deity of traffic safety and buy a lucky amulet. Further on, it's a short ride to either Habu or Karōto ports for connections to the Yumeshima Kaidō (p184).

04 Ikuchi-jima (生口島), the birthplace of domestic lemon cultivation, has the longest blue line on the Shimanami Kaidō. At 13km in length, there's plenty to linger for here. Allow ample time to explore the extensive 50,000-sq-metre temple grounds of Kōsan-ji (adult/student ¥1400/1000; 9am to 5pm), including its contemplative 'Cave of 1000 Buddhas' and striking 'Hill of Hope', a 5000-sq-metre sculptural garden made of glistening white Carrara marble.

The palm-tree-lined coastline around Setoda Sunset Beach is an especially pleasant stretch on two wheels. As you round the bottom of the island, you'll pass through Lemon Valley, where the bulk of the island's lemons are grown. Enjoy some playful photo opportunities with lemon-themed monuments (like 'Lemon Monster'), only reachable by foot or bicycle.

For those breaking up their ride over two (or more) days, Ikuchi-jima and neighbouring Ōmi-shima are popular locations for overnight stays. When you're finally ready to depart, make your way up to the 1480m-long Tatara Bridge.

05 The largest of the islands on the Shimanami Kaidō, Ōmi-shima (大三島) marks the switch to Ehime territory. The blue line only extends 5km along the eastern coast from Tatara Shimanami Park to Ōmi-shima Bridge, but detours call here.

Of particular note, and a 6km ride away, is Ōyamazumi-jinja, one of Japan's most historically important shrines. Since ancient times, military leaders have visited the shrine to pray for success in battle. Upon victory, they would return and offer their weaponry to the gods in gratitude. As a result, the Treasure House (adult/child ¥1000/400; 9am to 4.30pm, last admission 4pm) contains an astounding 80% of historical armour listed as cultural properties and national treasures in Japan. Outdoors, the oldest tree in the camphor grove is more than 2600 years old

Near the shrine, find accommodation options, restaurants and the

MYPIXELDIARIES/SHUTTERSTOCK

The blue line, Mukai-shima

The Blue Line

When in doubt, follow the 'blue line'. This literal blue line painted on the road marks the recommended cycling route (and remaining distance) between Onomichi and Imabari, making it almost impossible to lose your way on the Shimanami Kaidō. While you're free to stray from the lined route to explore, expect some tough uphill sections requiring above-average levels of fitness. Along the way, find around 150 'Cycling Oasis' locations denoted by a blue-and-white sign. These rest stops offer varying services to cyclists, such as benches, drinking water, toilets, bike racks and pumps, as well as area information.

YOSHINORI OKADA/SHUTTERSTOCK

Murakami Pirates

Before modern-day bridges, it wasn't so easy to traverse this strategic archipelago across the Inland Sea. Known as the Geiyo Islands, its narrow passages and strong currents presented perilous conditions for ships and an opportunity for enterprising seafarers to control them. The Murakami Kaizoku, a familial sea tribe formed in the 14th century, were sole guarantors of a safe passage in the centuries that followed. By the time piracy was outlawed, the group had amassed such power they had morphed into a government-sanctioned navy (Murakami Suigun). Along the route, find museums, castles and annual festivals dedicated to this interesting maritime past.

Kurushima-kaikyō bridges, Kurushima Strait

Mare Grassia public bath by Utena Beach. Continuing along the island perimeter from here, encounter various museums and on the far-southwest corner, Yahoo Hill, a thrilling 1km stretch of downhill 's' bends.

From the largest to the smallest of the islands, the blue line skirts the western coast of Hakata-jima (伯方島), known for its salt, for only 3km. Over the hill and past the shipyard, stop at Hakata SC Park roadside station by Hakata Beach. The mildly sweet Hakata salt soft-serve ice cream here is mandatory. From the beach, view the 840m Hakata-Ōshima Bridge, the next bridge crossing.

If your visit to Hakata-jima feels too brief, the full 20km island loop is mostly flat. If you're prepared to pedal harder, head to Hiraki-yama Park in the north-west corner, especially in spring when the 1000 cherry trees are in bloom. It's a tough 2km climb to the summit car park of the 149m mountain, but the three observation decks provide glorious views all year round.

The 10km blue line on Ō-shima (大島) starts with a pleasant 2km coastal ride overlooking former pirate stronghold, No-shima. At Miyakubo Port, you'll cut inland and head down the island's middle. If you want to learn more about the area's naval history, continue straight on for another 1km to the Murakami Kaizoku Museum (adult/student/under-18s ¥310/160/free; 9am to 5pm Tuesday to Sunday).

Ō-shima's interior route is the toughest blue-line section of the Shimanami Kaidō with two long climbs. The flatter (but longer) west coast route is a good substitute. Alternatively, start your ride from the Imabari side and enjoy a downhill slope towards Hakata-jima instead.

If you can muster the energy for another hill detour, the views from Kirō-san Observatory Park (elevation 307.8m), designed by renowned Japanese architect Kengo Kuma, are often cited among the best on the entire ride. Challenging for even the most dedicated cyclists, this almost 3km climb has an average gradient of 9–10% (in contrast, ascents to Shimanami's bridges average 3%). Be prepared to walk your bike up or arrange a taxi.

Gloriously flat and protracted, the 4.1km-long stretch across the Kurushima-kaikyō bridges and Kurushima Strait is a dreamy end to a Shimanami Kaidō adventure. Lock the island-dotted view to memory before ending in Imabari (今治) at Sunrise Itoyama hotel. Nonguests can access the restaurant and free observatory, along with showers for a small fee.

If returning your bike here, be sure to first grab a photo by the outdoor Shimanami sign with bridge backdrop. For those continuing to JR Imabari Station, it's a further 6km. Attractions in the area include Imabari-jō (Imabari Castle) and the Towel Museum (Imabari towels are a signature local product). For post-cycle dinner and drinks, do a round of Imabari's *yakitori* joints, another Imabari speciality.

TOP TIP:

Spare Change

Carry small change for cash purchases such as ferries, bridge tolls and vending machines. Small tolls for cyclists (about ¥500 total) are to be paid for bridge crossings. These fees are waived until 31 March 2026; see jb-honshi.co.jp/english for updates.

Take a Break

At around the halfway point of the Shimanami Kaidō on Ōmi-shima, TATARA SHIMANAMI PARK (多々羅しまなみ公園) is the largest rest area on the route, with excellent lunch options, fresh-fruit vendors and souvenir shops. The 'Cyclist Sanctuary', a stone monument with the Tatara Bridge in the background, is a favourite photo spot. On weekends and public holidays, also find drinks van SHIMANAMI COFFEE. Nearby, accommodation facility WAKKA *(wakka.site/en)* has a seaside cafe and range of services for cyclists, including laundry and showers.

02

Best for

HISTORY & CULTURE

Tobishima Kaidō

DURATION	DIFFICULTY	DISTANCE	START/END
5hrs	Intermediate	30–50km	Kawajiri (Hiroshima)/ Okamura-jima (Ehime)
TERRAIN	Paved; road cycling		

PICMIN/SHUTTERSTOCK

The Tobishima Kaidō on Toyo-shima

Named after its resemblance to stepping stones in a Japanese garden, the Tobishima Kaidō (とびしま海道; Island Stepping Stone Road) connects mainland Honshū with seven islands in the Akinada archipelago. Just west of the popular Shimanami Kaidō, this quieter, coast-hugging 'sea road' is made possible by seven bridges that straddle the border between Hiroshima and Ehime prefectures. A direct route of 30km can take you from end to end, but at least a couple of sightseeing detours are required to capture the cycle's top attractions.

Bike Hire

JR Aki-Kawajiri Station (mainland) or Kajigahama (Shimo-kamagari island). Bikes can be returned at various points along the route depending on availability. Minimum three-day advance reservation (*kajigahama.jp/rentcycle*).

Starting Point

Begin at Kawajiri (Hiroshima side) and cross the Akinada Bridge to Shimo-kamagari, or take a ferry from Imabari (Ehime side) and start your ride from the island of Okamura.

Starting from Kawajiri, cross the 1175m Akinada Bridge, the only toll bridge on the route (cyclists exempt), to Shimo-kamagari-jima (下蒲刈島). The Sannose district on the island's northeast was an important sea checkpoint during the Edo period, welcoming travelling *daimyō* (feudal lords) and numerous Korean delegations.

It's only a 2.5km ride east from the bridge into Sannose's cultural precinct, where visitors can find Shōtō-en (9am to 5pm, closed Tuesday), a garden and historical museum (including an interesting

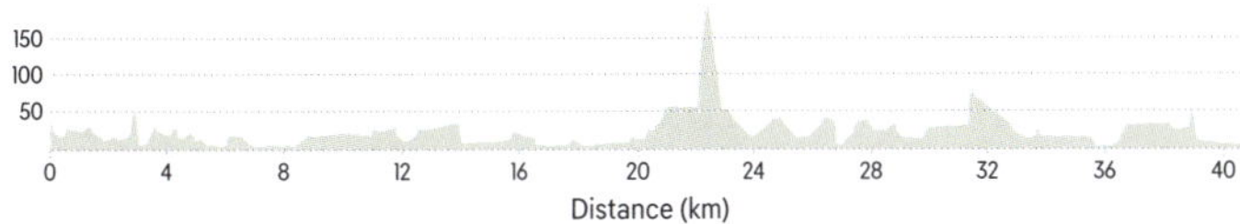

Korean envoy exhibit), along with two art museums and an insect house. Shirayuki-rō tearoom (9am to 5pm, closed Tuesday) offers Inland Sea views from its 2nd floor. From Sannose, the 480m Kamagari Bridge is conveniently placed for quick access to the island of Kami-kamagari.

02 According to folklore, the first islands on the Tobishima Kaidō were named *kama*, a reference to the aquatic 'cattail' plant, and *gari*, meaning 'to prune', after Empress Jingū dropped her comb and all the cattail brush was slashed to find it.

A pleasant 8km southern route will take you across Kami-kamagari-jima (上蒲刈島) via Koi-ga-hama beach. Instead of cutting inland for direct passage to the next bridge, take a 1.5km detour along the coast to sandy, palm tree–lined Kenmin-no-hama, considered one of the best 100 beaches in Japan. Nearby is Kamagari Onsen (3pm to 8pm, closed Tuesday), the Ancient Salt-Making Ruins Exhibition Hall (9am to 5pm, closed Monday and Tuesday; seaweed-salt-making workshops by reservation: moshionokai.jp/learning), and Kure Kamagari Observatory. Walk-in astronomical observation events are held on Saturdays from 7.30pm to 9pm *(kamaten.net/event.html)*.

Proceed back to Koi-ga-hama beach and rejoin Rte 287, taking Rte 356 at the fork. Prepare for a long and steep approach to the Toyo-shima Bridge (903m).

Kure in Film

A combination of quaint coastline, island-hopping bridges and historic townscapes has seen the islands on the Tobishima Kaidō, and other parts of Kure City, serve as a backdrop in numerous films, anime and live-action adaptations. In particular, Academy Award-winning feature film *Drive My Car* (2021), based on a short story by Japanese novelist Haruki Murakami, has drawn international attention to this endearing archipelago. Fans of the romance-drama can enjoy following in the footsteps of the film's protagonist, including crossing the Akinada Bridge and staying at Mitarai's Edo-period inn Kangetsu-an Shintoyo. The scenery from the film's poster is just outside.

03 It's a mostly flat, 5.5km northern coastal course on the fishing island of Toyo-shima (豊島). While the lack of big attractions means you can make quick time, the ride's defining low breakwaters and coast-clinging roads are on full display here, further accentuated by left-hand traffic that has you riding waterside.

If visiting on a Sunday, drop into Toyo-shima Ōhashi Produce Market (8am to 3pm) for exceedingly cheap citrus fruit. A detour into the island's interior will take you to Kūkai and Jūmonji-yama Observation Decks, but like many of the other viewing platforms on the route, they require narrow, steep and often unmaintained hill climbs, that may be outside the comfort zone of many casual cyclists. Be selective about which ones you deem worth the effort.

04 After crossing the Toyo-hama Bridge to Ōsaki-shimo-jima (大崎下島), follow the cycle's guiding 'blue line' (painted on the road) along the northern coast for 8km to the historic quarters of Mitarai, designated as an 'Important Preservation District for Groups of Historic Buildings'. A port of great esteem during feudal Japan, Mitarai flourished as an overnight merchant stopover with a prominent 'teahouse' (pleasure house) industry.

Among the historic landmarks is the former Wakaebisu-ya Teahouse (under refurbishment until March 2028), Otomeza Geisha Theatre (9am to 5pm, closed Tuesday) and Chisago Stone Pier. Compared to other scenic lookouts on the route, it's a relatively easy and gradual 1km slope to Historic Hill Park Viewpoint for panoramas over the entire town. If you'd prefer a break from pedalling, take the stairs from the historic precinct via the former elementary school and Oiran Park.

05 A series of three bridges spanning two uninhabited islands will transport you over the prefectural border to Ehime and the final destination of Okamura-jima (岡村島).

Take a 3.7km, mostly flat southern route to Okamura Port, where ferries depart for Imabari on the Shikoku mainland (one hour to one hour 20 minutes). Check the schedule online *(city.imabari.ehime.jp/chiiki/tosen/sekizen.html)* and confirm in person to prevent an unscheduled overnight stay. As a general rule, avoid doing the cycle on a Tuesday when most of the islands' attractions are closed.

Take a Break

Toyo-shima's eastern coast is a great midpoint for lunch. Head to local favourite MARI-CHAN (マリちゃん; 10.30am to 3pm, closed Wednesday) for house speciality Toyo-shima ramen, made with a flavourful hairtail fish broth, or Hiroshima-style *okonomiyaki* (savoury pancakes), with udon or soba noodles and lots of cabbage. You'll have to search for the tiny 10-seat eatery down a narrow alleyway by Onoura Community Center; look for the red awning. Nearby, SHIMA CAFE KITATANI (7am to 7pm) offers pizza, curry and ice-cream floats.

KOREKORE/GETTY IMAGES

Mitarai

Mitarai's Teahouses

The largest of the four main teahouses that operated in Mitarai during the Edo period, Wakaebisu-ya (circa 1724) is the only one still standing. Rivalling the finest pleasure houses in Kyoto and Edo (modern-day Tokyo), at its peak it employed as many as 100 *yūjo* (sex workers) and *oiran* (high-ranking courtesans), the latter adorned with exquisitely embroidered robes, tortoiseshell combs and gold hairpins. A mysticism, however, surrounded the house, ranging from ghost stories to unexplained deaths. It is said that the number of women employed was deliberately capped at 99, as whenever it reached 100, one of them would mysteriously perish.

Fukaya
Kumagaya
Hokota
Tsuchiura
Kasumigaura
05
Kashima
Suwa-ko
Chino
Chichibu
Tone Gawa
Kobushi-ga-take
Kawagoe
Saitama
Koshigaya
Kashiwa
Kobuchizawa
Chichibu-Tama-Kai National Park
Senjō-ga-take
Ōme
Kawaguchi
Narita
Sakura
Chōshi
Nirasaki
Enzan
Kōfu
Hachiōji
Chōfu
Tokyo
Funabashi
03
Yokoshiba
Ōtsuki
Chiba
Minami Alps National Park
04
Sagamihara
Tokyo Bay
Kawasaki
Tōgane
Fuji-Yoshida
Yamato
Fuji-Hakone-Izu National Park
Yamanaka-ko
Atsugi
Yokohama
Mobara
Minobu
Hadano
Mt Fuji
Chigasaki
Fujisawa
Kisarazu
Gotemba
Hiratsuka
Enoshima
Kamakura
Bōsō Peninsula
Odawara
Yokosuka
Fujinomiya
Hakone
Ōhara
Ashi-no-ko
Miura Peninsula
Fuji
Mishima
Katsuura
Numazu
06
Atami
Kamogawa
Shimizu
Sagami-wan
Shizuoka
Tateyama
Itō
Izu Peninsula
Yaizu
Shimada
Suruga-wan
Inatori
Izu-ōshima
PACIFIC OCEAN
Shimoda
To-shima
0 50 km
0 25 miles

PANUWAT DANGSUNGNOEN/GETTY IMAGES

Fuji Kawaguchiko (p44)

Around Tokyo

03 **Chōshi Geopark**
Catch the first seaside sunrise from Japan's easternmost cape, and ride past dramatic geological strata from the age of dinosaurs. **p38**

04 **Fuji Kawaguchiko**
View Mt Fuji spectacularly close up, while contouring a glimmering lake surrounded by novelty museums, gourmet cafes and seasonal flowers. **p44**

05 **Tsukuba Kasumigaura Ring Ring Road**
Immerse yourself in the natural wetlands and farmlands of Japan's second-largest lake, then explore its deep WWII history. **p48**

06 **Izu Peninsula: Numazu to Shuzen-ji Onsen**
Go on a riverside pilgrimage from the Edo-period port city of Numazu to the ancient spiritual retreat of Shuzen-ji Onsen. **p52**

Explore

Around Tokyo

The sprawling metropolis of Tokyo (東京) reaches out to include its suburban and more rural prefectural neighbours of Saitama, Ibaraki, Chiba and Kanagawa, bordered by the Pacific Ocean to the east, and to the south by Tokyo and Sagami bays. To the west in Yamanashi and Shizuoka prefectures, Mt Fuji (富士山) dominates the landscape like a ubiquitous deity rising above the horizon, so part of the fun is spotting it from different locations in varying landscapes. In clear weather, the sacred mountain can be seen from as far east as Chōshi.

Tokyo

Japan's capital city offers an urban kaleidoscope of places to stay, eat, shop, play and relax – from trendy Shibuya and Shinjuku nightlife, to classic Marunouchi around Tokyo Station and timeless Asakusa on the Sumida-gawa – plus major transport hubs to the surrounding areas. Central Tokyo may be crisscrossed by long avenues and highways, but it also has plenty of quieter side streets and alleys with only light car traffic, not to mention a wide range of landscaped gardens, public parks and playgrounds. The scenic Arakawa and Tama Rivers are best for long-distance cycling, although the riverside paths may turn to gravel in more remote sections.

Fujikawaguchiko

Fujikawaguchiko (富士河口湖) is the gateway to the Fuji Five Lakes (富士五湖) area in Yamanashi Prefecture, which covers Kawaguchi-ko, Saiko, Shōji-ko, Motosu-ko and Yamanaka-ko – each with its own unique views of Mt Fuji. Along with Yamanaka-ko, Kawaguchi-ko is the best for families, including plenty of accommodation, museums, restaurant-cafes and other lakeside activities. Kawaguchiko Station is where the regional buses and train line stop, right after the Fuji-Q Highland amusement park.

WHEN TO GO

Once the frosty winter warms to a milder crisp spring air, floral blossoms and birdlife abound, before the rainy season takes over in June. Summer in Tokyo is notoriously sweltering, but also filled with fireworks and night festivals. For less noise and balmier days, head to the eastern shores of the Pacific coast or the Izu Peninsula.

Chōshi

If you prefer a simple modern business hotel to the luxury onsen (hot springs) resorts on the cape, Chōshi (銚子) is the perfect base, with transport connections to the JR Sobu line through to Chiba and Tokyo, the leisurely Electric Railway line to Inubō, and even the Tone-gawa riverway leading inland past Itako and Lake Kasumigaura.

Numazu

Numazu (沼津) is the 12th post town on the Edo-period (1603–1868) Tōkaidō pilgrimage route from Tokyo to Kyoto, as well as the western entry point to the Izu Peninsula (伊豆半島). With a grandiose view of Mt Fuji on clear days, it's a hub town in more ways than one: cycle east to follow the Kano-gawa towards Shuzen-ji, west to ride along the Senbon Matsubara beachfront, or south to contour the peninsular coastline counterclockwise.

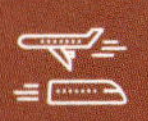

TRANSPORT

Tokyo's railways and highways reach out to all surrounding prefectures, with Limited Express trains running direct to Chōshi and Shuzen-ji, and direct buses from Shinjuku to Fujikawaguchiko. Train buffs will love riding the novelty train line between Ōarai and Kashima-jingū, or especially the vintage Chōshi Electric Railway that goes around the cape to Tokawa.

WHAT'S ON

Japan's First Sunrise

Sixty thousand people gather around Chōshi's Cape Inubōsaki to watch the first sunrise of the new year.

Itako Ayame Matsuri

One million irises bloom from late May to June, as brides float by on wooden sculling boats and ride rickshaws with the grooms.

Kawaguchiko Herb Festival

Lavender blossoms with a Mt Fuji backdrop at Ōishi Park from late June to mid-July.

Resources

Choshi Geopark *(choshi-geopark.jp)* Visitor-friendly geological info about Chōshi.

Explore Izu *(explore-izu.com)* Illustrated resource for routes, highlights, maps and more, with downloadable data.

Cycling Ibaraki *(cycling.pref.ibaraki.jp)* Official website for recommended routes, including the Kasumigaura Ring Ring Road and Hitachi Seaside Park.

WHERE TO STAY

There is no shortage of accommodation around Fujikawaguchiko, from mountain-side glampsites to lakeside luxury hotels, but you'll find the best views of Mt Fuji from the north shore. Several ryokan even have a view from their hot-spring baths. If you're onsen-hopping across the region, don't forget to reserve a room facing the ocean at Inubōsaki Onsen in Chōshi to catch the sunrise. In Shuzen-ji Onsen, many traditional ryokan (traditional Japanese inns) also serve exquisite *kaiseki* (Japanese haute cuisine) meals. At the cycling hub of the Ring Ring Road, BEB5 Tsuchiura welcomes bikes in a casual and creative atmosphere.

03

Chōshi Geopark

DURATION	DIFFICULTY	DISTANCE	START/END
2-3hrs	Intermediate	20km	Chōshi Station/ Inuboh Station

TERRAIN	Paved road

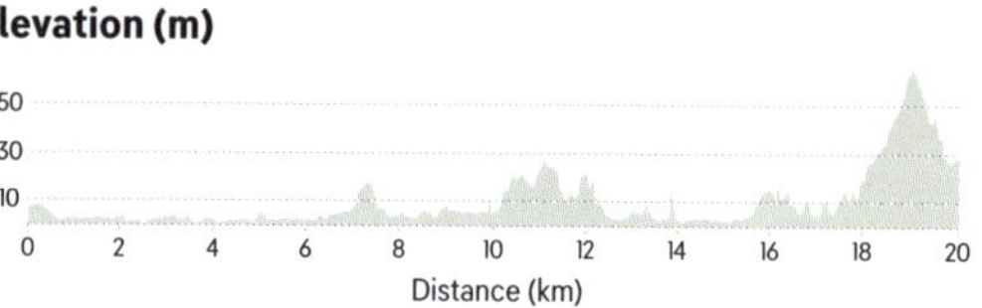

Poking out of Japan's Honshū into the Pacific Ocean, Chōshi is where you can see the first seaside sunrise, ancient strata from the age of dinosaurs, and the curve of the earth from a hill above the cape. Superlative fossils have been found here too: an ammonite shell with a 50cm diameter, the oldest Japanese amber and a megalodon tooth. But Chōshi is also where you'll find seagulls at fishing ports, sandpipers on the shore and starfish at low tide. Riding through this compact natural geopark is like caressing the edge of the earth, surrounded by the sea.

Bike Hire

Just outside Chōshi Station, Rentacycle Chōshi rents e-bikes that can also be returned in Inubō. You can even take them back on the Chōshi Electric Railway from Inuboh station.

Starting Point

Chōshi Station is directly accessible from central Tokyo on the JR Sobu line Limited Express 'Shiosai' to Chōshi. There are also direct trains from Chiba Station and Narita Airport.

Outside Chōshi Station, on the left side of Symbol St, is a red statue of Chiba-kun, Chiba Prefecture's official mascot, riding a bicycle. This spot marks the official starting point of the Pacific Cycling Road (太平洋岸自転車道), which continues along the coast for some 1400km to Wakayama. However, the PCR is more of a route than a path – many sections share a narrow road (sometimes even highway) with cars – so if you decide to pursue the route beyond Chōshi, proceed with caution. Meanwhile, you'll recognise the painted blue arrows along the road.

KO-TORI/SHUTTERSTOCK

Best for

SEASIDE SUNRISE

Cape Inubōsaki (p40)

02 From Kawagishi-kōen (河岸公園), you can see the red Chōshi suspension bridge stretching across to Ibaraki Prefecture at the mouth of the river. The Tone-gawa (利根川) originally flowed into Tokyo Bay, until it was redirected by the Edo Shogunate in order to improve the water transport network, protect the capital of Edo from water disasters, and develop new rice fields.

03 For the past four centuries, the Tone-gawa has flown into the Pacific Ocean at Chōshi's Outer Port. Just off the coast, the warm Kuroshio Current from the south meets the cold Oyashio Current from the north, where lots of plankton gather and attract many small and bigger fish. During the Edo period, Chōshi developed as a prosperous fishing port and distribution hub supplying fish, rice and other goods from the eastern provinces to the capital, thanks to the Tone-gawa waterway.

04 On your right, the octagonal observatory of the glass Chōshi Port Tower (銚子ポートタワー) offers a panoramic view of the city, the Pacific coastline and beyond. This is the spot where Japan's first successful wireless communication with a ship on the Pacific Ocean was established on 27 May 1908.

05 At the foot of the tower is Meotogahana (夫婦ヶ鼻), so-named because it's a cape that once contained a cave, which collapsed in 1959. Its strata include thin layers of fine-grained sandstone sandwiched between layers of fine-grained mudstone, which formed in the deep sea 17 million years ago, around the same time as the Sea of Japan.

06 Shortly after you go round the bend of Kurohaie Port (黒生港), you will see perched on the seashore the grey silhouette of Tombi Iwa (とんび岩), a black kite-shaped formation of dark rocks mixed with pebbles, distinguished by its square, hooked

Take a Break

INUBOW TERASU TERRACE (犬吠テラステラス) is a contemporary roadside station with a stylish observatory. When you're done shopping and eating on the ground floor, head upstairs to find a brighter, quieter open space also selling local products. The real attraction is by the windows: on one end, tables and chairs where you can sit down with your snacks; on the other, hammock-style nets ensconced in warm wooden furniture where you can lie back and gaze out to sea.

beak. All along the coastline, signs point to highlights of the nationally designated Chōshi Geopark.

07 Rejoining Rte 254, the path becomes a brick pavement with railing on both sides. After a stretch of rocky coastline you will pass Ashikajima Swimming Beach (海鹿島海水浴場).

08 Another curve brings you to Kimigahama Shiosai Park (君ヶ浜しおさい公園) and its long rocky beach separated from the ocean by a short rail fence. Instead of swimming here, go hiking in the Kimigahama Forest, which extends across the entire length of the park above the beach.

09 The path winds quickly uphill to Inubow Terasu Terrace and Chōshi's main tourist attraction of Cape Inubōsaki (犬吠埼). The Inubōsaki Lighthouse is a Western-style lighthouse built in 1874. At a height of almost 32m, it is the second-tallest brick building currently standing in Japan. Climb the 99 steps of the corkscrew staircase for a commanding view of the cape jutting out into the Pacific.

10 Chōshi's eastern shore is formed by rock made of sand and mud that accumulated in the ocean some 120 million years ago, before the entire landmass gradually moved several thousands of kilometres north to its current position. Walk down the stairs and along the paths to the shoreline to examine the Cretaceous shallow sea deposits that form the cliffside and touch the layered Chōshi stone, while listening to the sound of waves eroding ancient strata. Japan's easternmost cape of Inubōsaki is where you can catch the archipelago's first sunrise at seaside. Watch for brown warblers nibbling on golden pampas grass as you follow the walking paths around the cape.

11 Keep following Rte 254 down the coast, then turn left and continue around the shoreline to Cape Nagasakibana (長崎鼻) with its own little lighthouse. Look for marine life, cactus plants and light porous volcanic rock formations on the shore. The cape is made of rocks from three distinct eras: alternating layers of sandstone and mudstone deposited on the deep seafloor about 100 million years ago; the rare high-magnesium andesite Hōman (宝満) rocks formed from solidified magma that erupted about 20 million years ago; and pebble rocks that formed about five million years ago. Cretaceous fossils such as shark teeth, whale bones and elephant molars have been discovered in these nodules.

DREAMNIKON/GETTY IMAGES

Byōbugaura

Byōbugaura

This dramatic 10km-long cliffside, ranging in height from 20m to 60m, was created by cutting waves that uplifted sea sediments over millions of years. Byōbugaura's (屏風ヶ浦) lower strata, formed up to 3.1 million years ago, contains fossils of deep-sea creatures such as sea urchins and shellfish. The upper strata formed about 100,000 years ago when Chōshi was surrounded by a shallow sea, as an isolated island centred around Atago-yama. Byōbugaura has long been a favourite spot for artists and writers, and was also portrayed in *ukiyo-e* by Utagawa Hiroshige, as a famous tourist destination since the Edo period.

HIT1912/SHUTTERSTOCK

Chōshi Electric Railway

The vintage 6.4km electric-powered Chōshi Electric Railway (銚子電気鉄道) line from the 1920s may be just as much a source of pride for local residents as it is a sightseeing ride for slow-travellers. You will encounter both, from curious trainspotters at the old-fashioned Tokawa terminus to families getting on at Inuboh or Kannon stations. The entire journey takes 20 minutes, with views of farmlands and spiffy young train attendants coming through the two cars to check tickets. Once you hop on, don't forget to set aside ¥200 to buy a hot sweet potato on board before pulling into Chōshi.

Chōshi Electric Railway

12 Continue along the coastline past Tokawa (外川), a fishing port whose annual seafood catch consistently ranks among the highest landing weights in Japan. The area is known for preserving its traditional fishing village atmosphere. Just up the street is the quaint Tokawa train station, a small wooden building filled with miscellaneous artefacts that date back to 1921. Right outside behind a retro red postbox, a restored antique black-and-red Deha 801 train car is permanently parked at the end of the tracks.

13 Near the end of Tokawa Port, turn left onto the jetty towards Sengaiwa (千騎ケ岩), a huge rock mass that was once an island. It contains the oldest stratum in Chiba Prefecture, a mix of dark mudstone and whitish sandstone estimated to be from the Jurassic period. Near the end in the softer mudstone, you can see its distinctive hole eroded from the waves over millennia.

14 Head back up the road and turn left onto the edge of Inuwaka Port. Then walk down to the shore to view Inuiwa (犬岩), another Jurassic-period rock that weathering and erosion have formed into the shape of a dog lying with its ears perked up. This is the easternmost point from which you can view Mt Fuji on the western horizon, making it an otherworldly place to watch the sunset on a clear evening.

15 Back on the road, continue past the Chiba Institute of Science and uphill to the main road, then follow the signs left down to Byōbugaura. Along the shoreline, a paved concrete path extends several hundred metres in either direction above the seawall, for unparalleled close-up viewing of the spectacular cliffside. The dark brown, cracked stratum at the very top of Byōbugaura is the 20-million-year-old Kanto Loam layer, consisting of volcanic ash turned to clay soil that makes up the fertile Shimousa Plateau (下総台地) on the Kanto Plain.

16 Follow Rte 286 uphill for a couple kilometres across the forest and farmlands, before making a sharp turn right down the mountain. Soon you will see a sign pointing the way to the entrance of the Horizon Observatory perched atop Atago-yama. Keep going until you see a large abstract sculpture overlooking a landscaped park extending down the hill. Even if you don't enter the observatory, the outdoor platform is a spectacular place to rest, with a wide-angle view from the ocean to Tsukuba-san.

TOP TIP:

Extend Your Ride

If you want to go further, consider extending your ride about 40km from Chōshi to Itako via the dedicated bike path on the southern bank of the Tone-gawa. From Itako, you can segue directly to the Tsukuba Kasumigaura Ring Ring Road.

17 After marvelling at the sweeping view of Byōbugaura and beyond from the peak, there are at least a couple of options on how to get back from here. Either ride downhill a straightforward 4.5km from the observatory directly back to Chōshi Station, or roll downhill about 1km to Inubō, return your bike (or not) at one of the designated hotels, then take the vintage electric railway back to Chōshi from Inuboh Station (犬吠駅).

Take a Break

The Japanese name of the **HORIZON OBSERVATORY** (地球の丸く見える丘展望館) translates more poetically as 'Observation hill from which you can see the curve of the earth'. Go up to the rooftop. If you can't see the global curve, you will see 360 degrees all the way around the cape from Tsukuba-san to the Tone-gawa to Byōbugaura to Tokyo Bay, of which a mesmerising 330 degrees is pure ocean. Downstairs is a cafe where you can contemplate the sea view from indoors.

04

Best for

MT FUJI VIEWS & FLOWERS

Fuji Kawagu-chiko

DURATION	DIFFICULTY	DISTANCE	START/END
1–2hrs	Easy	19km	Mt Fuji Panoramic Ropeway/ Kawaguchiko Station

TERRAIN	Paved road

STEVE TRAVELGUIDE/SHUTTERSTOCK

Mt Fuji Panoramic Ropeway

Among Mt Fuji's famous five lakes, Kawaguchi-ko (河口湖) is the most developed and easiest to access. It also has arguably the most spectacular view of the 3776m-high sacred mountain. Kawaguchi-ko's peaceful lakeside is a place of both culture and leisure, with landscaped flower gardens, cafe terraces, art museums, music concerts, shrines, luxury onsen hotels and mountainside glampsites. For more remote adventures, Kawaguchi-ko is also the gateway to the less-developed lakes of Sai-ko, Shōji-ko and Motosu-ko to the west.

Bike Hire

Hello Cycling has thousands of public e-bikes available in the Greater Tokyo region through its smartphone app. Many of the hotels on Kawaguchi-ko also have bicycles available for guests.

Starting Point

The Mt Fuji Panoramic Ropeway is on the east side of the lake, where most of the hotels are. Hello Cycling has docks at Kawaguchiko Station, the Ropeway and Music Forest Museum.

01 The Mt Fuji Panoramic Ropeway takes you up to the hillside Tenjōyama-kōen (天上山公園) and its commanding views of Kawaguchi-ko looking west. It's a good spot to get an overview of the lakeside landscape before diving in.

02 Back down by the shore, leave the pleasure boats behind as you begin riding counter-clockwise around Kawaguchi-ko. You will pass several hotels before coming to a tunnel. Turn left and contour Cape Ubuya, merging with the Kawaguchiko Bridge off-ramp pavement to continue northwards.

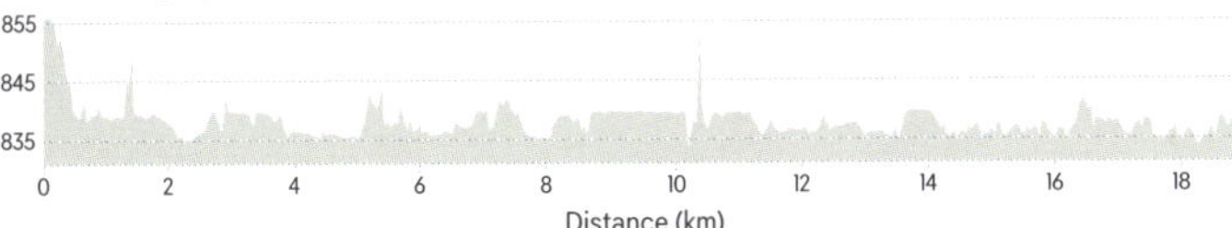

03 From here the road passes in front of several novelty museums on the left. The Kawaguchiko Museum of Art (河口湖美術館) primarily exhibits contemporary art picturing Mt Fuji and the surrounding area, alongside a lakeside observation lounge surrounded by 9m-high glass. Across the street, Houtou Labo serves the famous hot-pot dish with noodles handmade on-site. The Music Forest Museum (音楽と森の美術館) specialises in historical musical automatons as well as classical concerts and gourmet dining around a European-style flower garden and cafe. The Konohana Museum (木ノ花美術館) is the personal theme castle for artist Akiko Ikeda's Dayan the Cat, with a sunny restaurant patio.

04 If you're ready to stretch your legs on the water, the Kawaguchiko Boat House is a hub for renting swan paddle boats, kayaks, row boats and more from various companies. In autumn, don't miss the Maple Corridor (もみじ回廊) of fiery foliage fluttering over the lake canal. Further up the canal, the Kubota Itchiku Art Museum (久保田一竹美術館) exhibits exquisitely dyed silk kimonos by its namesake master.

05 Follow the paved path contouring Kawaguchi-ko past Nagasaki-kōen. Soon you will pass the Nasubiza (なすび座) theatre on the right. Five times a day, local musicians perform a lively concert featuring traditional Japanese instruments such as the *Tsugaru shamisen* (three-stringed

More Lakes: Sai-ko & Motosu-ko

When you reach the west end of Kawaguchi-ko, consider extending your ride to Sai-ko and Motosu-ko lakes (西湖・本栖湖). Further away from the crowds, you will be rewarded with a more immersive journey into the landscape, seeing Mt Fuji from different viewpoints. There are a few climbs and narrow pavement paths along a busy road, especially passing through the huge Aokigahara Forest. Push on towards the Motosuko Observation Park to see the famous view of Mt Fuji as illustrated on the back of old ¥1000 banknotes, then savour a hot *hōtō* (noodle dish) at the lodge just above Koan (浩庵) campsite.

instrument resembling a lute or a banjo), *taiko* (drum) and *shakuhachi* (bamboo flute).

06 A bit further, turn left into the large car park at Ōishi Park. This is another popular tourist spot to pause and admire the view of Mt Fuji directly from the lakeshore. The Kawaguchiko Natural Living Center (河口湖自然生活館) serves Fuji-themed refreshments above its lovingly cultivated flower gardens. Looking back at the mountain, you will see the cubic luxury units of Hoshinoya Fuji hotel.

07 Keep riding across the north side of the lake on Rte 21 to the quieter, more forested west side. When you reach the three-way intersection with Nagahama Pocket Park (長浜ポケットパーク) on the left, you will have the option of turning right onto the road that leads (uphill) to Sai-ko lake. To continue around Kawaguchi-ko, keep following the road ahead, passing through small neighbourhoods along the shadier south side, with a view of the lake.

08 Round the bend that cradles Fujiomurosengenjinja (冨士御室淺間神社), a Shintō shrine complex in the village of Katsuyama (勝山).

09 After passing under the southern end of the Kawaguchiko Bridge, you will pass the Happy Days Cafe and Nostalgic Toys Museum (おもちゃ博物館), founded by Teruhisa Kitahara based on his personal collection of antique tin toys. A few steps away, the thatched roof Fudo Chaya serves tea and udon, but only until they run out in the early afternoon.

10 Around the corner and across the street from Ōike-kōen (大池公園), feel free to soak your feet in the long wooden foot bath (足湯) right outside the Shiki no Yado Fujisan (四季の宿　富士山) hotel.

11 Continue around the lake to complete your loop at the Mt Fuji Panoramic Ropeway, return to your hotel, or take the backstreets to Kawaguchiko Station. If you're feeling peckish by the end of your ride, there is a Houtou Fudou restaurant right across from the station. The Fujikyū Railway (富士急行線) goes to the Fuji-Q Highland amusement park and Ōtsuki (大月), where you can transfer to the JR Chuo line back to Tokyo. There are also direct buses to Shinjuku (新宿).

Take a Break

Hōtō (ほうとう) is a regional speciality of Yamanashi Prefecture that is particularly prized around Mt Fuji. This hearty soup noodle dish, often served in an iron pot, features thick, chewy, flat wheat noodles simmered in a sweet miso-based broth. Traditional ingredients include pumpkin, potatoes, mushrooms, carrots and other seasonal roots and vegetables, but some local variants also add meat or seafood. HOUTOU FUDOU (ほうとう不動) has four different charismatic shops around Kawaguchi-ko. Be sure to arrive early before they sell out.

NAOKITA/SHUTTERSTOCK

Ōishi Park

Ōishi Park

About halfway across the north shore, Ōishi Park (大石公園) is an ideal place to stop and smell the flowers. The park may be best known for the Kawaguchiko Herb Festival with its extensive lavender fields, framing an excellent view of Mt Fuji reflected on the lake among swaying pampas grass. Lavender blooms from late June to mid-July, but the cafe serves lavender ice cream all year round. The lakeside promenade is lined with various colourful seasonal flora, from pink moss in late April to scarlet kochia in October. Lake Bake specialises in French breads and scones with patio seating.

05

Tsukuba Kasumi-gaura Ring Ring Road

Best for

LAKE VIEWS & HISTORY

DURATION	DIFFICULTY	DISTANCE	START/END
4–5hrs	Easy	55km	Tsuchiura/ Itako

TERRAIN	Paved bike path

KOREKORE/GETTY IMAGES

Wada Park (p50)

Kasumigaura (霞ヶ浦) is Japan's second-largest lake, and its quiet, rural wetlands are located within the Suigo-Tsukuba Quasi-National Park. The Tsukuba Kasumigaura Ring Ring Road (つくば霞ヶ浦りんりんロード) is one of Japan's designated national cycle routes. This section of the route takes you from Kasumigaura's cycling hub of Tsuchiura (土浦), past wartime artefacts, swaying pampas grass, sunbathing cormorants, jumping fish and stone jetties, to the Edo-period waterway town of Itako (潮来). Just follow the bright blue arrows.

Bike Hire

At Ring Ring Sq inside Tsuchiura Station, Ibaraki Wide-Area Rental Cycle has road bikes, hybrids and e-bikes that can be rented for multiple days and returned at 11 locations.

Starting Point

Tsuchiura Station is a 50-minute train ride from Tokyo Station, with bikes, showers, lockers, maps and more. You can also begin in Itako, but rental options will be limited.

01 Above and around Tsuchiura Station (土浦駅) is a towering commercial complex that includes the bicycle-friendly BEB5 hotel, a food court, and shops selling any supplies you might need for the ride. You can even roll your bike right through the mall on the indoor path. It's a good transition from urban Tokyo; the road ahead gets rural pretty fast.

02 Still within the urban bounds of Tsuchiura, Kasumigaura Comprehensive Park (霞ヶ浦総合公園) is immediately recognisable by its iconic Dutch windmill. The aquatic botanical garden is

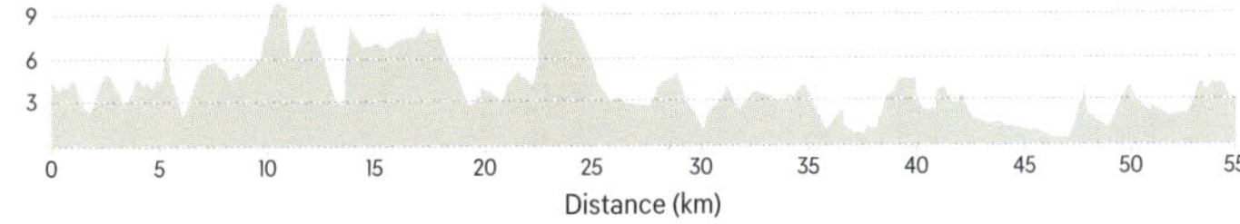

zigzagged with wooden walkways and old watermills. In spring, look out for colourful stripes of 30,000 tulips and other seasonal blossoms such as lotus flowers in summer. Climb to the top of the windmill for a panoramic view of the lake.

03 Further eastwards along the path, just around a grassy corner, stands a large contemporary concrete building with a chequered architecture that is open to the sky. This is the Yokaren Peace Memorial Museum, which commemorates tens of thousands of teenage boys who enlisted as trainees for the Kasumigaura Navy Air Corps between 1930 and 1945. Outside the museum you will see a full-scale model of a 14.75m-long Kaiten Type 1 human fish tank used for suicide missions.

04 For the next 40km or so, the path becomes more of a rural immersion ride, safely separated from the quiet country road, where you can take in the tranquil lakeside scenery at your own pace. Follow the gently curving path, often stretching out to the horizon, with the lake, fishing boats and the occasional shrine on one side, farmlands and wetlands on the other.

05 Just before rounding a sharper bend, you will pass the crumbling, overgrown ruins of the Kashima Naval Air Squadron Site (鹿島海軍航空隊跡), which served as a training ground for the Yokaren up until the end of WWII. After being abandoned for decades, the former military site finally opened to the public in July 2023.

Yokaren Peace Memorial Museum

The excellent Yokaren Peace Memorial Museum (予科練平和記念館), full of period artefacts, photographs, letters, diaries and dioramas, commemorates Kasumigaura's significant role in modern history. It was here, in the lakeside town of Ami, that some 240,000 boys aged 14½ to 17 years old, selected from a highly competitive exam, trained as Yokaren (Naval Aviator Preparatory Course Trainees). During the 15 years leading up to the end of WWII, around 24,000 of them graduated to become combat pilots on the front. Many Yokaren were assigned to kamikaze missions, and 80% of them – more than 19,000 teenage boys – died in the war.

It's a rare chance to explore the ghostly structures and history of a key wartime location, while marvelling at how nature has since reclaimed it.

06 Continue along the curve of the lake, narrowing to a short neck before crossing the straight Futto Bridge (古渡橋) and heading back up around a sharp corner, then turning right onto another long stretch.

07 Shortly after passing a solar panel park and single sheltered bench at Cape Nishinosu (西の洲岬), you will come to Ukishima Kōshin-zuka (浮島庚申塚), an ancient stone monument that portrays a standing Buddhist figure with four waving arms. The monument pays tribute to the local practice of nighttime rituals that were once popular among Kasumigaura's farming communities, who traditionally prayed here for protection against misfortune, good harvests and favourable weather.

08 The path rolls past discreet underwater sewage-treatment plants, stopping temporarily at Wada Park (和田公園) on the dramatic cape; famous in spring for its 120,000 tulips in 21 varieties.

09 Continue past Kasumigaura Ukishima Marsh (霞ヶ浦浮島湿原), also known as Myōgi-no-hana (妙岐ノ鼻), where an educational wooden birdwatching hut invites you to survey the surrounding wetlands. Look out for Japanese bush warblers, bitterns and ospreys.

10 Turn right onto the Hitachitone-gawa path, cross the bridge and glide into Itako, rolling on tiled streets lined with the old shops and inns of this ancient water town. If you arrive in late May or June, look for thousands of white, purple and pink irises in full bloom at Suigō Itako Iris Garden (水郷潮来あやめ園). This is also when the Ayame Matsuri re-enacts local Edo-period rituals, such as newlywed brides floating down the canal on traditional wooden sculling boats, before joining the groom for a rickshaw ride. From Itako, you can continue riding the Ring Ring Road counterclockwise around the less-travelled north side of the lake.

11 If you're ending your ride here, return your bike at the Itako Station Information Center (水郷潮来観光協会), then take the JR Kanto highway bus back to Tokyo Station (70 minutes).

Take a Break

Once outside Tsuchiura, be sure to stock up on snacks to eat along the way. There are some minimalist, sometimes floral rest areas where you can pull over for a pause, such as the **ŌSUKAZU AGRICULTURAL VILLAGE PARK** (大須賀津農村公園), situated about one-third into the ride. You will find picnic benches on the hill, *sakura* (cherry blossoms) in spring, and an observation deck where you can put your journey into perspective as you gaze out across the still lake and fertile agricultural lands.

AMANA IMAGES INC./ALAMY

Kashima-jingū

Kashima-jingū

If you follow the bike path from Itako along the Wani-gawa towards Lake Kitaura (北浦), you will see a giant red *torii* gate standing 18.5m tall above the surface of the lake. This majestic water *torii* is the westernmost gate of Kashima-jingū (鹿島神宮) – the oldest Shintō shrine in the Kantō region established in 660 BCE, revered for its powerful spiritual energy. Detour from the path about 2.5km east of the *torii* to find the vast forested shrine grounds, home to a crystal-clear koi pond, sacred deer and an enshrined mystical sword.

06

Izu Peninsula: Numazu to Shuzen-ji Onsen

LILYROSEPHOTOS/SHUTTERSTOCK

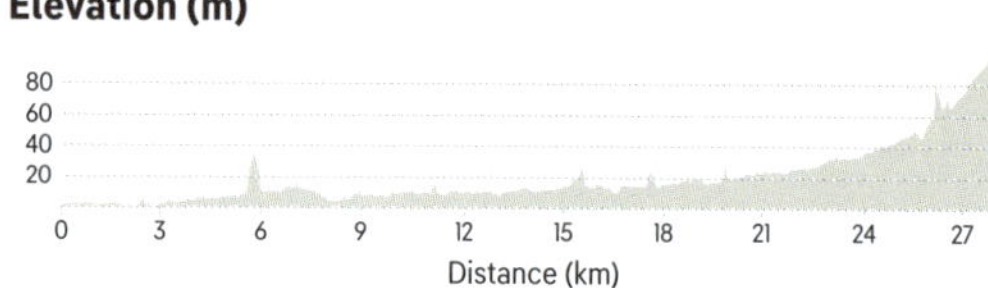

DURATION	DIFFICULTY	DISTANCE	START/END
2.5–3.5hrs	Easy	28km	Numazu Port Observatory/ Shuzen-ji Onsen
TERRAIN	Paved bike path		

Izu has long been a cycling destination, as witnessed by its well-maintained paths and ever-developing bicycle infrastructure. Travel from Numazu, the northern coastal gateway city, to the Izu Peninsula, on urban bike paths and along the banks of the Kano-gawa (狩野川), down to the spiritual town of Shuzen-ji Onsen (修善寺温泉). Along the way, Mt Fuji will be watching over you, whether from behind the hills, behind the clouds or in plain magnificent sight.

Bike Hire

Hello Cycling offers a public e-bike sharing service through its smartphone app. Look for docks at Numazu Station, Numazu Port, Shuzenji Station and at Shuzenji in Shuzen-ji Onsen.

Starting Point

The Numazu Port Observatory Water Gate is about a 12-minute ride from Numazu Station. You could also start at Shuzen-ji Onsen, about a 12-minute ride from Shuzenji Station.

01 The Kano-gawa originates in the central Izu Peninsula and goes north into Suruga Bay at Numazu, where the ride begins. The Numazu Port Observatory Water Gate (沼津港大型展望水門) overlooks the city port, the bay and the mountains, including Mt Fuji, with sweeping views all around. If you enter on the Fish Market side of the gate, walk across to the Park Side tower and look down at the beach. There's a clear view of the long Senbon Matsubara (千本松原) strip of pine trees and paved beach path. Take the bike path on the west side of the Kano-gawa, cruising through the city as black kites circle overhead.

Numazu and Mt Fuji

Best for

MT FUJI VIEWS & COUNTRYSIDE

Izu for Serious Cyclists

Perched in the mountains of eastern Izu is Japan's only military-style school dedicated to Keirin (競輪), the highly competitive sport and multi-billion-yen gambling industry. Established in 1948, now an official Olympic event, Keirin is a typically Japanese form of strictly regulated bike racing with its own techniques and strategies. Every Keirin bicycle is unique, with a handmade steel frame, fixed gear and no brakes. The Izu Velodrome, opened in 2011 in the same area, hosted international cycling events during the 2020 Tokyo Olympics. Just outside it, the Cycle Sports Center contains kid-friendly cycling circuits, mountain-bike trails and a pedal-powered monorail.

02 At Kurose Bridge (黒瀬橋), if not before, cross over to the south side of the river. The bridge has a separate, tiled path for bicycles and pedestrians. Then continue on a relatively seamless route through the city, following or running parallel to the river.

03 By the time you get to Kanogawa Fureai Sq, you will be back on the riverbank. From here onwards, the riverside bike path becomes much more rural, opening up on all sides to reveal beautiful agricultural landscapes. Even in winter, the dry grasses reflect the sunlight in various hues, as the wind rustles through the trees. Don't forget to look back now and then – the views of snowcapped Mt Fuji rising above the horizon never get old.

04 In the distance on your left, what looks like a bright red sausage resting on top of a blue-and-white building is Kanefuku Mentai Park, a factory/theme park celebrating *mentai* (walleye pollack roe). Along the path you will also see at various points a small square sign indicating the Kano-gawa and a 'number of kilometres' below an illustration of swimming fish. This is the distance from the mouth of the river (河口より), which you have also travelled.

05 When you get to the green metal Ishidō Bridge (石堂橋), cross over to the east side of the Kano-gawa to continue your riverside route southwards. The long, well-paved bike path now runs through more residential neighbourhoods, roughly parallel to the highway and the Izuhakone Railway Sunzu line to the east.

06 As you roll into Kanogawa Kamishima Undō-kōen, you may see an old-school yellow school bus parked on the left side of the path. It's actually a food-truck cafe, so don't hesitate to get a drink to go if it's open.

07 Just past the bend around Ōhito Station stands the red metal Ōhito Bridge (大仁橋), with a bench and viewing platform below. Just behind it is Suishōzan (水晶山) or 'Quartz Hill', a designated geopark mound of accumulated submarine volcanic deposits and quartz crystals that were extracted from it in the 19th century. The original Ōhito Bridge was built in 1880 to connect Suishōzan to the former Ōhito Gold Mine on the other side of the river.

08 As the roads around you get busier, you will soon arrive at Shuzenji Station. Inside the building is a small tourist information centre.

09 Cross the red Shuzenji Bridge onto the main road and continue a bit uphill until you come to the big overpass interchange, marked on the ground by the big block characters for Shuzenji (修善寺). Continue straight along the same road for a few hundred metres into the hot-spring enclave of Shuzen-ji Onsen.

Take a Break

Izu celebrates its strawberries, and IZU-NO-HESO (伊豆のへそ) in Izunokuni is a great place to taste the local harvest. The roadside station sells seasonal fresh produce, while its Ichigo BonBonBerry cafe serves everything made with regional varieties of strawberries and more, from strawberry jams and pastries to an individually glazed strawberry bavarois. The lunch menu also includes beef stew, curry and pasta. If you're after treats to go, there are riverside benches at the nearby Kamishima Undō-kōen.

PRINCESS_ANMITSU/SHUTTERSTOCK

Shuzen-ji Onsen

10 The quiet main street that follows the Katsura-gawa (桂川) leads to the landmark temple of Shuzen-ji. Although the ride ends here, it's worth spending some time in this ancient hot-spring town, if only to walk along the peaceful Bamboo Forest Path. Shuzen-ji Onsen was established in 807 by Kūkai, the founder of Shingon Buddhism in Japan; you can even see the legendary Tokko-no-Yu (独鈷の湯) where Kūkai is said to have struck a rock with his staff to heal a sick person, and a hot spring gushed forth. Don't touch the sacred water, but do soak your feet in the warm foot bath on the walking path above it.

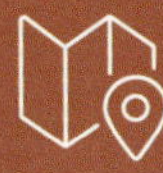

Choose Your Own Adventure

Depending on your greater itinerary or personal preference, this ride can be done in either direction. Depart from Shuzen-ji (with limited direct trains from Tokyo) to face Mt Fuji as you ride towards the mountain, with options to extend the ride from Numazu along the peninsula or the forested Senbon Matsubara path on the Pacific Cycling Road. Or, start with Numazu's panoramic port view and enjoy the backlit rural ride southwards, concluding with a soothing bath followed by a buffet dinner in Shuzen-ji Onsen (and face Mt Fuji on the train ride back up the peninsula).

Also Try...

Windsurfers, Kamakura

KAZUNO WILLIAM EMPSON/SHUTTERSTOCK

Kamakura to Ōiso

DURATION	DIFFICULTY	DISTANCE
2hrs	Easy	25km

This scenic section of the Pacific Cycling Road starts in Kamakura (鎌倉), one of Japan's ancient capitals and site of the Great Buddha, also known locally as a laid-back beach town. Begin at Yuigahama beach, where windsurfers dot the bay behind cormorants perched on breakwaters in Sagami Bay. Round Cape Inamura and continue towards Shōnan Kaigan Park facing Enoshima with its iconic Sea Candle rising above the densely forested island. Ride along the sand dunes of Tsujidō, as surfers ride the waves. Rejoin the ancient Tōkaidō pilgrimage route on the coast in Ōiso (大磯), just beyond graffiti art and tepees on the beach, at the gourmet Ōiso Connect port roadside station. Hello Cycling has docks around Kamakura and at Ōiso Station.

Hitachi Seaside Park

DURATION	DIFFICULTY	DISTANCE
2–3hrs	Intermediate	30km

Hitachi Seaside Park (ひたち海浜公園) is most famous for its immersive, landscaped hills that bloom in season with colourful flora, but it also includes an extensive and scenic cycling course. The refreshing ride northwards from Ōarai (大洗) follows the Pacific coast in Ibaraki Prefecture, passing family-friendly attractions such as the Ōarai Marine Tower, Kamiiso-no-Torii water shrine and Aqua World. However, the seaside route leading up to the park also has narrow and uphill sections without dedicated bike paths. Rent a Mini Velo e-bike at Ōarai Station's Umimachi Terrace and return it at Nakaminato Station (那珂湊; 7km south of the park on the way back to Ōarai). Alternatively, Hitachi Seaside Park offers rental bikes for use exclusively inside the park.

JOHN S LANDER/LIGHTROCKET VIA GETTY IMAGES

Edo-Tokyo Open Air Architectural Museum

Arakawa

DURATION	DIFFICULTY	DISTANCE
1–2hrs	Easy	25km

From the panoramic Arakawa River Sky View tower inside the Arakawa Museum of Aqua (荒川知水資料館), across from the Old Iwabuchi Watergate, take in your surroundings from above and observe the complete course heading south towards the mouth of the river. Then enjoy gliding along the wide, well-paved paths on either side of the Arakawa, passing bridges, recreation grounds and flower fields, all the way down to the harbour. At the scenic Ōjima-Komatsugawa-kōen (大島小松川公園) on the west bank of the Arakawa, turn onto the bridge that also crosses the Nakagawa and continue straight down to the expansive Kasai-Rinkai Park (葛西臨海公園). Hello Cycling has docks at Akabane-Iwabuchi (赤羽岩淵) Station and Kasai-Rinkai Park Station.

Tama-ko

DURATION	DIFFICULTY	DISTANCE
2–3hrs	Easy	25km

Start from either end of the forested Sayama Park, with a peaceful view of Tama-ko (多摩湖). Further along the quiet, shaded 12km path that winds around Tama-ko, the lake will be out of sight behind the trees, but plenty of twists and turns keep it interesting. The Murayamaue Dam cuts across the middle of the lake for a scenic stopping point. Looping back on the north side, you will see the red Ferris wheel of the retro Seibuen Amusement Park. Head south towards Musashi-Yamato Station to segue into the 10km straightaway, passing the Edo-Tokyo Open Air Architectural Museum and finally into Mitaka (三鷹), home of the Ghibli Museum inside Inokashira Park. Hello Cycling has several docks around Tama-ko and Mitaka.

0
50 km
0
25 miles
07
08
09
10
Sea of Japan
Noto Peninsula
Suzu
Anamizu
Noto-jima
Nanao
Hakui
Himi
Toyama Bay
Takaoka
Toyama
Kurobe
Itoigawa
Jōetsu
Kashiwazaki
Tokamachi
Tsunan
Iiyama
Nakano
Nagano
Kusatsu
Shirouma-dake
O-yama
Chūbusangaku National Park
Yariga-take
Hotaka-dake
Norikura-dake
Kanazawa
Komatsu
Haku-san National Park
Haku-san
Fukui
Takayama
Shiojiri
Matsumoto
Ueda
Asama-yama
Karuizawa
Saku
Chino
Kobushi-ga-take
Chichibu-Tama-Kai National Park
Shiratori
Ontake-san
Ina
Kiso-komagatake
Senjō-ga-take
Kōfu
Tsuruga
Mino
Nakatsugawa
Iida
Minami Alps National Park
Nagahama
Lake Biwa
Sekigahara
Gifu
Ogaki
Hikone
Tajimi
Fuji-Hakone-Izu National Park
Mt Fuji
Nagoya
Toyota
Kuwana
Yokkaichi
Okazaki
Fuji
Tokoname
Handa
Suzuka
Shizuoka
Yaizu
Suruga-wan
Shimada
Ise-wan
Tsu
Toyohashi
Atsumi Peninsula
Hamamatsu

HIDEO T / 500PX/GETTY IMAGES

Shukunegi (p63), Sado

Central Honshū (Chūbu)

07 Sado

Head to this island off the coast of Niigata for rides along rugged coastline and through bucolic countryside that's home to wildlife like the protected Japanese crested ibis. p62

08 Toyama Bay

Cycle around one of Japan's most scenic yet under-visited bays, with sandy beaches and rocky shoreline set against a mountainous backdrop. p66

09 Karuizawa

Enjoy a gentle pedal around this upscale resort town – a cool summer retreat for wealthy Tokyoites and Japan's Imperial family. p72

10 Lake Hamana

Follow the shoreline of this brackish lake in Shizuoka on a family-friendly ride that takes in gardens, hot springs and an old-school amusement park. p76

Explore

Central Honshū (Chūbu)

Filling the centre of Japan's main island, the Chūbu region stretches across nine of the country's 47 prefectures. With Kansai to its west and Kantō to the east, Chūbu runs from the Japan Sea coast down to the Pacific, punctuated by everything from mountain ranges and windswept coastline to timeless hot-spring towns and sprawling modern cities. There's enough here to fill a cycling book of its own, so just think of this chapter as a Chūbu sampler menu – something that will hopefully inspire you to hang around and delve deeper into the region.

Kanazawa

The largest city in northern Chūbu, Kanazawa (金沢) has been likened to Kyoto because of traditional sights such as Kenroku Garden, Ōmi-chō Market and Higashi-chaya geisha district. We don't have a Kanazawa ride in this book, but the city is easy to pedal around independently. As a regional transport hub with a great range of accommodation and nightlife, it also makes an excellent base for rides in the Noto Peninsula and (thanks to smooth bullet-train connections) in Toyama and Niigata.

Toyama

On the Japan Sea coast, the eponymous capital city of Toyama Prefecture is a handy place to stay for the rides in Toyama Bay and Itoigawa. While Toyama (富山) is far quieter than Kanazawa, there is a good selection of hotels and restaurants near Toyama Station, as well as plenty of things to see and do in the wider Toyama prefectural area when not cycling. That could include a scenic train ride through the Kurobe Gorge, learning to blow glass in Toyama City, and unwinding in the hot-spring baths of Unazaki Onsen.

Sado

Fifty kilometres off the coast of Niigata, Sado (佐渡) was once a place of exile for aristocrats and intellectuals and the site of an Edo-era gold rush. Today, this laid-back island is home to performing arts such as *nō* theatre and *taiko* drumming, but also delivers glimpses of a slower way of life and scenic rides

WHEN TO GO

With clear skies and comfortable temperatures, spring and autumn are best for all the rides in this chapter. Midsummer can often be very hot and humid even on the north coast, although with its shaded roads Karuizawa can still be enjoyed in summer. Most bike-rental shops will be closed in winter, although Lake Hamana remains open in good weather.

that range from sedate half-day excursions to an epic 210km loop around the entire island.

Karuizawa

For generations, Karuizawa (軽井沢) in Nagano Prefecture has been a holiday retreat for well-heeled Tokyoites and even the Imperial family – especially popular in summer when its cooler climate offers respite from the stifling heat of the capital. No surprises then that the area is known for its upscale cosmopolitan vibe, plush holiday homes, and fashionable ateliers and bistros. While you can do a Karuizawa ride en route to other stops on the Hokuriku Shinkansen (including Itoigawa, Toyama and Kanazawa), it's worth stopping for a night and taking it all in slowly.

Shizuoka

In the south of Chūbu, Shizuoka Prefecture is best known for up-close views of Mt Fuji and picturesque tea fields – although it also has a great range of rides available. For the Lake Hamana ride in this chapter, consider staying 15km away by Hamamatsu Station for a good selection of hotels, things to do at night and bullet-train connections. Another handy hub is Shizuoka Station, 80km away.

TRANSPORT

The starting points of all the main rides in this chapter can be reached by public transport. From Tokyo, the Hokuriku Shinkansen (bullet train) stops at Karuizawa and Toyama (you'll then take a local train to Himi), while Lake Hamana is reached by Tōkaidō Shinkansen and local train. For Sado, get the bullet train to Niigata, then take a ferry.

WHAT'S ON

Earth Celebration

On the final weekend of August, Sado hosts Japan's top world-music festival, featuring major concerts, fringe events and workshops.

Hyakumangoku

Kanazawa's biggest festival takes place on the first weekend of June, centred on a parade of traditional acrobatics, dancers and people in samurai attire.

Hamamatsu Matsuri

From 3 May to 5 May, Hamamatsu sees a giant kite-flying competition combined with a procession of temple-like floats bearing musicians.

WHERE TO STAY

The Chūbu region has every budget and type of accommodation covered. Except for Sado, the rides in this chapter start near (or a short train ride from) bullet-train stations, so you'll have access to plenty of midrange Western-style hotels, as well as some ryokan (traditional Japanese inns) and boutique hotels – many are bookable in English via major booking sites. On Sado, you could opt for a family-run *minshuku* (Japanese guesthouse). Book well ahead if travelling in spring and autumn, and be prepared to pay a premium during Japanese holidays like Golden Week (29 April to 5 May) or when the cherry blossoms are in full bloom in April.

Resources

Explore Shizuoka *(exploreshizuoka.jp/en)* Shizuoka Tourism's official website has a section dedicated to rides in the prefecture.

Sado Tourism Navi *(visitsado.com/en)* Covers all the cycling routes on Sado, plus information on getting to and around the island.

Toyama Cycling Navi *(cycling-toyama.jp/en)* Toyama Prefecture's in-depth website detailing its cycling routes.

07

Best for

GOING OFF THE BEATEN PATH

Sado

DURATION	DIFFICULTY	DISTANCE	START/END
2.5hrs	Intermediate	18km	Minami Sado Tourist Information Centre, Ogi
TERRAIN	Paved but hilly		

DAVORLOVINCIC/GETTY IMAGES

A *toki*

Despite being Japan's sixth-biggest island, Sado (佐渡) manages to feel peaceful and remote. Spread over 855 sq km, this rugged isle off the coast of Niigata was once a place of exile for aristocrats and intellectuals, before an Edo-era gold rush temporarily transformed it from backwater to bustling commercial centre. On this ride along Sado's Ogi Coast, you'll get glimpses of rural life, while also taking in pristine nature and remnants of the island's past – from mining heritage through to performing arts such as *nō* theatre and *taiko* drumming.

Bike Hire

The Minami Sado Tourist Information Centre rents sport-type e-bikes for ¥2000 for two hours, plus ¥500 per additional hour. Alternatively, you can do a 24-hour rental for ¥4500. Cash only.

Starting Point

Begin in Ogi, in Sado's southwest, at the Minami Sado Tourist Information Centre. From the main ferry terminal in Ryotsu, take a bus an hour to Sawata, then transfer to an Ogi-bound bus for another hour.

01 From Ogi's Minami Sado Tourist Information Centre, take the road leading behind the neighbouring Hotel Ogi, then go 150m (passing a post office) before turning right onto Rte 45 at the T-junction; it's the road you'll follow for much of this ride. For the first several kilometres, you'll be on a windy, up-and-down stretch that takes in ocean views, farmland and rice paddies. If you spot any white birds in the fields, you are in luck: it might be a rare *toki* (Japanese crested ibis), a bird listed as extinct in the wild in Japan after Sado's remaining five were taken

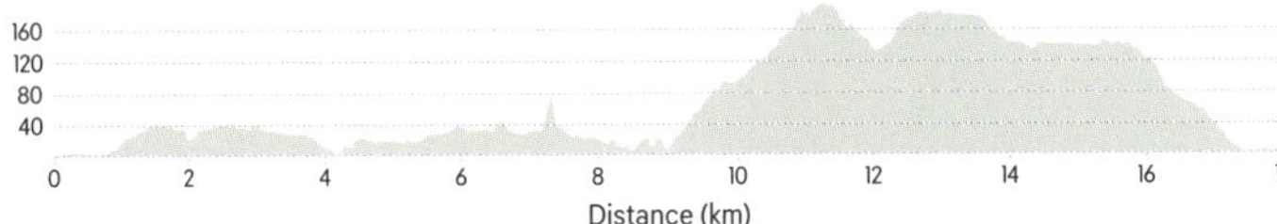

into captivity in 1981. After a successful artificial breeding programme, the *toki* are one of Japan's conservation success stories – and a symbol of Sado – with 400 or so now living here in the wild again.

02 After 4km, you'll reach the Ogi Folk Museum (小木民俗博物館), a former elementary school that now documents Sado's traditional fishing and shipbuilding industries, with exhibits including a restored wooden freight ship that in the 1800s used to haul cargo between Sado and the mainland.

03 A couple of hundred metres down the road comes one of the highlights of the ride: the preserved Shukunegi (宿根木) district. This hamlet of 100 or so creaking wooden houses connected by a maze of cramped alleyways was once home to shipwrights and merchant seamen who prospered during Sado's gold rush. While many houses here are still lived in, several are open as restaurants and museums. To get a sense of the wealth that gold brought to Sado, check out the lacquered wooden interiors and open hearth of the Seikurou's Residence, which was built by a ship's captain. It's also well worth stopping by the Triangle House – named because of the way it's squished into an alley corner – to learn about its most recent resident, Asa-san, who was doing the Shukunegi paper round well into her 90s.

Island Theatre

Among Sado's exiles, you could argue that actor and playwright Zeami left the greatest mark. Banished in 1434 after falling out of favour with the emperor, it was Zeami who brought a then-new form of theatre called *nō* to the island – a dance-drama performed by masked actors. Remarkably, almost a third of Japan's *nō* stages are found on Sado today, and between mid-April and mid-October local troupes regularly perform fire-lit outdoor shows. You can find out more at any of the island's tourist information centres or at visitsado.com.

04 Before leaving Shukunegi, you could also head across the road to the small bay for a ride in a *hangiri* (washtub boat). Barely big enough to hold four people, these little tubs made of cedar and bamboo were traditionally used for fishing along the rocky coast – today, you find them at Shukunegi and elsewhere offering short rides for travellers.

05 Back on the bike, cycling another several kilometres on Rte 45 will bring you to the Chōjaga Bridge (長者ヶ橋), where you get a lovely coastal view.

06 After another couple of kilometres, you could then take a very brief detour (you'll see the signs) to see the Sawasakihana Lighthouse (沢崎鼻灯台), a striking white tower set on a grass-covered lava plateau.

07 Continuing on Rte 45, you'll then soon pass a small shrine. Take the first right after this and you'll be on a winding road that in places gets quite steep on the 3.5km pedal to the Sado Island Taiko Centre (たたこう館). The centre is run by the internationally acclaimed Kodo drum ensemble, who as well as organising Sado's world-music festival in August (the Earth Celebration) also teach *taiko* drumming workshops here. These can be done in English, but it's best to call ahead and book, as learning to pound these big drums is a popular Sado experience.

08 From here, arms very possibly still vibrating from banging the *taiko*, it's an easy cycle several more kilometres along the road until it reconnects with Rte 45 on the outskirts of Ogi. Take a left here and you can retrace the first 500m of the ride back to the tourist information centre.

Take a Break

Once you get out of Ogi, refreshments are scarce. Shukunegi is one exception. Tucked away in the hamlet's old houses are several small restaurants. For a splurge, ANAGUCHI-TEI *(anaguchi.com)* does French lunch and dinner courses in laid-back surrounds, while the counter-only TAKOBOSHI cooks up no-frills dishes like curry and rice (albeit with limited opening hours). For lunch, YOSHIKAWA-YA – by the car park with a purple curtain over the door – serves Japanese classics like soba (buckwheat noodles) and *donburi* (dishes served over rice).

CHARLY TRIBALLEAU/AFP VIA GETTY IMAGES

***Taiko* drumming**

The Sadoichi

If this ride whets the appetite for more, check out visitsado.com for other routes. The longest, the Sadoichi, is a 210km loop around the entire island – possible in a very long day, but even better if spread over two or three days. There are also shorter rides, such as the 23km Satoyama Course, which visits rice fields, temples and beaches in the Sawata area, and the 20km Lake Kamo Course, which starts and ends at the main ferry port (Ryōtsu). As well as circling Lake Kamo, this route also stops at hot springs, a shrine, a *nō* stage and a Japanese crested ibis conservation park.

08

Toyama Bay

DURATION	DIFFICULTY	DISTANCE	START/END
2.5hrs	Easy	18km	Himi Station/ Amaharashi Station
TERRAIN	Flat and paved		

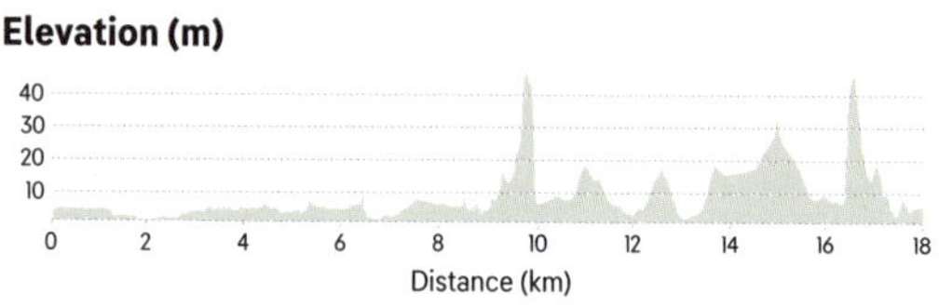

While parts of Japan are feeling the impact of overtourism, areas like Toyama remain almost entirely off most travellers' radars. That's especially true of Toyama Bay on the Japan Sea coast. On this unhurried ride around part of the bay, you'll see the coastal beauty that inspired a legendary haikuist, explore a warren of small-town backstreets, visit local temples and shrines...and see where the creators of Doraemon grew up. You could stop to try some of Japan's best seafood too.

Bike Hire

The tourist information centre at Himi Station rents push bikes for ¥300 per day or three-geared e-bikes for ¥700 per day. Fees include helmets. Bikes can be dropped off at Amaharashi Station at the end of the ride.

Starting Point

Himi Station on the Himi line. If you are staying in Toyama, take the Ainokaze line to Takaoka (20 minutes), then transfer to the Himi line (28 minutes). Amaharashi is also on the Himi line.

01 Go west from Himi Station for three blocks until hitting Rte 415, where you turn right and follow Rte 415 as it passes through Himi's main shopping street.

02 If you are wondering why there are statues of cartoon characters along the covered pavement, that's because one of Japan's most famous manga artists – Fujiko Fujio A (real name Motō Abiko) – was from Himi. These statues are all

Best for

BAY VIEWS

I LOVE PHOTO AND APPLE./GETTY IMAGES

Woman Rock (p68)

characters from the series *Ninja Hattori-kun*, created with longtime manga partner, Takaoka-born Fujiko F Fujio (Hiroshi Fujimoto). Although *Ninja Hattori-kun* might not be well known outside Japan, one of their other characters is: they also created *Doraemon*, one of the highest selling manga series of all time, starring a robotic cat from the 22nd century, who travels back in time to help a boy, Nobita Nobi.

03 You don't have Doraemon's Dokodemo Door (Anywhere Door), so you'll need to keep cycling. After the Fujiko Fujio A Gallery, turn right, go three blocks, then right again. You'll now be heading southeast on Rte 302.

04 On your left here, you'll see Himi Fishing Port (氷見魚港). If you've not eaten, you could pop into the port's fish market – a large, two-storey warehouse on the far side of the water – and grab something at the 2nd-floor seafood restaurant. Exactly what's on the menu will depend on the season and the day's catches, but there'll be options for sashimi set meals and filling seafood *donburi*. Look for the blue banners outside with '魚市場食堂' written on them.

05 Back on Rte 302, continue southeast for a few hundred metres until crossing a small bridge. Just afterwards, move over to the Isaribi Rd that runs alongside the bay. Now you'll be cycling with views of the curved Toyama Bay on your left and small-town Japan on your right. After a couple of kilometres, you'll see Himi Seaside Botanical Garden (氷見市海浜植物園) to your right, although at the time of writing most of this was closed for major renovations.

06 About 500m further along Isaribi Rd, you'll cross another tiny bridge. There are no signs in English here, but turn left immediately after the bridge (into a beachfront car park) and you'll be at the prettiest part of the ride so far: the long and narrow

Take a Break

Should you get the urge to linger on the beach at Shimao, early in the ride, grab refreshments at the BOON. On the sweet side of the menu at this smart, but laid-back cafe are cream-filled doughnuts and decadent Basque cheesecake, while lunch could be a healthy set meal centred on salad and quiche, or perhaps a bowl of ramen. They also have a kid-sized portion of curry. Drinks include espressos, matcha latte and juices. The cafe is closed on Monday and some irregular days.

band of sand that is Shimao Beach (島尾海岸). You could grab a coffee from the Boon cafe, or if travelling with small kids, further along the beach (in trees on your right) there's a well-maintained park with slides and play equipment.

07 From here, follow the bike path southeast for another 2km to a marina. Down the coast, far off in the distance, you'll see a rock formation sticking out of the bay, with the peaks of the Tateyama Mountain Range off behind. This is the Amaharashi Coast (雨晴海岸). Stay on the path for another few hundred metres and you'll see a sign for the Toyama Bay Course cycling route. A right and left here will take you to Amaharashi Station, where the ride ends.

08 For now, cycle past the station. In a couple of hundred metres, you'll see a long white building: Amaharashi Michi-no-Eki (雨晴道の駅), a roadside rest area. Like other *michi-no-eki* around Japan, you can stop here for snacks and drinks from the cafe but also pick up local souvenirs and produce. Here, you can also walk across the road (and over a railway crossing) to a rocky beach where you'll get great views of the tufted rock in the bay. Called Woman Rock (女岩), it inspired wandering poet Matsuo Bashō (1644–94) to write the following haiku when travelling through northern Japan on the journey that would be immortalised in his haiku-punctuated travelogue, *The Narrow Road to the Deep North*: the scent of rice fields/pushing through, to our right/the Ariso sea.

09 If you've had enough cycling, now would be a convenient time to head back to Amaharashi Station, return the bike and take a train back towards Toyama. If not, keep following the road from the *michi-no-eki* (now Rte 415) for 3km to the area around Fushiki Station. There's no bike path on this part of the route, so you'll be on the main road, unless you use the pavement. When you get to an Eneos petrol station, go left and prepare to enter the quiet maze of Fushiki's backstreets. Just under 1km down this road, you'll meet a school crossing with a white sign (in English) pointing right to the Kitamae-bune Museum (北前船資料館). This 19th-century merchant's house justifies a look just for the architecture – its gabled roof, aged tatami rooms and courtyard garden – but it is also dotted with exhibits on Fushiki's time as a thriving port in the Edo era.

10 Continue along the museum's backstreet and keep following it when it bends right. You'll soon be at Shōkō-ji Temple (勝興寺). An Important Cultural Property that's been here since the late 1500s – though it was

TAKASHI IMAGES/SHUTTERSTOCK

Shōkō-ji Temple

More Toyama Rides

This ride touches upon part of the Toyama Bay Cycling Route – one of Japan's six official National Cycling roads – which runs 102km on flat terrain across the full length of the bay, from Himi Town to Asahi Town. With a good road bike, the ride is doable in a day. You can find details of that at cycling-toyama.jp, which also lists rental shops and a bunch of shorter rides, including a 20km, family-friendly trip along the east side of the bay and a 50km journey through countryside close to the foot of the Tateyama Mountain Range.

Bay Bounty

Toyama Bay is one of Japan's richest fishing grounds, home to 500 of the 800 or so species that live in the Japan Sea. Some 200 of them end up at the stalls of local markets such as Himi Fish Market and Shinminato Kitokito Market, located a little further along the coast from Fushiki. Among the most sought-after specialities, you'll find *benizuwaigani* (red snow crab) from September to May and *hotaruika* (firefly squid) between March and June. Or there's *amaebi* (pink shrimp) in winter, which is known for its sweetness and melt-in-the-mouth texture when eaten raw.

CYRUS_2000/SHUTTERSTOCK

Hotaruika (firefly squid)

founded elsewhere in the 1400s – the temple's main hall and secondary buildings were recently given an extensive renovation, but alongside these impressive examples of temple architecture are minor features worth searching out. Seven of these are collectively known as the Seven Wonders of Shōkō-ji: 'the stone that fell from the sky', 'the pond that never dries', 'the fruitless gingko tree', 'the monkey that holds up the roof', 'the pillar that wards off evil', 'the three-leafed pin' and 'the flying dragon inkstone'.

11 Leaving the temple, start heading back the way you came but take the right-hand fork in the road, which leads to Fushiki Station (伏木駅). If you want to explore Fushiki more without getting lost, you can pick up an English map of the area here that will help you find a few craft and sweet shops, historic buildings, and other small temples and shrines.

12 When you are done in Fushiki, you need to return to Rte 415. From the station, that means cycling south, taking the second right (west) for 200m, then turning right (north) on Rte 415. From here you'll be headed back towards Amaharashi, albeit with a potential detour. That comes two blocks after the intersection with the Eneos petrol station you passed earlier, where you'll see an overhead road sign pointed left to Keta Shrine (気多神社): If you make the short, uphill pedal here, you'll find a collection of buildings, *torii* gateways, and stone lanterns spread out among tall cedars.

TOP TIP:

Cash Only

Bring cash. From bike hire to train tickets back to Toyama and cafes to museums, many places on this ride accept cash only. When buying tickets at Amaharashi Station in particular, it helps to have coins or small bills.

13 After this, you just need to return to Rte 415 and follow it a couple of kilometres until you are back at Amaharashi Station, where you can return the rental bike and helmet to the station staff. Just be aware that trains only leave once or twice an hour – if you want to check the timetables in advance, the Japan Transit Planner app (by Jorudan) will tell you the next train time.

Take a Break

In a building that almost resembles a white ocean liner, the AMAHARASHI MICHI-NO-EKI rest stop makes a good mid-ride break. The cafe here serves coffee, soda floats, ice-cream sundaes and pancakes, with some seats overlooking the bay. The souvenir shop sells local crafts such as lacquerware, painted candles and metalware alongside sake and sweet snacks. Don't buy straight away and weigh your bike down – you'll also pass by here again near the very end of the ride.

09

Karuizawa

DURATION	DIFFICULTY	DISTANCE	START/END
1.5hrs	Easy	11km	JR Karuizawa Station
TERRAIN	Flat and paved		

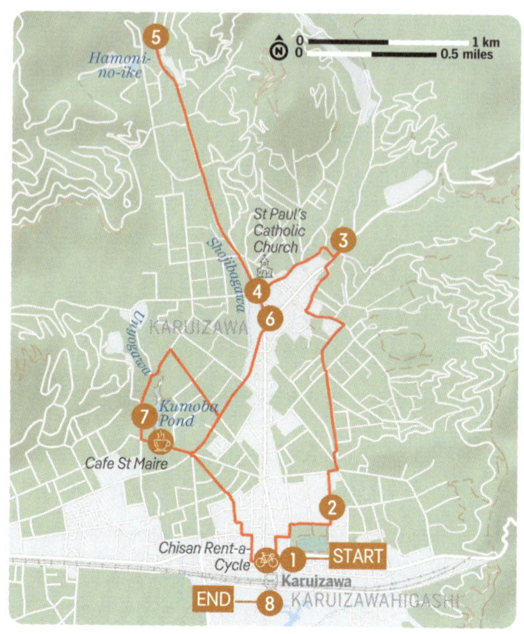

CHENG FENG CHIANG/GETTY IMAGES

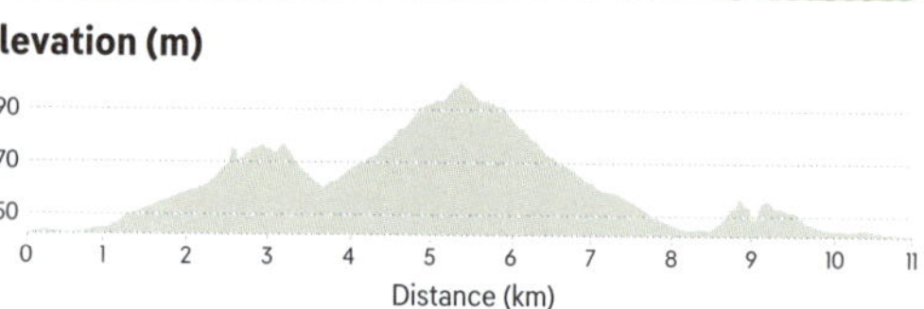

Once a staging post on the Nakasendō road that connected Tokyo and Kyoto in the Edo era (1603–1868), Karuizawa (軽井沢) began to develop an international feel in the 1880s, when foreign missionaries like Alexander Croft Shaw started summering in the area's cooler climes. In the years that followed, Karuizawa built a reputation as a cosmopolitan summer resort for well-heeled Tokyoites and even the Imperial family. A couple of hours on a bike is a great way to take in everything that continues to make this part of Nagano Prefecture a popular retreat.

Bike Hire

You'll find bike rentals by the north exit of Karuizawa Station, including Chisan, which offers simple shopping bikes, three-geared e-bikes and tandems. It's cash only, with rates from ¥600 per hour to ¥3400 per day.

Starting Point

Start on the north side of JR Karuizawa Station, but before setting off stop by the 2nd-floor tourist information office to pick up a cycling map of the area.

01 Once you've sorted your bike rentals by Karuizawa Station, head a block north, turn right at the Patagonia store and follow the broad road a few hundred metres until you pass a pond on your left.

02 After a left turn here, you'll soon arrive at the Musée Andō (安東美術館). Stop to see the 180-piece Tsuguharu Foujita (1886–1968) collection, covering the influential artist's early landscapes, distinctive cat paintings and the milky nudes that made him the darling of Paris in the 1920s.

Kumoba Pond (p74)

Best for

LAID-BACK GETAWAYS

Tag on an Extra Ride

The tourist information booth at Karuizawa Station (2F, north exit) has a handy walking and cycling map in English, with multiple routes in the area. To add a couple of hours to your Karuizawa ride, follow the 14km Minami Karuizawa Course from the south side of the station. The route is mostly flat and on paved roads as it takes in the outlet stores of Prince Shopping Plaza, the seasonal blooms of Karuizawa Lake Garden and the local produce at Karuizawa Hotchi Market. If you rent an e-bike by the station, you should have enough battery to combine the two rides.

03 Next, be ready for a few twists and turns, as you cycle through the wooded shade of Karuizawa's largely residential backstreets. Start by cycling north of the museum for several hundred metres, then turn right at the end of the street, first left, and then next right over the river. Now you can go left (north) and follow the river for about a kilometre. When you reach a T-junction, go left for a couple of hundred metres, passing tennis courts on your right, then turn right and follow the narrow Shaw St a few hundred metres until it joins up with the far end of Kyū-Karuizawa Shopping St. One hundred metres to the right here is to the Shaw Memorial Church (ショー記念礼拝堂), the first church in Karuizawa when it was built by Anglican missionary Alexander Croft Shaw in 1895. Just behind it, you'll also be able to enter a reconstruction of Shaw's modest Western summer home.

04 Backtracking down the street, take the first right onto a road that will curve for 500m, passing St Paul's Catholic Church and then meeting a main road called Mikasa-dōri (三笠通り). Go right here and follow the long row of larches, passing a succession of summer homes tucked into the woods.

05 After 1.5km, you'll reach the historic Mikasa Hotel (旧三笠ホテル). This wooden Western-style building from the early 1900s is open to the public as a beautifully preserved example of the European architecture and interiors – complete with touches like electric chandeliers – that began to appear in Japan in the decades after the country fully reopened to the world. At the time of writing, the hotel was undergoing conservation work, but it is due to fully reopen in late 2025.

06 From the Mikasa Hotel, retrace your route south and then continue another 100m to a crossroads. On the left is the southern end of Kyū-Karuizawa Shopping St (旧軽井沢銀座通り). The street is bike-free, so park up (the free bicycle parking area to your right is well signposted) and then have a stroll. In the Edo era, this street was part of the Nakasendō road and would have been a focal point for merchants passing through the area. Today, Kyū-Karuizawa is better known for artisanal produce and sweet treats, cafes, bakeries, tiny galleries, and an interesting mix of interior and fashion boutiques.

07 Back on your bike, follow the old Nakasendō west on a bending road that will soon come to a small roundabout (a rarity given there are only 80 across Japan), where you can turn right to one of Karuizawa's scenic spots, Kumoba Pond (雲場池). It only takes 15 to 20 minutes to walk around the pond, but it's an

Take a Break

There are plenty of cafes and restaurants along the route, especially on Kyu-Karuizawa Shopping St. But if you want to wait until the ride is almost done, try CAFE ST MAIRE next to Kumoba Pond. You could get a takeaway coffee for a walk around the pond, sit down for a decadent parfait or opt for a ¥2500 lunch course that includes an antipasto plate and choice of three spaghettis: at the time of writing, bacon and mozzarella in tomato sauce, tuna and mushroom in a lemony cream sauce, or a summer vegetable *peperoncino*.

LIU YU SHAN/SHUTTERSTOCK

Kyu-Karuizawa Shopping St

especially pretty stroll when the summer greenery or autumnal foliage is reflecting upon the water.

08 To wrap up the ride, return to the roundabout, go straight across it, and then take a right when you get to the main street that leads south 300m to Karuizawa Station. If you fancy some shopping after returning your bike, you could stop by the Prince Shopping Plaza (プリンスショッピングプラザ) on the other side of the station. Be warned: it can be busy – unlike the ride – but you'll find more than 200 outlet stores for brands such as Bally, Burberry, Disney, Iittala, Lego, L'Occitane and Nike, plus restaurants and cafes.

An Imperial Love Story

When you cycle by the tennis courts opposite the Union Church, you'll pass a spot that played a role in the modern history of Japan. This is where then crown prince Akihito – the future emperor – first met Michiko Shōda in a tennis tournament. As the story goes, the two fell in love, but Michiko was deemed 'too lowly' by some to marry into royalty and was sent to study in Belgium. Akihito would send letters to Michiko via the king of Belgium, who later helped negotiate the pair's engagement. They married in 1959. Now known as the Emperor Emeritus and Empress Emerita, they celebrated their 65th anniversary in 2024.

10

Lake Hamana

DURATION	DIFFICULTY	DISTANCE	START/END
2.5hrs	Easy	23km	Bentenjima Station/Kiga Station

TERRAIN	Flat and paved; some dedicated bike paths

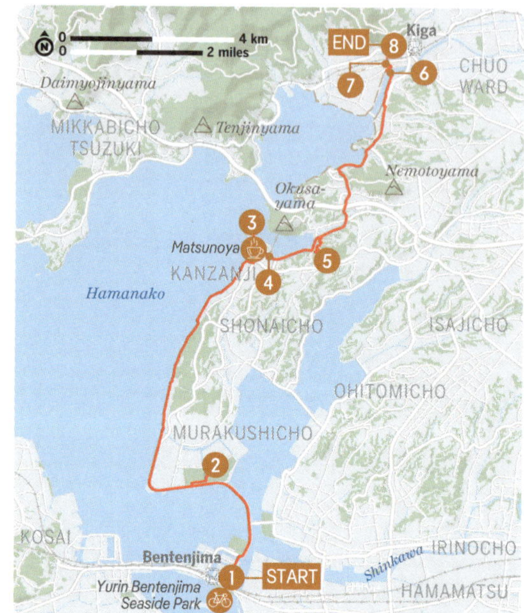

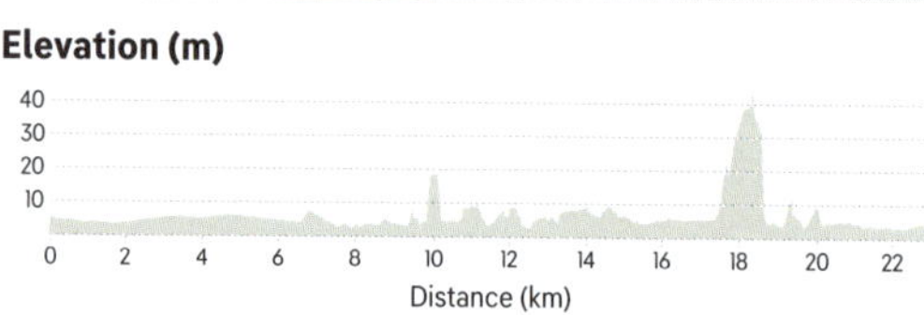

TOP PHOTO CORPORATION/SHUTTERSTOCK

Cycling around Lake Hamana (浜名湖) in Shizuoka Prefecture offers something for everyone. For committed cyclists, the full 67km loop of the brackish lake – known as the Hamaichi – is a popular full-day ride. In this section, we've opted for a shorter, family-friendly excursion on the lake's eastern shore. It's the kind of trip you can do on a shopping bike, and it combines wonderful views of the lake with a historic temple, a retro amusement park, flower gardens, and plenty of other stops in a part of Shizuoka that most non-Japanese travellers overlook.

Bike Hire

Push bikes from Yurin rental station near Bentenjima Station are ¥520 per day plus a ¥1000 deposit. You can return at seven rental stations, including Kiga, but you'll lose the deposit if not returning to Bentenjima.

Starting Point

From Tokyo, take the Tōkaidō Shinkansen's Hikari or Kodama services to Hamamatsu (85 minutes or one hour 50 minutes), then transfer to the local Tōkaidō Main Line to Bentenjima Station (12 minutes).

01 Once you've got your bike, head north from Bentenjima Station (弁天島駅). You'll cross several small bridges – alongside which will be dozens of little fishing boats – before reaching Rte 323, where you need to go right and follow the road (as it then loops left) over a pair of long, low bridges.

02 Shortly after crossing the final bridge, you'll pass Lake Hamana Garden Park (浜名湖ガーデンパーク), home to 56 hectares of seasonal gardens that range from an expanse of sunflowers in summer to tulips in spring. It isn't an essential

Onsen, Lake Hamana

A Bath Break in Kanzanji

In the 1950s, Kanzanji Town discovered and drilled into a natural hot-spring source that now fills a collection of soothing onsen (hot-spring baths). In all, there are a dozen ryokan and resort hotels scattered around town that open their bathhouses to nonguests, some with communal outdoor baths offering lake views. Opening times vary, so if you'd like a post-ride soak, stop by Kanzanji's tourist information centre, in the car park just south of Pal Pal's blue rollercoaster. Staff can give you a map with the baths marked and tell you which are currently open. There's also information on the town's website: hamanako-kanzanji.com.

stop, but for a contrast to this ride's lake scenery, you could add a couple of kilometres to the ride with a loop of the park's bike paths.

03 Next, keep following the lakeside road west. It will soon turn north and connect to a dedicated bike path that runs 7km alongside the lake. You don't have to think about directions here, just follow the path and enjoy the lake views. At the end of the bike path, you'll see a blue sign in Japanese saying 'Kanzanji 0.5km'. Follow it through a narrow residential street, then go left onto the main road at the other end and you'll soon be at Kanzan-ji temple (舘山寺), said to have been first built in 810 by the legendary monk Kōbō Daishi. Leave your bike in the car park to the right of Kanzan-ji's gateway, then give yourself 30 minutes to stroll the temple grounds. The main hall is quite modest, but there's a tall statue of the goddess of mercy and an observation deck with sweeping lake views. Almost hidden on one stretch of trail, you'll also find a candlelit cave called Ana Daishi, in the gloom of which Kōbō Daishi supposedly spent 37 days meditating and carving statues. Nowadays, people come to the cave to pray for help with eye ailments.

04 From the temple, cycle back down the main street, then take a left onto Rte 320 (it's well signposted). You'll pass a Family Mart before getting to the Pal Pal amusement park (浜名湖パルパル) – home to the Ferris wheel you would have seen in the distance earlier in the ride, as well as go-karts, an adventure castle, a couple of small roller-coasters, and other rides aimed at families. Next to Pal Pal, you could also take a ropeway up 113m to Mt Okusa for more lake views or hop aboard a boat for a short sightseeing cruise. If at this point you don't have the urge to keep cycling, you could return the bike to the tourist information centre in the car park south of Pal Pal and then catch one of the twice-hourly buses to Hamamatsu (45 minutes) for the shinkansen. Before getting the bus, staff at the information centre could also point you to one of the day-use hot springs in town.

05 If you want to keep going to Kiga (another 8km), cycle east along Rte 320. You'll soon pass Hamamatsu Flower Park (はままつフラワーパーク), where you could stop to take in a collection of pretty gardens and a small zoo.

06 After that, pedal north on Rte 320, which will wind inland for a couple of kilometres before rejoining the lakeshore near a small temple called Juraku-ji. For the next 3km, you'll be mostly on a dedicated bike path alongside Rte 320, tracing the shoreline until reaching the bike-only Miotsukushi Bridge.

PATCHIYA WASITWORAPOL/SHUTTERSTOCK

Hamamatsu Flower Park

Take a Break

One thing you might notice travelling around Japan is how most areas have a signature food. Around Lake Hamana, it's *unagi* (freshwater eel). The lake has been Japan's largest producer of it for 100 years, and you'll find numerous *unagi* restaurants on the street leading to Kanzan-ji temple. That includes MATSUNOYA (松の家), where like elsewhere around the lake, the eel is covered in a sweetened soy-based sauce and then char-grilled, before being placed atop a bowl of rice. To help with ordering, they have a picture menu.

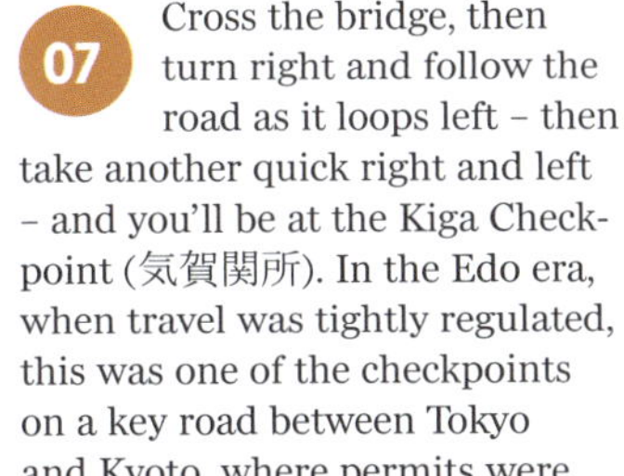

07 Cross the bridge, then turn right and follow the road as it loops left – then take another quick right and left – and you'll be at the Kiga Checkpoint (気賀関所). In the Edo era, when travel was tightly regulated, this was one of the checkpoints on a key road between Tokyo and Kyoto, where permits were scrutinised and taxes collected. Now it's a small history museum, with mannequins of Edo merchants and shogunate officials.

08 A couple of blocks east, return the bike at Kiga Station (気賀駅). Trains go to Hamamatsu via Nishi Kajima Station in around an hour.

More About Rentals

While you can return the push bikes from Bentenjima at Kiga and elsewhere around the lake, they also rent out e-bikes (¥2500 for four hours) that can be returned to Bentenjima only. If you'd prefer one of these, you can still follow this ride to Kanzanji, but from there return to Bentenjima without retracing the lakeside route: instead, take Rte 323 south (inland) for 5km, then turn left onto Rte 319, which will cut through the quiet residential district of Murakushicho and back to Rte 323 near Lake Hamana Garden Park.

Also Try...

Hokuriku Railway tunnel, Kubiki Cycling Road

TAKASHI ISOBE/GETTY IMAGES

Kubiki Cycling Road, Niigata

DURATION	DIFFICULTY	DISTANCE
3.5hrs	Easy	32km

Starting at Itoigawa (two shinkansen stops east of Toyama) and ending in Jōetsu, the coastal Kubiki Cycling Road is an easy half-day ride that passes through small fishing communities, takes in local temples and shrines, and follows the tracks of the abandoned Hokuriku Railway – dark tunnels and all. The route is well paved and there are several cycling stations where you can borrow a pump or make repairs. If you aren't travelling with your own bike, the drawback is that rentals are only available at the Itoigawa end of the trail, so you'll need to do a lot of backtracking. Given how cold and wind-swept this part of Niigata Prefecture's coast gets in winter, rentals are also seasonal from spring to autumn. Find out more at discover-itoigawa.com.

Noto Satohama Route, Ishikawa

DURATION	DIFFICULTY	DISTANCE
3hrs	Easy	34km

The largely rural Noto Peninsula in Ishikawa Prefecture was rocked by a major earthquake on 1 January 2024 that left a trail of damage in its wake. With things returning to normal, now is a great time to support the local economy by visiting. For serious cyclists, Noto has a 373km course that covers the entire peninsula, but you could also opt for a far easier 34km coastal ride between Uchinada and Hakui. Called the Noto Satohama Route, this mostly flat journey includes an 8km section on a sandy beach, plus the option to add a hilly 10km detour and cycle up 573m Mt Hōdatsu – a quad-busting addition that delivers sweeping views across the peninsula.

TWENTY47STUDIO/GETTY IMAGES

Lake Suwa, Nagano

Hida Satoyama, Gifu

DURATION	DIFFICULTY	DISTANCE
2.5hrs	Easy	22km

Cycling around Hida (飛騨) in the Gifu countryside – within easy reach of the popular sightseeing spots and hotels of Takayama – is a great way to get off the beaten path and connect with rural Japan. Here you can pedal through swathes of rice paddies, check out the local shrine and the town's historic architecture, and do a spot of shopping at the farmers market. The area gets snowy in winter, so this ride is only possible from late March to November. If you want to do it with a local guide who can help you chat with locals and tell you about rural life, Satoyama Experience offers half-day group and private tours with bike rental included.

Nakasendō Road, Nagano

DURATION	DIFFICULTY	DISTANCE
6hrs	Difficult	54km

In the Edo era, the Nakasendō was the key inland road connecting Kyoto and Edo (Tokyo), weaving a route through a succession of post towns where weary travellers could rest on the long walk. While you can easily visit beautifully preserved post towns like neighbouring Magome and Tsumago on the Gifu–Nagano border, this ride between Iwamurata and Lake Suwa focuses on the challenging 1000m climb through Nagano's Wada Pass. Along the way, it also visits a traditional garden, historic teahouse, sake brewery and remnants of old post towns. For more information, Gifu and Nagano tourist boards have a booklet with multiple Nakasendō routes that can be downloaded at visitgifu.com.

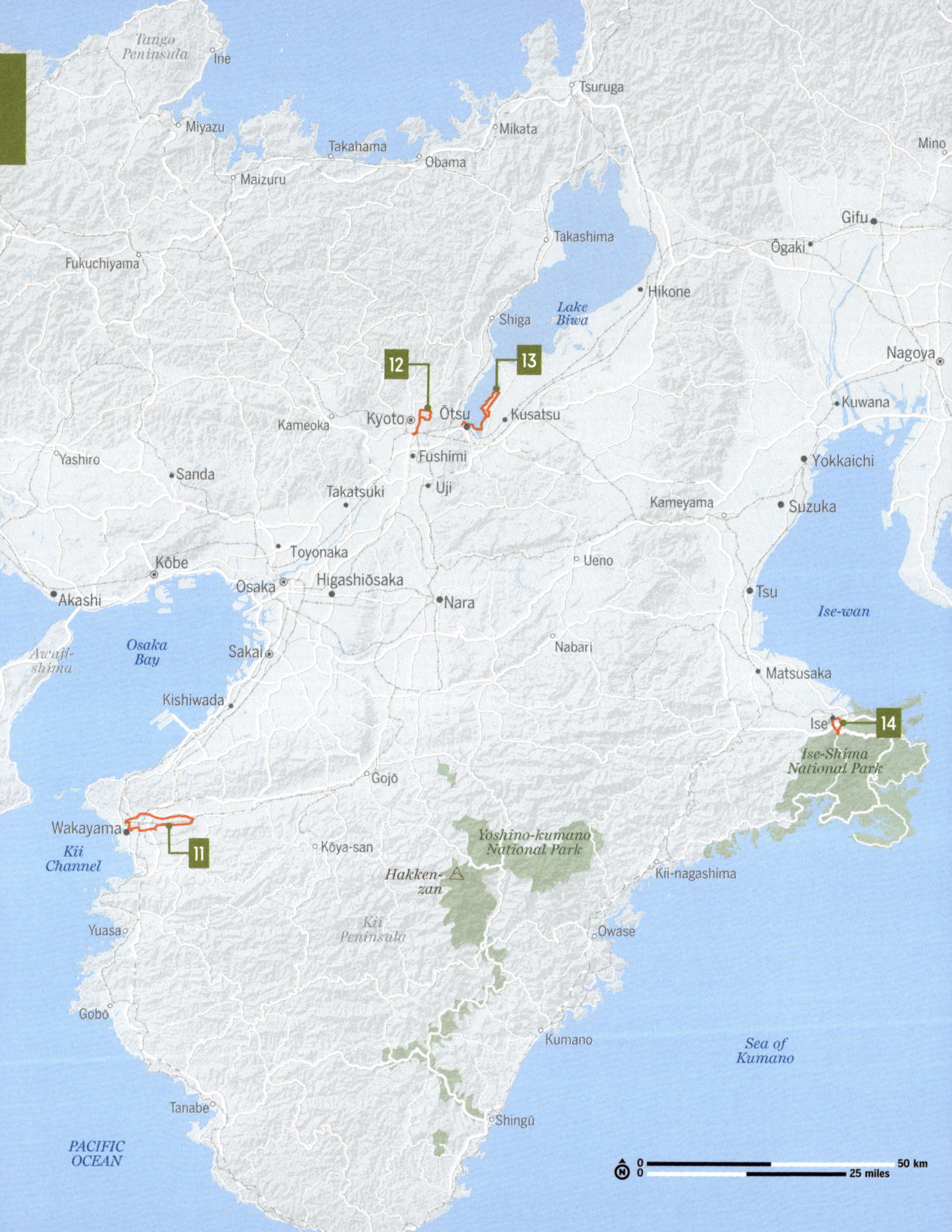
Tango Peninsula
Ine
Tsuruga
Miyazu
Mikata
Takahama
Obama
Mino
Maizuru
Gifu
Takashima
Ōgaki
Fukuchiyama
Hikone
Lake Biwa
Shiga
Nagoya
12
13
Kuwana
Kyoto
Ōtsu
Kusatsu
Kameoka
Yashiro
Fushimi
Yokkaichi
Sanda
Uji
Takatsuki
Kameyama
Suzuka
Toyonaka
Ueno
Kōbe
Osaka
Higashiōsaka
Tsu
Akashi
Nara
Ise-wan
Awaji-shima
Osaka Bay
Sakai
Nabari
Matsusaka
Kishiwada
Ise
14
Ise-Shima National Park
Gojō
Wakayama
Yoshino-kumano National Park
Kii Channel
11
Kōya-san
Hakken-zan
Kii-nagashima
Kii Peninsula
Yuasa
Owase
Gobō
Kumano
Sea of Kumano
Tanabe
Shingū
PACIFIC OCEAN
0
50 km
0
25 miles
N

WENILIOU/SHUTTERSTOCK

Kamo-gawa, Kyoto (p90)

Kansai

11 Wakayama & the Kinokawa

Get a brief taste of the Wakayama 800km cycling route on a ride that visits Wakayama's imposing castle before following a meandering riverside bike path. **p86**

12 Kyoto Without the Crowds

Enjoy a different view of central Kyoto, with a ride along the quiet banks of the Kamo-gawa, en route to a spot of temple-hopping in northern Higashiyama. **p90**

13 Lake Biwa

From the quad-busting 200km Biwaichi route to multiple half-day outings, Lake Biwa offers something for all levels of cyclist. **p96**

14 Ise

Head to the far south of Kansai for a cycle to the serene inner and outer precincts of Japan's most sacred shrine, Ise-jingū. **p100**

Explore

Kansai

Comprised of seven prefectures in the southern-central part of Japan's main island, Honshū, Kansai is as varied as it is large. On the one hand, the region is home to Japan's vibrant second city, Osaka, while nearby are the historic sights of two former capitals – Kyoto and Nara. Away from those hugely popular destinations, you'll also find scenic rides around Lake Biwa and on the island of Awajishima, not to mention rides that take in historic sites like the grand shrine of Ise-jingū in Mie Prefecture. This chapter is just the tip of the iceberg for an area of Japan that you could spend weeks exploring.

Kyoto

Japan's former capital, Kyoto (京都), is one of the country's most popular destinations, its World Heritage temples and shrines (and other historic attractions) drawing 75 million visitors annually. With that, the city has every type of accommodation covered, from ¥100,000-per-night traditional inns to the most basic of youth hostels. Yes, Kyoto is suffering from overtourism, but exploring the city by bike is a great way to beat the crowds; pedalling between sights you'll see an entirely different Kyoto to travellers who squeeze onto the overburdened bus network. As well as being home to rides of its own, Kyoto also makes a good base for lots of the rides in this chapter – Lake Biwa, Wakayama and Ise are all within day-trip distance by train.

Osaka

We don't have any Osaka (大阪) rides listed in this chapter, but that doesn't mean Japan's second city isn't a good place to stay. Like Kyoto, the city has weeks' worth of things to see and do when not riding, a multitude of accommodation options, great nightlife and dining, and is a major transport hub for the Kansai region: by train you could be in Kyoto in as little as 25 minutes (without splurging on the bullet train), and reach many of this chapter's main rides and 'Also Try' rides within an hour or two.

Wakayama

In the south of Kansai, Wakayama is home to plenty of potential rides, including the long-distance Wakayama 800

WHEN TO GO

With comfortable cycling temperatures and plenty of sunny days, spring and autumn are the best times for pedalling around Kansai. In winter, it is typically dry and cold, but rides are still possible in most areas. If you can, avoid summer – the heat and suffocating humidity make being outdoors for extended periods dangerous.

and a bunch of far easier routes in Wakayama City. Around Wakayama Station are many places to stay and enjoy a night out, and from there you could take the express train down the coast for the hot springs and white sandy beach of Shirahama. If you wanted to linger longer, public transport could also take you (albeit slowly) inland to the ancient Kumano Kodō pilgrimage trails and the temples of sacred Kōya-san.

Lake Biwa

While Lake Biwa is an easy side trip from Kyoto, you could also base yourself there. Located on the bullet-train route between Kyoto and Tokyo, one option is Maibara on the eastern shore. Or for the lake's southern loop, there's Ōtsu. Both have a selection of business hotels near their respective stations, and tourist information centres with bike rentals.

TRANSPORT

Kyoto, Osaka (Shin Osaka) and Maibara are served by shinkansen (bullet train) routes, and all other locations in this chapter can be reached by rail. If visiting multiple parts of Kansai, it's worth getting JR West's Kansai Wide Area Pass. It gives five consecutive days of travel on bullet trains, express trains and other transportation within the region for ¥12,000. That includes all the main areas in this chapter.

WHAT'S ON

Aoi Matsuri

Held on 15 May, this parade featuring hundreds of people in Heian-era (794–1185) dress is one of Kyoto's 'big three' festivals, along with the Gion Matsuri in July and Jidai Matsuri in October.

Ōtsu Matsuri

In early October, large, decorated floats are paraded around Ōtsu on the southern shores of Lake Biwa.

Ise-jingū Fireworks Festival

Ise-jingū's annual fireworks display In mid-July sees 7000 rockets lighting up the night sky.

Resources

Biwaichi *(en.biwako1.jp)* Route maps, rental information and everything else you need to plan a ride around Lake Biwa.

Kyoto Bicycle *(kyoto-bicycle.com/en)* The city's official cycling guide covers road rules, rental shops and sightseeing information.

Ise Tourism *(en.ise-kanko.jp)* Ise's official website has details on bike rentals, routes and the town's main attractions.

WHERE TO STAY

In Kyoto and Osaka, you could choose anything from five-star international brands to traditional ryokan (Japanese inns) or budget hostels. Outside of the biggest cities – in places like Maibara and Ōtsu around Lake Biwa – you'll find business hotels near the main stations, and *minshuku* (family-run guesthouses) and ryokan away from the main hubs. With Kyoto in particular, expect big premiums when the cherry blossoms are in full bloom in April and when the leaves turn a fiery red in autumn. The same applies to major holidays such as Golden Week (29 April to 5 May). For these periods, book many months in advance.

11

Best for

RIVERSIDE CYCLING

Wakayama & the Kinokawa

DURATION	DIFFICULTY	DISTANCE	START/END
3.5hrs	Easy	35km	Wakayama Station

TERRAIN	Flat and paved; some dedicated bike paths

SEANPAVONEPHOTO/GETTY IMAGES

Wakayama Castle

You'll find a host of reasons to head to Wakayama in southern Kansai, from the Kumano Kodō pilgrimage trails to the temples of sacred Kōya-san and the ancient Kumano Sanzan shrines. To add to that, the prefecture is also an emerging cycling destination, home to the Wakayama 800 (km) route. This ride gives a brief taster of the Wakayama 800, on a journey that takes in Wakayama Castle, traces the peaceful Kinokawa River and then visits a few unheralded sights in the outskirts of Wakayama City.

Bike Hire

The tourist information centre, in the basement on the west side of Wakayama Station (Central Exit), rents push bikes and power-assisted bikes from ¥600 to ¥1100 a day.

Starting Point

Wakayama Station. From Osaka Station, the Kuroshio Express gets to Wakayama in an hour. A few Kuroshio also connect to Kyoto, although there are plenty of other options for the Kyoto–Osaka route.

01 From Wakayama Station (和歌山駅), follow the broad main road (Rte 17) west, either on the road's bike lane or the bike path on the pavement. After 1.5km, you'll see the towering white keep of Wakayama Castle (和歌山城) appearing on your left, like you've stumbled onto the set of *Shōgun*.

02 You can't park on this side of the castle, so instead turn left and follow the moat south, then turn right and cycle along the castle's south side (Rte 138), where there's a parking area. The three-tiered castle itself is a faithful 1950s

Elevation (m)

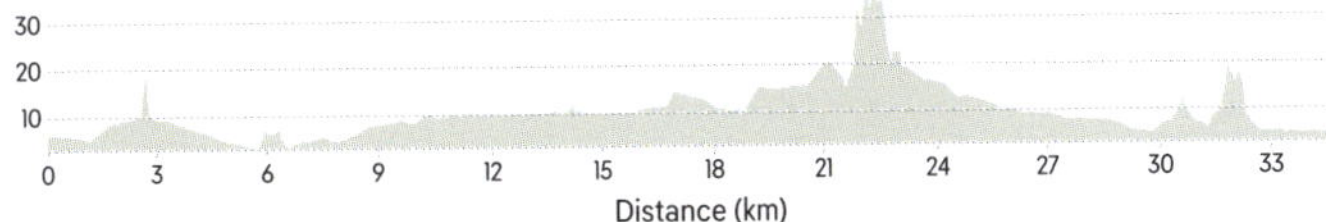

rebuild of the 16th-century original and across the sprawling grounds you'll also find a teahouse serving green tea and sweets, a history museum, and a traditional garden known for its red foliage in autumn.

03 Next, keep riding along the castle's south side, where on the opposite side of the road you'll see the Museum of Modern Art (和歌山県立近代美術館). At the time of research, the museum was closed for renovations, but if it's open when you are visiting, the 10,000-piece collection includes Wakayama-born artists and also some Picasso and Rothko works.

04 Just ahead is an intersection, where you turn right, cycle by the castle's west side and continue for 1.5km – passing Wakayamashi Station – until you reach the Kitajima Bridge (北島橋). Bikes can't take the main road up on to the bridge, but there's a lane to the left leading to the bridge's footpath and your first views of the wide Kino River.

05 On the other side of the bridge, take the first left and follow the road 400m until you reach a slope down to the riverside. Now you are on the Kinokawa Cycling Road (紀の川サイクリングロード), where you'll be cycling for the next 15km. Other than the occasional sports pitch and the bridges you'll pass under, there are no outstanding points of interest. This section is all about having a ride and getting some fresh air along the river.

The Wakayama 800

At 800km, the Wakayama 800 is a beast of a ride. Covering Wakayama Prefecture's coastline and heading inland for sights like Kōya-san (home of Shingon Buddhism), it includes everything from challenging hill climbs to relaxing seaside paths. The good news is that there is an official website *(wakayama800.jp)*, which breaks it down into dozens of manageable shorter sections. The not so good news...the website is currently in Japanese only, apart from an automated translation feature that produces some curious results.

06 After 15km – or 10 bridges, if you fancy counting – leave the cycling path and cross the Iwade Bridge (岩出橋). There's a jumble of roads on the other side but just go straight through the busy intersection and you'll then be following Rte 9. You'll be on the road here, so keep well left and ride single file. After several hundred metres, Rte 9 will calm down as it passes through rice paddies and low-rise clusters of urbanity. In most places you'll have lined-off space to ride on directly next to the road, and then pavement as the fields gradually give way to the scruffy outskirts of central Wakayama.

07 In 7km, when you see an overhead sign pointed left for Akizuki on Rte 144, follow it for a few potential stops en route to Wakayama Station. The first is Kii-fudoki-no-oka Museum of Archaeology and Folklore (紀伊風土記の丘), a few hundred metres off the main road (it's signposted in English), where you can see 5th- to 7th-century burial mounds and rebuilt pit dwellings, and visit a museum of related relics.

08 Another 1.5km further on, you can then stop at Hanayama Onsen Yakushi no Yu (花山温泉-薬師の湯), a traditional ryokan with onsen (hot-spring baths) open to nonguests; it's the white and green building immediately after passing under an expressway bridge. Unlike typical hot-spring baths, the piping-hot waters here are a cloudy reddish-brown and the bath itself looks almost coated in clay because of all the minerals in the water.

09 For the final stop, take the single lane across from Hanayama, and follow it as it winds 1km through quiet residential streets to the adjoining Hinokuma-jingū and Kunikakasu-jingū shrines. Set among trees, these understated shrines don't have the glitz of Kyoto's World Heritage Sites but instead offer a tranquil, everyday view of a local Japanese shrine. They are historic too, having been documented as far back as the 8th-century *Nihon Shoki* chronicles.

10 From the shrine, keep following the road west. After crossing two sets of rail tracks, turn right. Wakayama Station is a few hundred metres to the north.

Take a Break

With much of this ride on the riverbank, you won't find many great restaurants along the route – at least, not outside of central Wakayama. Instead, pack a lunch for the river. The basement floor of KINTETSU DEPARTMENT STORE next to Wakayama Station has bakeries, *bentō* shops and SEIJO ISHII sells ready-made meals. If you'd rather sit down in a restaurant, look out for a ramen joint. Most cook up the local variation of Japan's favourite noodle, Wakayama ramen, which features a soy- and bone-based stock and thinner-than-usual noodles.

Wakayama City and the Kino River

The Waka-matsuri

Warm and sunny, May is a lovely time of year for cycling in Wakayama. If you do come then, the second Sunday of the month is when one of the area's most vibrant festivals takes place. Called the Waka-matsuri, it's held at Kishū Tōshō-gū shrine, a few kilometres south of Wakayama Castle, and features traditional dancing, *taiko* drumming and mock sword fights. The highlight of proceedings sees dozens of locals in white robes barrelling down the shrine's 108 stone steps with a large portable shrine on their backs, before heading off on a parade around the coastal Wakaura area.

12

Kyoto Without the Crowds

DURATION	DIFFICULTY	DISTANCE	START/END
2hrs	Easy	18km	Kyoto Station

TERRAIN	Flat and paved

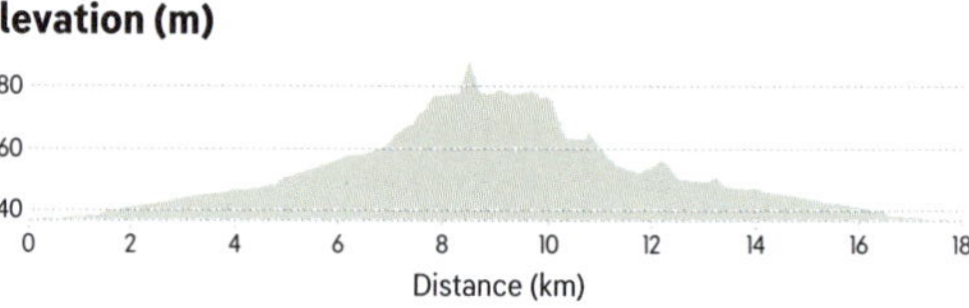

From World Heritage temples to exquisite gardens, Kyoto is peppered with remnants from almost 1000 years as Japan's capital. While that has made Kyoto one of the busiest destinations in Japan, it's still possible to escape the crowds. Exploring by bike is a great way to do it. On this ride, you'll start with a peaceful pedal along the Kamo-gawa, then hop between temples, shrines and museums in northern Higashiyama – all without adding to the growing burden on the city's trains and buses.

Bike Hire

Kyoto Eco Trip, just south of Kyoto Station, has 11 types of bikes for rental and accepts online reservations *(kyoto-option.com)*. It also has a detailed English-language cycling map of Kyoto.

Starting Point

The south side of Kyoto Station. On the Tōkaidō Shinkansen's Nozomi service, Kyoto Station is two hours and 10 minutes from Tokyo and 23 minutes from Shin Osaka.

01 The first few minutes of this ride are about navigating the concrete sprawl around Kyoto Station (京都駅) and getting to the Kamo-gawa. From the bike rental just south of the station, follow the street east for five blocks, when you should come to a busy road (Rte 27) and see the Almont Hotel on your left. Cross the road, head left (north) under the underpass, then take a right at the *kōban* (police box). You are now going east on Shiokoji-dōri, which has a clearly marked bike lane. In 300m, you'll reach the Kamo-gawa (鴨川).

MISTERVLAD/SHUTTERSTOCK

Best for

WORLD HERITAGE

Heian-jingū (p95)

02 Cross the bridge and go left to the slope that leads down to the river. Now you can start heading north along the riverside path. As you pedal north, you'll pass through some of the busiest parts of Kyoto, but down on the riverbank, next to the ducks bobbing on the gently flowing water, you'd barely know it. Sometimes you'll see crowds on the bridges above, but the Kamo itself is a place for cyclists, joggers, picnics and sedate strolls. It offers up calm and a completely different perspective on Kyoto. After 6km of peace and quiet, you'll pass under a bridge where the river forks into two. This is where you'll leave the river and head into the northern Higashiyama area for a collection of temples, shrines and museums. To do that, head up the slope after the bridge, then go back to the road (Imadegawa-dōri) that crosses that bridge. Follow this road east, making sure to stick closely to the bike lane. Admittedly, passing through this section of Kyoto isn't the most exciting part of the ride – the road is busy, the buildings grey and bland – but you'll only be on it for 2km. And you will be seeing a normal part of the city, warts and all, that often doesn't get highlighted in travel brochures.

03 As you approach the end of Imadegawa-dōri, you'll see wooded hills in the distance. Then you'll reach the pedestrian approach to Ginkaku-ji (銀閣寺). You can park in the Ginkaku-ji car park using a ¥200 one-day parking pass – it's 100m down the road to your right. As for the temple, it was initially built as a shogun's retirement villa in 1482 but then converted into a Zen temple upon the shogun's death. It features several standout features, the first of which you'll see being a Zen garden called the Ginshadan, comprised of a raked sea of silver sand upon which sits a 2m mountain of sand known as the Kōgetsu-dai (moon-viewing mound). Then there are pathways that lead to a hillside viewpoint over the northern Higashiyama district, before

Take a Break

The area around Nanzen-ji is known for its tofu restaurants; specifically, *yudōfu* (simmered tofu). At JUNSEI *(to-fu.co.jp/en)*, on the road leading west from the Sanmon Gate, lunch is an affordable way to try a *yudōfu*-centred meal that also features other tofu variations, pickles, rice and a light portion of tempura. It's set in an Edo-era building with views of a traditional garden. Courses start at ¥3600. While lunch reservations aren't essential, you can book online in English.

visiting a mossy garden and finally the main attraction, the two-storey Silver Pavilion (although there's no silver on it), which casts a reflection onto the pond before it.

04 On the way to Ginkaku-ji, you should have seen signs pointing to the Philosopher's Path (哲学の道). When you are finished at the temple, go grab your bike and push it through the pedestrian zone to the start of that path. This 2km canal-side route is engulfed by pink cherry blossoms in spring, but at any time of year it's a mellow place to hop between cafes and small craft shops. You can cycle alongside the pathway, although if it's busy it's best to push (or skip it altogether for the road that runs parallel a block over).

05 At the end of the Philosopher's Path, take a right, then left, and you'll be at Eikan-dō (永観堂), one of the finest *kōyō* (autumn foliage) sites in Kyoto when the maples repaint its grounds a fiery red in November. If you pop in, make sure to visit the Shaka-dō Hall, a lovely old building that creaks underfoot. Arranged around an inner courtyard, it has a collection of tatami-mat rooms exhibiting screen-door paintings.

06 Keep going south from Eikan-dō and in several hundred metres you'll be at the Sanmon, the towering, roofed gateway to Nanzen-ji (南禅寺). There's bike parking next to it. Like Ginkaku-ji, Nanzen-ji started out as a shogun's retirement villa, but then morphed into a Zen complex with numerous sub temples. Also like Ginkaku-ji, it's now one of the 17 sites that make up Kyoto's UNESCO World Heritage listing. You could spend hours exploring all the sub temples here, but if you want a quick visit, walk east of the Sanmon to the former abbot's residence, the Hōjo, for its screen-door paintings and landscaped rock gardens. The main garden is a *karesansui* (dry landscaped garden) dating from the early 1600s that employs a bed of raked gravel and rock formations to represent a tigress and her cubs crossing a river. Inside, you'll also find a varied collection of 17th-century paintings on gold-leaf backdrops – from images of cherry blossoms to stylised tigers prowling through a bamboo grove and scenes capturing daily moments of the upper classes.

07 Next, cycle west from the Sanmon for 400m, head over the small bridge and take Niōmon-dōri (on your right) west. You'll have part of a canal and Kyoto Zoo on your right and up ahead you should soon see the 24m-high *torii* gateway of Heian-jingū. This is Okazaki Park (岡崎公園) and it's full of things to do. As

LEOCHEN66/SHUTTERSTOCK

Nanzen-ji

Bike Rules

Japan has bike rules, but Kyoto has more. The city is especially strict when it comes to parking, which is only allowed in designated zones. Any bike left in the wrong place (including in car-only car parks) can be towed, and you'll need to take a trip to the depot and pay a ¥3500 fine to get your bike back. Cycling on pavements is prohibited unless you see a circular blue sign with the image of a bicycle alongside a man walking with a child. For more rules and etiquette, check out kyoto-bicycle.com/en.

ALAN DREHER/SHUTTERSTOCK

The Silver Mystery

Curiously, Ginkaku-ji, aka the Temple of the Silver Pavilion, is entirely devoid of silver. Nobody is sure why, but there are theories. A strong possibility is that the Silver Pavilion was originally coated in a kind of black lacquer – now long since worn off – that could have lent the building a silvery shimmer in the right light. Another is that the project ran out of money before any silver could be added. Or it could be a nod to Kinkaku-ji (the Temple of the Golden Pavilion) on the other side of Kyoto, which was built for the grandfather of Ginkaku-ji's builder and partially inspired Ginkaku-ji's design.

Ginkaku-ji (p91)

you cycle under the vivid vermillion *torii,* the Kyocera Museum of Art (京セラ美術館) will be on your right and the National Museum of Modern Art, Kyoto (京都国立近代美術館) on your left. The larger Kyocera is always worth a stop for its contemporary exhibitions, which have recently included a collection of Yayoi Kusama prints and a street art retrospective featuring work by Banksy. The NMMA Kyoto is more modest, but still puts on interesting exhibitions, such as a retrospective of early-20th-century Polish art. Nearby is also the Kyoto Museum of Crafts and Design (京都伝統産業ミュージアム), home to a floor of well-curated displays focusing on Kyoto's traditional crafts, from *kyō-yuzen* silk dyeing to *nishijin-ori* woven textiles and *kyō-tsuzura* lacquered boxes.

08 Then there's Heian-jingū (平安神宮), just north of the *torii.* You can park here free of charge, just behind the purification fountain to the left of the entrance. The shrine was built in 1895 to commemorate the 1100th anniversary of Kyoto's establishment as Japan's capital, as a scaled down replica of Kyoto's original Imperial Palace, with vermillion-coloured buildings arranged around a spacious courtyard. To see that is free and only takes a few minutes. If you feel like lingering, for a fee there are also more than 3 hectares of gardens behind the shrine buildings, divided into four sections that each represent a different style of landscaping from Kyoto's past – including areas where weeping cherry blossoms bloom in spring and irises come alive in early summer.

TOP TIP:

Eye on the Sky

The banks of the Kamo-gawa are lovely for a peaceful picnic but watch out for the birds of prey that sometimes hover above the river. They aren't shy about swooping to steal food straight from the hand...and maybe taking a bit of hand with it.

09 From here, head back to the Kamo-gawa. The easiest way to do that is to go west from Heian-jingū until seeing the canal, then follow that west for several hundred metres. At the riverbank, you can take one of the slopes down to the riverside path. Then all you need do is retrace the route to Kyoto Station, 4km away.

Take a Break

Down a side street just south of Kyoto Zoo is the MURIN-AN VILLA (無鄰菴). Built in 1896 as the private residence of prime minister Yamagata Aritomo, it features a traditional Japanese building where you can enjoy tea and sweets with views over a garden that uses the distant Higashiyama mountains as *shakkei* (borrowed scenery). The villa only admits 15 people every hour – you can book a spot online at murin-an.jp/en. There are bicycle parking spaces just inside the main gate.

13

Lake Biwa

BEEBOYS/SHUTTERSTOCK

DURATION	DIFFICULTY	DISTANCE	START/END
3hrs	Easy	32km	Ōtsu Station

TERRAIN	Flat, paved and mostly on dedicated bike lanes

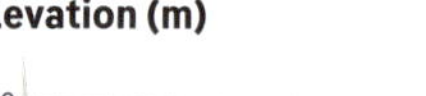

Elevation (m)

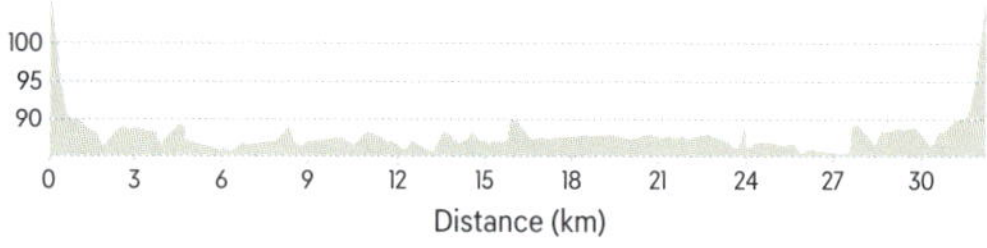

Over the last couple of decades, Lake Biwa (琵琶湖) in Shiga Prefecture has become known for its cycling route, the 200km Biwaichi loop ride. With well-developed cycling infrastructure, including bike lanes and a plethora of rental stores, the lake is incredibly cyclist-friendly. On this ride, you'll get a short taster of the Biwaichi, riding along its southeastern shore and then looping back through farmland – with opportunities en route to stop at a local market, visit the lake's natural history museum or just chill in a lakeside park.

Bike Hire

The tourist information centre at Ōtsu Station rents cross bikes and e-bikes for ¥250 per hour or ¥1800 per day/overnight. They also accept reservations via email. See otsu-guide.jp/cycle_en.php.

Starting Point

Ōtsu Station, 10 minutes from Kyoto Station on the JR Biwa line. From Tokyo, take the Tōkaidō Shinkansen's Hikari service to Maibara (2¼ hours). From there, Ōtsu is 45 minutes on the Biwa line.

One joy of this ride – for the most part – is the simplicity of the journey itself. Begin by heading 800m north from Ōtsu Station, until the road bends right and starts to lead you along the lakeside. As the lake portion of the ride progresses, all you need to do is keep the lake to your left, make sure you are on the bike path (or bike lane on the road initially), and keep pedalling.

After hugging the lakeside for 2.5km, you'll come to a long, low bridge. Cross on the pavement, then you'll see signs pointing

Mizu no Mori Water Botanical Garden (p98)

Best for

LAKE VIEWS

Biwaichi Cycling Navi

Shiga Prefecture's free Biwaichi cycling app is a handy resource to take with you on a ride. While not every model route on the app is currently available in English, the English content includes helpful guides to multiple areas around the lake, and search functions for things such as cafes, restaurants, rentals and wi-fi hotspots. There's also a route-planning function where you can create your own ride. Just take care when checking the app mid-ride. Japan's newly strengthened bicycle laws prohibit the use of phones while riding and now come with penalties of up to six months in prison and a ¥100,000 fine.

left for the main cycling path. Heading north here, you'll soon cross another bridge onto a small island – reclaimed from the lake – called Yabase Kihan (矢橋帰帆島), which has benches and grass to picnic on, plus great lake views. If you don't feel like a stop now, don't worry: over the next several kilometres you'll come across many similar lakeside parks.

03 Roughly 8km on from Yabase Kihan – with the lake remaining close on your left – you'll reach Karasuma Peninsula (烏丸半島), home to several connected sights. It all revolves around the Lake Biwa Museum (琵琶湖博物館), a well-put-together facility that covers the natural history of the lake, with a varied array of exhibits. There are sections devoted to the lake's geological developments and fossil finds; to the species of elephant that roamed here 1.8 million years ago and the crocodiles two million years before that; and to human life around the lake, from the earliest known settlers to current festivals. Next door, consider popping into the museum's aquarium, which showcases the biodiversity of the lake and ongoing conservation work. The only thing to bear in mind is that (like many Japanese museums) it all closes on Mondays.

04 Once you've checked out the museum and aquarium, you could also stop at the neighbouring Mizu no Mori Water Botanical Garden (水生植物公園 みずの森) where the focus is on aquatic plants such as waterlilies and lotuses. In all, you could easily spend an hour or more in the Karasumahan area.

05 If you were to keep heading north here, you could cross the Biwako Bridge and ride down the other side of the lake to complete the 50km southern loop ride. But, given the bike paths are less well-developed on the southwest shore, our ride is going to take a different way back to Ōtsu. For that, take the road (Yubae-dōri) leading east away from Lake Biwa Museum. In 300m, you'll see Roadside Station Kusatsu (道の駅草津) on your left. Like *michi-no-eki* (roadside stations) across Japan, it's fairly no-frills, with a local farm produce shop that also has sweet-toothed souvenirs, plus a couple of places to buy hot drinks, ice cream or simple meals such as udon noodles. Behind it, if you are here from mid-December to early May, there's a strawberry farm called Rock Bay Garden, where you could try some strawberry-picking.

06 Next, you need to take the third right after the *michi-no-eki* onto the sweetly named Melon Rd (メロン街道). This is where the ride

Take a Break

For a boost at the halfway point of the ride, stop by CAFE ROB (カフェロブ) for some extra-fluffy pancakes. You could order them plain or ramp up the calories with toppings of cream, chocolate, banana and caramel. That could be washed down with coffee or Taiwanese bubble tea. And if pancakes aren't your thing, they also have ice-cream sundaes on the menu. You'll find it right next to the Roadside Station Kusatsu and Rock Bay Garden.

BEEBOYS/SHUTTERSTOCK

Shirahige-jinja's 'floating' *torii* gate on the Biwaichi

replaces lake with farmland, and you get to take in a view of Japan many visitors miss, as you head southwest on a quiet route through a sea of rice paddies and greenhouses. After about 4km of arrow-straight cycling, the road will turn left and (soon after) right – just ignore the side streets and keep going until you reach a small river. Here, turn right (west) and you'll be heading back to the lake, where you can rejoin the bike path you were on earlier.

07 All you need do from here is cycle south, on the same route you previously followed north. In 10km, you'll be back at Ōtsu Station.

The Biwaichi

At 200km, the full loop ride of Lake Biwa – the Biwaichi – is on many Japanese riders' bucket lists. It's a great ride, largely on dedicated bike lanes, that offers plenty of reasons to stop or take a detour en route: to Hikone Castle and the 'floating' *torii* gate of Shirahige-jinja to name just a couple of spots. To plan the full loop, visit the official Biwaichi website (en.biwako1.jp) for information on bike rentals – overnight is possible – bike-friendly accommodation, route maps and road rules. Give yourself at least two days, but ideally three.

14

Ise

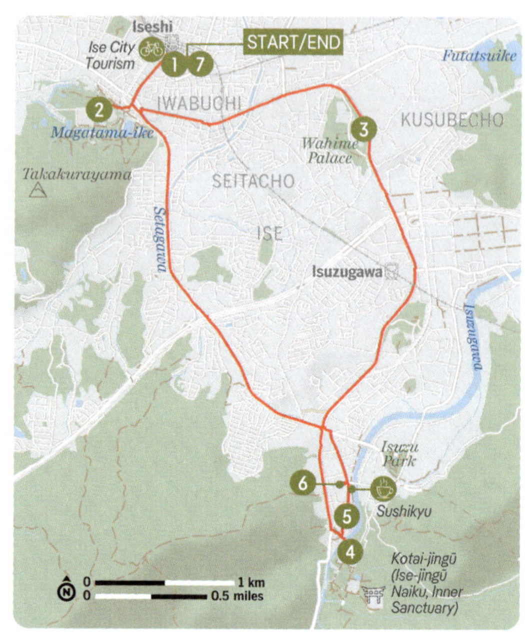

DURATION	DIFFICULTY	DISTANCE	START/END
1hr	Easy	10km	Iseshi Station

TERRAIN | Paved, but with no dedicated cycling path

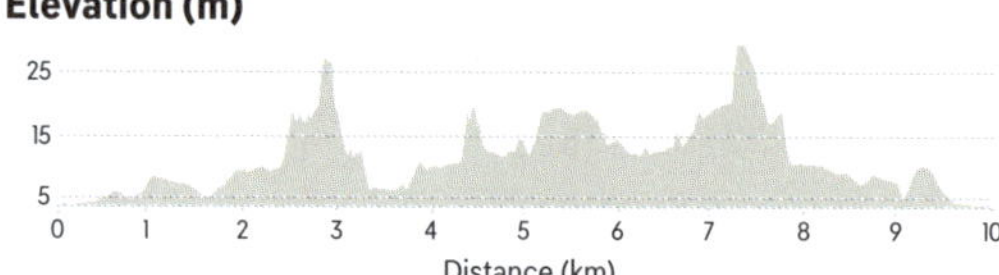

The grand shrine of Ise-jingū is the most important Shintō site in Japan, said to have been in existence since at least the third century. Its inner shrine (Naikū) and outer shrine (Gekū), set several kilometres apart in the small city of Ise, are remarkable for the hushed calm of their vast wooded surrounds and the craftsmanship of the buildings, which incredibly are fully rebuilt every 20 years. This ride visits both, in the process taking in several history and art museums that offer a deeper perspective on Japanese spirituality.

Bike Hire

Ise City Tourism runs several rental spots, including one next to Iseshi Station, with push bikes and e-bikes available from ¥800 for four hours and ¥1500 for four hours, respectively.

Starting Point

Iseshi Station. You can get here on Kintetsu express trains from Nagoya in 80 minutes. From Kyoto, take a Kintetsu express train two hours to Uji Yamada Station, also in Ise, a 10-minute walk from Iseshi Station.

01 From Iseshi Station (伊勢市駅), take the road south for 500m and you'll already be at the first stop, Ise-jingū's outer shrine, the Gekū (外宮). You can't take your bike over the bridge into the shrine, but there is parking off to the right.

02 Once across that bridge, the Gekū is a calming sanctuary that, while more modest than the inner shrine later in the ride, is nonetheless well worth a stroll: for the calm surroundings, the minimalist architecture of its thatched buildings, and the Sengūkan Museum, which does an excellent job of

SEREE TANSRISAWAI/SHUTTERSTOCK

Naikū (inner shrine), Ise-jingū

Best for

SACRED SITES

Rebuild & Rebirth

Walking around Ise-jingū, you'll notice empty lots adjacent to some buildings. They are there because both the Gekū and Naikū are rebuilt every 20 years; something that's been happening since the year 690. It's not just the structures, but the furnishings and sacred relics too. While it might sound sacrilegious to pull down a place of worship, it's part of a Shintō belief called *tokowaka* and the idea of continued re-birth and renewal. It also helps pass down Shintō traditions and the craftsmanship to future generations. The 63rd rebuild is set to take place in 2033.

documenting Ise-jingū's 20-year rebuilds and the accompanying Shikinen Sengū ritual to transfer the gods to the new structures.

03 From the Gekū, two roads initially head east. You are going to take Miyuki-dōri (the left of the two), a looping 5km stretch of road built to connect the inner and outer shrines ahead of an Imperial visit in the Meiji era (1868–1912). Like the entire route, there's no dedicated bike path, but you can either use the two-lane road or ride the pavement next to it. After just under 2km, you'll reach a crossroads, where on the right is the entrance (down a long road) to a group of small museums: the Jingū Chōkokan Museum (神宮徴古館), in a Renaissance-style stone building, documents the history and rituals of Ise-Jingū; the Jingū Art Museum (神宮美術館) houses works of art from the shrine; and the Jingū Agriculture Museum (神宮農業館) covers exactly what it says – agriculture. If you plan on visiting all three, the combo admission ticket almost cuts the costs in half. Just time for one? Jingū Art Museum.

04 After another 3km, Miyuki-dōri will lead you to the entrance of the Naikū (内宮), the most impressive part of Ise-jingū. This inner shrine complex, dedicated to the ancestral goddess of the Imperial family, is set among ancient cedar and cypress forests, with pebble stone pathways running between a collection of wooden shrine buildings with tightly thatched roofs. Some of the most sacred buildings are off-limits to all but priests and members of the Imperial family, but take a walk around the sprawling grounds and you'll still get a strong sense of Ise-jingū's importance – not least that people from all walks of life come to pray.

05 Back on your bike, leave the Naikū not via Miyuki-dōri, but on the street to its right – on Google Maps, it's labelled Ise Hwy, though it's a single street. This will take you through the Oharaimachi (おはらい町) area, the central street of the old town that was once the gateway to Ise-jingū. Roughly 800m in length, it's now home to a mix of restaurants and souvenir stores, but also retains some historic buildings.

06 After 400m along Oharaimachi, you get to Okage-yokochō (おかげ横丁), an Edo-style cluster of streets designed to give a sense of the area's heyday. It is (like parts of Oharaimachi) a bit touristy, but fun for a spot of shopping. The shops here sell all sorts of traditional crafts, from wooden spinning tops to ceramic lucky cats and painted candles to household Shintō altars. Unique items include the Okage-inu dog figurines. These

Take a Break

At the midpoint of the ride, along Oharaimachi, SUSHIKYU has been serving a local favourite called *tekonezushi* for more than 120 years. Initially designed to be quickly put together on fishing boats, *tekonezushi* is simply bonito (a tuna-like fish) sashimi soaked in soy sauce, then arranged on a bed of warm rice with a topping of dried seaweed. Here, it comes as part of a set meal, the simplest of which features a palate-cleansing soup and pickles, although you could opt for larger sets that include tempura and small hotpots.

AMSTK/SHUTTERSTOCK

Gekū (outer shrine), Ise-jingū

honour the 'substitute dogs' that some Edo-era people would send (with handlers) on pilgrimages to Ise-jingū, where the dogs would collect amulets for their owners. The figurines are white, as sending a white dog was seen as more auspicious, and they have little money bags hung around their necks – offerings to the shrine.

The Gods of Ise-jingū

The reason Ise-jingū is so important is because of the main god believed to reside in the Naikū (inner shrine). That would be the sun goddess, Amaterasu-no-Ōmikami, the chief *kami* (god) of Shintōism, who in Japanese mythology is also said to be the ancestress of Japan's Imperial family. Over in the Gekū (outer shrine), the main deity is Toyo'uke-no-Ōmikami, residing there to provide Amaterasu with companionship and sacred foods. As such, Toyo'uke is prayed to as a guardian of wellbeing who grants clothing, food and shelter.

07 Another 400m along Oharaimachi will be the end of the street, and almost the end of the ride. Turn left here onto Rte 32, and it will take you all the way back to the Gekū in 3km. From here, it's easy to retrace your steps to Iseshi Station.

Also Try...

Whirlpools, Naruto Strait, Awaichi Ride

AINES/SHUTTERSTOCK

Awaichi Ride, Hyōgo

DURATION	DIFFICULTY	DISTANCE
3–10hrs	Moderate	38–150km

With its varied terrain and sights that range from the whirlpools of the Naruto Strait to Izanagi-jingū shrine and the remains of Sumoto Castle, this 150km loop of the island of Awajishima (淡路島) in the Inland Sea is one of Japan's classic bike rides. To do the full ride, you'd ideally be bringing your own bike, but you could tackle shorter sections on the rental bikes available around the island. The website of the local tourism board *(awajishima-kanko.jp/cycling/en)* has details of the full ride and other routes, including a 38km loop ride for beginners on Awajishima's southern coast. The site also lists rentals and all the information you'll need for reaching and navigating the island.

Tanichi Ride, Kyoto

DURATION	DIFFICULTY	DISTANCE
6hrs	Difficult	80km

Following a loop around northern Kyoto Prefecture, the Tanichi offers an entirely different perspective to Kyoto than the busier sights in the often crowded city centre. The ride visits the scenic Amanohashidate sandbar, follows the coast to the pretty harbour village of Ine and rugged cape Kyōga, and then ventures inland to the rice paddies and rural scenery of Kyōtango. On the way, you could stop for a soothing hot-spring bath. A good starting point is Amanohashidate Station, next to which is an e-bike rental store. Buses run here from Kyoto Station in two to three hours, depending on traffic. Alternatively, stay a night in one of Ine's charming old *funaya* (boathouses) and rent an e-bike from Ine's tourist information centre. For more: kyoto-ocean.com/tan-ichi.

AVANT VISUAL/SHUTTERSTOCK

Ninai Falls, Akame 48 Waterfalls, Mie

Nabari, Mie

DURATION	DIFFICULTY	DISTANCE
2hrs	Easy	20km

Fifty kilometres east of Nara City, the quiet surrounds of Nabari (名張) offer up a collection of unhurried rides. From Nabari Station, you could do a 20km loop called the Ninja Route, which visits areas connected to the legendary Iga ninjas, including castle remains and the Akame 48 Waterfalls. From late March to early April, another option is the 18km Mahoroba Sakura Route, which starts and ends at Haibara Station and takes in the area's best cherry-blossom spots. There are bike rentals available, but bike numbers are limited, so it's best to make a reservation. For details of how to do that, plus maps, route descriptions and more, visit enntourism.com/enn-yamanami-rides.

Wakaura, Wakayama

DURATION	DIFFICULTY	DISTANCE
2hrs	Easy	22km

If you are visiting Wakayama City for the Kinokawa ride earlier in the chapter, a journey to the coastal Wakaura area would make for a good second day of riding – or even as an addition to the Kinokawa. It follows the same route to Wakayama Castle, but then you go south for 4km along Rte 42 to a scenic part of the coast that's home to small fishing ports, several historic shrines and a garden with views of the emerald waters of Wakaura Bay. Staff at Wakayama Station's tourist information centre can give you a map. You can also rent bikes here. Just be aware that this ride is entirely on road and pavement, without designated cycling roads.

0 50 km
0 25 miles
Nishino-shima
Dōgo
Nakano-shima
Oki Islands
Chiburi-jima
Naka-umi
15
Matsue
Sakaiminato
Shinji-ko
Sea of Japan
Izumo
Yasugi
Tottori
Kurayoshi
Daisen
16
Daisen-Oki National Park
Ōda
Chizu
Gotsu
Tsuyama
Hamada
Niimi
Sayo
Miyoshi
Shōbara
Masuda
Akō
Okayama
Kurashiki
Nagato
Hagi
17
Hiroshima
Fukuyama
Shōdo-shima
Sea of Harima-nada
Hatsukaichi
Mihara
Onomichi
Miyajima
Innoshima
Takamatsu
Mine
Yamaguchi
Kure
Ikuchi-jima
Marugame
Inland Sea
Eta-jima
Ōmi-shima
Iwakuni
Hakata-jima
Seto-nai-kai National Park
Shimonoseki
Kanmon Straits
Hōfu
Sea of Aki
Inland Sea
Ō-shima
Sea of Hiuchi
Naruto
Kitakyūshū
Ube
Yanai
Imabari
Kawanoe
Mima
Tokushima
Inland Sea
Niihama
Sea of Suo
Yashiro-shima
Saijō
Matsuyama
Yukuhashi
Iizuka
Tsurugi-san
Bungo-Takada
Sea of Iyo
Ishizuchi-san
Kunisaki

SEAN PAVONE/SHUTTERSTOCK

Hiroshima-jō (p120)

Hiroshima & Western Honshū

15 Matsue, Shinji-ko & Izumo

Journey through lakeside scenery to Japan's oldest shrine and a sacred beach. **p110**

16 Tottori's Yumigahama

Ride along white sand and pine groves to enjoy salty soaks and fresh seafood. **p114**

17 Hiroshima Peace Ride

Learn about the city's history and recovery on this off-the-beaten-path tour. **p118**

Explore

Hiroshima & Western Honshū

The prefectures of Hiroshima, Okayama, Tottori, Shimane and Yamaguchi comprise Chūgoku, the largely rural region also known as 'San'in-San'yō'. The alternative moniker reflects the region's two parts: one facing the Sea of Japan, called 'yin of the mountains', and one facing the Seto Inland Sea, called 'yang of the mountains'. Mountains run east to west through the region, with rolling hills, plains and scenic coastline to the north and south. Natural beauty is abundant, from volcanic peaks like Daisen to the sand dunes of Tottori, while historic sites include the 'floating' shrine Itsukushima-jinja on Miyajima and Izumo-taisha, Japan's oldest shrine.

Hiroshima

Though most known for its Peace Memorial Park and Atomic Bomb Dome, which serve as a memorial to those killed in the WWII bombing of the city, Hiroshima (広島) is also bustling with energetic shopping districts like Hondori St, contemporary architecture and a rich culinary culture. Okonomi Village offers *okonomiyaki* (savoury pancakes) local style on a bed of noodles, while Shukkeien Garden presents fresh sushi and Miyajima serves local oysters raw, grilled or deep-fried with tartar sauce.

Okayama

With fewer rainy days than anywhere else in Japan, Okayama (岡山) is called 'the land of sunshine'. As a political and economic centre in the region from the 14th to 16th centuries, the city enjoyed significant development, evidenced by remaining sites such as Okayama-jō (Okayama Castle) and Kōraku-en, one of Japan's three greatest gardens. The northern area comprises gentle hills, where the city's renowned white peaches and grapes are cultivated, while the southern area includes art island Inujima.

Matsue

The capital of Shimane Prefecture, Matsue (松江) sits between Shinji-ko (Lake Shinji) and Nakaumi lagoon, providing a tranquil environment and an ample supply of eel, a local speciality that can be enjoyed in Ginza. This vibrant district is packed with small eateries and shops. For a relaxed atmosphere, visit Koraimachi, with its

WHEN TO GO

The region has a temperate climate, but the Japan Sea coast (Shimane, Tottori and northern Yamaguchi) is slightly colder and wetter than the Inland Sea coast (Hiroshima, Okayama and southern Yamaguchi). Rainy season (June and mid-July) is followed by humidity and temperatures of 35°C (mid-July to August). Shimane and Tottori can experience heavy snowfall and high winds from December to February.

traditional restaurants serving local soba (buckwheat noodles) and *mochi* (rice cakes). Sites such as Matsue-jō (Matsue Castle), the samurai district and Adachi Museum of Art offer chances to uncover Japan in a scenic setting.

Tottori

Tottori (鳥取) is renowned for its sand dunes, which cover 30 sq km to the north of the city centre and offer sandboarding and paragliding. The nearby Tottori Sand Museum exhibits giant sand sculptures that are designed and made annually. The main street, Wakasa Kaidō, offers a lively mix of shops and eateries and runs to the oldest part of the city, home to the ruins of Tottori-jō (Tottori Castle), as well as temples, museums and parks. These include the Watanabe Art Museum, which houses the largest collection of armour in Japan.

Yamaguchi

Yamaguchi (山口) prospered as a centre of culture, having welcomed intellectuals escaping Kyoto in the 15th century. Much development was modelled on Kyoto, resulting in craftsmanship and temples still seen today, such as Jōe-ji, a National Place of Scenic Beauty. Businesses offer experiences in Ōuchi-nuri, a lacquerware of multiple layers and gold leaf, and Yamaguchi Hagi-yaki pottery, which changes colour with use due to the properties of the coarse clay used.

TRANSPORT

On the JR Tōkaidō-Sanyō Shinkansen line from Tokyo, the Nozomi train stops at Okayama and Hiroshima, the two gateways into the region. Both of these cities are also served by direct flights from South Korea, Hong Kong, Taiwan and China (plus Vietnam for Hiroshima). Yonago Kitaro Airport in Tottori has direct flights to South Korea and Hong Kong.

WHAT'S ON

Matsue Samurai Parade

(visit-matsue.com) The first Saturday in April sees hundreds of people don samurai armour and depart Matsue-jō for a procession.

Izumo Taisha Grand Festival

(ankou-shimane.com) Shrine priests perform archery to dispel evil, and plant rice as part of this religious event on 14 May.

Kumano Brush Matsuri

(fudematsuri.jp) Performances, including giant calligraphy, *kagura* (sacred dance) and boat spinning, celebrate brushes during this festival in mid-September.

WHERE TO STAY

Most accommodation options can be found on the coasts, where visitor traffic is higher. Popular spots such as Hiroshima, Miyajima and Matsue offer all kinds of places to stay, from mid- and high-end Western and Japanese hotels to ryokan (traditional Japanese inns), business hotels, guesthouses, capsule hotels and campsites. In Hagi and Izumo, which are renowned for their historic and cultural sites, expect traditional accommodation, while the scenic areas of Hiruzen Highland and Daisen offer more luxury hotels. Higher-end hotels are located on the shores of the Seto Inland Sea, with cheaper options inland or in cities such as Kurashiki and Fukuyama.

Resources

Shimane Cycling Navi *(kankou-shimane.com/cycling/en)* Routes, bike rental, news, events and tips.

Tottori Bike Tour *(tottori-tour.jp/en/bike-tour)* Routes, rental, sightseeing spots and maps.

Hare Iro Cycling Okayama *(okayama-kanko.jp/hareiro-cycling/en)* Routes and bike rental.

Dive Hiroshima *(dive-hiroshima.com/en/feature/cycling)* Routes and maps of cycling infrastructure.

15

Best for

LOCAL DELICACIES, HISTORIC SITES

Matsue, Shinji-ko & Izumo

CARLA SILENE/SHUTTERSTOCK

Matsue Vogel Park (p112)

DURATION	DIFFICULTY	DISTANCE	START/END
5–6hrs	Intermediate	39km	Matsue Shinjiko-Onsen Station/ Izumotaisha-Mae Station

TERRAIN	Mostly flat, on cycle paths or pavement

Running alongside Shinji-ko (宍道湖), known for scenery, seafood and birdwatching, to one of Japan's most sacred beaches, Inasa (稲佐), this ride is ideal for fans of nature, history, culture and cuisine. It is part of a network of cycle routes in the area, with several cycling stations with bicycle stands and simple maintenance gear. From Izumotaisha-Mae Station, near the end of the route, it's possible to return with your bicycle to Matsue Shinjiko-Onsen Station in about one hour via the Ichibata Electric Railway by purchasing an additional ticket.

Bike Hire

Giant Cycle Shop Matsue, at Matsue Shinjiko-Onsen Station, rents bicycles and e-bikes from ¥3960 per day (helmet and insurance included). You can reserve on their website up to two days beforehand.

Starting Point

Take a bus from JR Matsue Station bound for Matsue Shinjiko-Onsen Station. It is a 15-minute bus ride.

01 Turn right out of Matsue Shinjiko-Onsen Station (松江宍道湖温泉駅), following the road westbound with the railway tracks on the right. After 600m, turn left to join Rte 431. The convenience store at this crossroads is a good spot to stock up on supplies for the ride, but there are also a couple more convenience stores in the upcoming few kilometres.

02 The route hugs Shinji-ko for the next 1.5km before turning slightly inland. After a further 1.3km, go over the level crossing at the

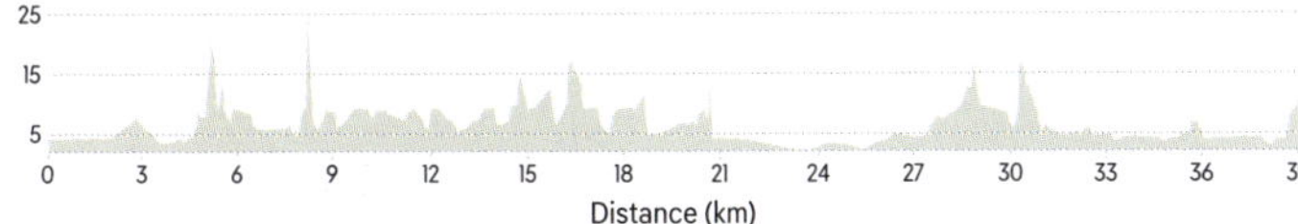

junction for Rte 264 and join the Shinjiko-Kohoku Cycling Road. This wide tarmac path offers close-up views of the adjacent rice fields, which support lush green plants in summer that turn golden in autumn as harvest approaches.

03 At the end of the road, turn left, cross the railway tracks and turn right to rejoin Rte 431. After climbing to the crest of a hill, Shinji-ko will appear in view. Travel downhill and turn right at the sign for Shinjiko-Kohoku Cycling Road. Take the narrower road on the right, along the train tracks, to turn right onto Rte 431 in 1.6km.

04 This marks the start of the longest unbroken stretch of cycling alongside Shinji-ko, the brackish body of water responsible for Matsue's alternative moniker, the City of Water. As a significant wintering ground for waterfowl and a wetland of international importance for bird conservation, the lake is listed under the Ramsar Convention and is a popular spot for birdwatchers. Rich in both fish and shellfish, including *unagi* (eel), the lake is also one of Japan's largest sources of *shijimi* (Japanese basket clam).

05 After 3km, you'll reach Roadside Station Aika Nagisa Park, a rest stop located on the shore with refreshments and toilets. From here, you can walk to the waterside to take in the view or spot local wildlife.

Unveiling Mythology, Unsheathing Swords

Shimane Museum of Ancient Izumo is a stylish facility that displays the history and culture of Shimane prefecture, particularly the heritage of ancient Izumo. Three galleries introduce Izumo-taisha, the mythology related to Izumo and the locally excavated bronze artefacts that are designated national treasures. Highlights include a huge pillar that supported the main shrine of Izumo-taisha in the 13th century, a model of the shrine as it once looked that has been reconstructed at a 1/10 scale, and a display of the 358 bronze swords unearthed at the Kojindani ruins in Izumo. More swords were found at this one site than in the rest of Japan combined.

06 Riding another 1km brings you to Matsue Vogel Park, a bird and flower attraction that offers events year-round. In addition to a waterfowl pond and aviary for tropical birds, there is a petting zoo, seasonal flower displays and two restaurants.

07 Return to the ride for unparalleled views of the lake and rolling hills on the shores beyond. In 7km, you'll approach a gradual hill and a signpost indicating to take the right-hand road for Izumo Route Cycling Road, a winding southeasterly route that reaches Inasa Beach in 31km. To stay on your current, shorter course, take the left-hand road (Rte 431) up the hill and over the bridge.

08 The next point of interest is Unshu-hirata, home to a district of old storehouses, merchant homes and breweries dating from the 19th century. You'll pass by the train station, from where it is a 10-minute walk. There are no shops or eateries after passing through this town, making it a good place to pick up what you need before you continue.

09 From here, it's a 14km well-signposted ride along the wide Kohoku Plain and some residential areas to reach the Shimane Museum of Ancient Izumo. Call into this modern structure for an introduction to the history and archaeology of the area. A little further along, you'll reach a massive *torii* gate, the entrance to Izumo-taisha (出雲大社). Continue around the corner and downhill and you will reach the parking area, from where you can enter the shrine grounds.

10 From the car park, continue on Rte 431 towards the coast. After around 1km, the Sea of Japan and Inasa Beach will appear below. Bentensan, the huge rock in the sea, houses a shrine dedicated to the god of the sea and is a popular view at sunset.

11 Return to the *torii* gate at Izumo-taisha and turn right, heading downhill. After around 350m, you'll reach Izumotaisha-Mae Station (出雲大社前駅) for a train back to Matsue Shinjiko-Onsen Station, where you can enjoy a warming soak in an *ashi-yu* (foot bath).

Take a Break

Numerous restaurants along the lakeshore, such as ALASKA, serve eel-based dishes like *unajū* (grilled eel over rice). YOHUKIYA, near the end of the lake, specialises in fresh fish and seafood served over rice, and miso soup brimming with local *shijimi,* which can be enjoyed at tables or on tatami matting overlooking the lake. The hillside road between Izumo-taisha shrine and Izumotaisha-Mae Station is flanked by cafes serving traditional sweets and restaurants specialising in Izumo soba noodles served with a thick, sweet soup.

HUGO TREMOLIERE/500PX

***Shimenawa,* Izumo-taisha**

Where the Gods Hang Out

As the gathering place for all Japanese deities, Izumo-taisha is one of the most important Shintō shrines in the country. The main shrine, which is a national treasure, houses the deity of marriage who is said to create bonds between all living things. The grounds are expansive, with three large *torii* gates to pass through on your approach to the main building. Check out the giant *shimenawa* (straw rope) hung from the main sanctuary to ward off evil and the little statues of white rabbits that commemorate a deity who delayed his travels to help a rabbit in distress.

16

Best for

SALTWATER SOAKS

Tottori's Yumigahama

ITASUN/GETTY IMAGES

View of Daisen

DURATION	DIFFICULTY	DISTANCE	START/END
2–3hrs	Easy	16km (32km return)	Yonago City Tourist Centre/ Sakai Yumeminato Terminal

TERRAIN	Paved cycle paths

The most westerly section of the Tottori Uminami Road (鳥取うみなみロード), a 143km-long course that runs the length of Tottori Prefecture's coast, the Yumigahama Cycling Route offers a journey by white-sand beaches and through pine tree groves to Sakaiminato, a port city brimming with fresh seafood. A summer ride presents *hamanasu* (Japanese rose) in bloom and swims in the Sea of Japan, while a cycle in winter affords views of majestic Daisen, the region's highest peak. The route is well marked and easy to navigate, even without a map.

Bike Hire

Yonago City Tourist Centre (米子市観光センター) rents bikes from 8.30am to 6pm. An e-bike is ¥2000 per day (with a helmet and insurance included). Identification, such as a passport, is required.

Starting Point

Take the 21 bus (20 minutes) bound for Kaike Onsen Kanko Center from JR Yonago Station, served by the San-in, Hakubi and Sakai lines. Yonago City Tourist Centre adjoins Kaike Onsen Kanko Center.

01 There are no shops along the Yumigahama Cycling Route until you reach Sakaiminato, so the area around Yonago City Tourist Centre is ideal for picking up any snacks or drinks before you depart. The convenience store across the road is the closest place to do this. From the tourist centre, turn right and ride 300m to reach the beachside statue of Arimoto Matsutaro, the local man who developed Kaike Onsen as a resort town during the late 19th century. Ahead lies the Sea of Japan and Kaike Onsen Beach, a popular swimming spot due to its clean sand and clear waters.

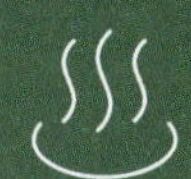

The Salt Springs of Kaike Onsen

Kaike Onsen is a rare saltwater hot-spring resort. First discovered in the early 1900s by a fisherman who spotted bubbles rising from the ocean floor about 200m off the coast, the natural onsen in the area are beneficial to health. There are more than 20 day-use hot-spring facilities with indoor and outdoor bathing that provide towels and other amenities. Options include Ocean One Day Onsen, Ou Land and Bayside Square Kaike Hotel, which are all on the route. For a quick dip, try soaking your feet in the Kaike Onsen foot bath at Yonago City Tourist Centre.

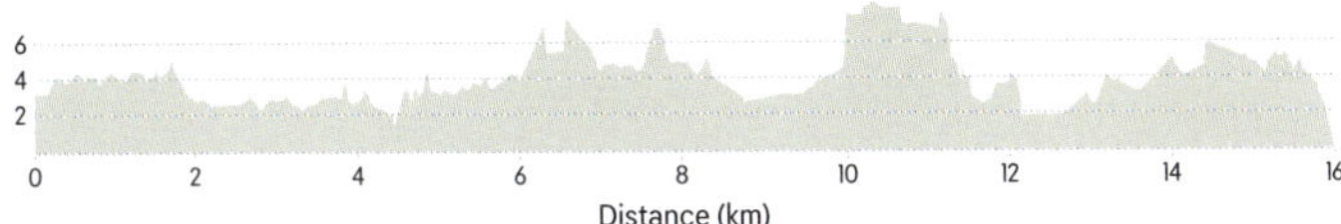

02 Turn right and go straight for 1km to arrive at the start of the Yumigahama Cycling Route, at the mouth of the Hino-gawa. On a clear day, the raised gazebo offers spectacular views of Daisen, a dormant stratovolcano and the highest mountain in the Chūgoku region, and its neighbouring peaks. There are toilets here too.

03 Setting off, you'll now head west, back the way you came, alongside various seafront hotels, onsen (hot springs) and restaurants. A few metres after the statue of Arimoto Matsutaro, the path opens up on the left to reveal Kaike Seaside Park, which comprises some shady areas equipped with picnic tables, a vending machine and a free covered *ashi-yu* drawing from the town's warm saltwater hot spring; ideal for a refreshing break.

04 Riding 1.7km brings you to Kaike fishing port, where small boats are lined up along the harbour walls. Clearly marked blue signage on the road will lead you slightly inland to skirt around the port, cross a bridge and return to the coastal route via a narrow path. Bollards are fixed to the entrance here, making the route inaccessible to vehicles.

05 Continue for your first glimpse of the combination of white sandy beaches and green pine trees that characterise this route, which stretches on for kilometres, offering unparalleled views of the coast, both ahead and behind. The next landmark is Yumigahama Park, a wide expanse to take a break, with a helpful information board and public toilets.

06 From here, cross the bridge over the river and enter Pine Grove Rd, an area recognised as among the country's top 100 scenic areas for white sand and pine trees. Tall green pines line this secluded, quiet path, which is reserved for bicycles and pedestrians. After about 1km you'll cross Ondochigawa at another small fishing port and return to the coast at Yomi Beach, another beautiful stretch of white sand.

07 Following the markings, the path turns inland to run alongside Rte 431 towards Sakaiminato (境港), one of Japan's leading fishing ports for crab. A sign at a crossroads marks the entrance to Yumigahama Observatory, where there is a gazebo, toilets and a vending machine. This spot is halfway along the route and affords excellent views of Daisen to the east, particularly on a fine day.

08 From here, you'll ride alongside Rte 431 for 1.8km before returning to the coast for around 5km of coastal views flanked by white sand, blue sea and green pines. Several observatories are dotted along the path, and with Yonago Airport nearby, this part of the ride offers close-ups of low-flying aircraft.

09 On the outskirts of Sakaiminato, the path joins Rte 431 and winds into the port area, passing the public marina and into Yumeminato Park. Where the route splits, take the right path to enjoy views from the observation deck, or park your bicycle for a walk along the boardwalk. Returning to the route, carry on past Yumeminato Tower to reach Sakai Yumeminato Terminal. This facility is equipped with tourist information, free wifi, a selfie stick for taking photos, and a large observation deck with both indoor and outdoor seating. It's also possible to rent bicycles and helmets should you wish to ride this route in the other direction.

Take a Break

Located across the road from Yumigahama Observatory, ORANG LAUT is one of the most accessible dedicated 'cycle cafes' on the route. It serves breakfast, lunch and dinner ranging from pizza and pasta to rice, noodles and seafood dishes as well as sweets and drinks. Kogane, on Rte 431 on the outskirts of Sakaiminato, offers ramen, *gyōza* (dumplings) and *yaki-soba* (soba noodle stir-fry). For freshly caught sushi and other seafood, the Sakaiminato port area has plenty of options including SUSHIWAKA and KAIDO, both near Sakai Yumeminato Terminal.

NAZRA ZAHRI/GETTY IMAGES

Seafood, Sakaiminato

Seafood & Spirits in Sakaiminato

The westernmost city of Tottori Prefecture, Sakaiminato is surrounded on three sides by Nakaumi lagoon, the Sea of Japan and the Sakai Channel, creating scenic waterfront views. At Sakaiminato Fish Centre, you can see catches of snow crabs, white squid and bluefin tuna being prepared for market, and buy or try some fresh produce. Along the 800m Mizuki Shigeru Rd, named after manga artist Mizuki Shigeru, there are 153 bronze statues of Mizuki's *yōkai* (spirit monsters), including details on each character, as well as spooky shops, cafes, public art and a Yōkai Postbox that issues a *yōkai* postmark.

17

Hiroshima Peace Ride

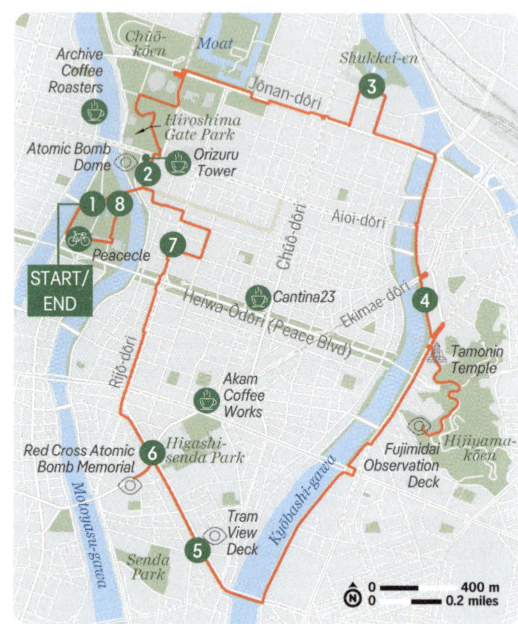

DURATION	DIFFICULTY	DISTANCE	START/END
2–3hrs	Easy	13km	Hiroshima Peace Park

TERRAIN	Paved

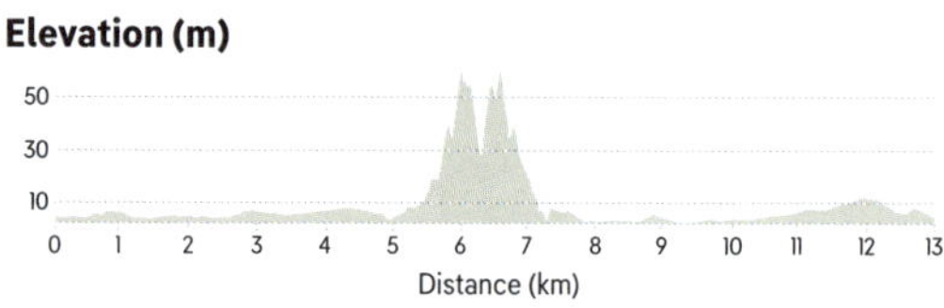

Millions of people visit the sombre Hiroshima Peace Memorial Park and Museum, but few think about the expanse of the city that was damaged by the atomic bomb. This is largely due to the determination of the city's residents to overcome the tragedy of the bombing. This tour visits lesser-known monuments that provide perspective on both the breadth of devastation and the miraculous rebirth of Hiroshima City after WWII.

Bike Hire

There are many Hiroshima Peacecle *(docomo-cycle.jp/hiroshima)* rental stations in the city. The stations at the Hiroshima Peace Memorial Museum or International Conference Center Hiroshima are closest to the start point.

Starting Point

The ride begins and ends in Hiroshima Peace Park. Combine the ride with the Hiroshima Peace Memorial Museum and a visit to the park's many monuments for a full-day experience.

01 Your first stop is within the Hiroshima Peace Park, along the west bank of the Motoyasu-gawa across from the remains of the Atomic Bomb Dome (原爆ドーム). This is one of the best views of the dome, its ravaged shell a sharp contrast to the beautiful riverside park constructed around it. Don't assume this monument will be here forever in this state; challenges in making the site earthquake-resistant have clouded its future.

02 Cross the Motoyasu Bridge and get a closer look at the Atomic Bomb Dome. The bomb exploded about 600m above it, creating a

Tram 651 (p120)

Best for

HISTORY

A Guided Tour with Local Commentary

While the ride is simple enough to do on your own, you'll get more depth and local context on a guided tour led by sokoiko! *(sokoiko-mint.com/en)*. With tour guides who are local to Hiroshima, you'll hear the stories of survivors of the atomic bombing and receive first-hand accounts of the city's rebirth. The guides are passionate about sharing the tragic history of Hiroshima with visitors from around the world, as well as conveying that the hardships endured by its residents contribute to Hiroshima's bright future as a city of peace.

fiery explosion that crushed the building with wind speeds of nearly 1000mph and a force of over 3 tonnes per square foot. The inspiration to preserve the building was the words contained in the diary of 16-year-old Hiroko Kajiyama, who died from leukaemia 15 years after being exposed to the blast.

03 Ride roughly north through Hiroshima Gate Park, heading towards the Omotemon (main gate) of Hiroshima-jō (広島城; Hiroshima Castle). Head east on Jōnan-dōri, watching for the left-turn sign directing you to Shukkei-en (縮景園). This historic garden was partially destroyed by the bomb but was used as a refuge for injured survivors. A large ginkgo tree leans heavily and bears scars from the bombing but lives on to provide a carpet of golden leaves each autumn.

04 Return to Jōnan-dōri and ride east, crossing Kyōbashi-gawa at Kamiyanagi Bridge. Follow the path along the eastern bank of the river about 1km south to Tamonin temple at the foot of Hijiyama-kōen (比治山公園). Ride up the winding road to Fujimidai Observation Deck, which offers a sweeping view of modern Hiroshima and looks west towards Peace Memorial Park. Just after the bombing, much of what you see was a wasteland. Only through the determination of the city's residents was the area rebuilt so thoroughly that it is now difficult to imagine the extent of the destruction.

05 Ride back down the hill and follow the path along the east bank of the Kyōbashi-gawa. Cross Miyuki Bridge, in about 1.5km, and follow the main street with the tram line up to the side street on the right just before Hiroden Honsha-mae tram station. Down this street, a small viewing deck looks over the Hiroden tram yard. Three trams that survived the bombing (651, 652 and 653) are still in service; the last is only used for special events and might be seen from the viewing deck.

06 Follow the main street with the tram line (Senda-dōri) about 600m further until you see the Hiroshima Red Cross Hospital on the left. Turn left here and ride about 100m to the Red Cross Atomic Bomb Memorial. This sombre site includes a melted window frame and the scarred wall of the original hospital, severely damaged by the blast despite being 1.6km from the hypocentre. Although 10% of the staff were killed in the bombing and nearly half received injuries, they continued to provide care for the flood of victims who came in desperate need after the blast.

07 Follow Senda-dōri northwards until you reach the Fukuromachi tram

Take a Break

Hiroshima is filled with incredible cafes. Try ARCHIVE COFFEE ROASTERS near the Peace Park or AKAM COFFEE WORKS near the Red Cross Hospital for a caffeinated boost during your ride. More substantial meals can be had at CANTINA23 with an eclectic menu of fish and chips, pulled pork sandwiches and Tex-Mex fare. Head to the rooftop of ORIZURU TOWER to enjoy an after-ride celebratory drink and light dessert with a panoramic view of the Peace Memorial Park and Atomic Bomb Dome.

TARO HAMA @ E-KAMAKURA/GETTY IMAGES

Atomic Bomb Dome

station. Turn right for the Fukuromachi Elementary School Peace Museum. The wooden buildings here were instantly destroyed in the blast, claiming the lives of 160 students and staff. The West Wing, made of concrete, survived and was used to shelter and care for survivors before becoming a school again a year after the bombing. It has been preserved for its collection of messages left by people searching for lost loved ones right after the tragedy, scrawled in chalk on the charred walls.

The Hiroshima Peace Park lies due west, just a few minutes' ride crossing the river at Motoyasu Bridge located close to the Atomic Bomb Dome. If you haven't already explored the park, visit the highlights: the Memorial Cenotaph, Flame of Peace, the Children's Peace Monument and the Hiroshima Peace Memorial Museum (広島平和記念資料館) itself.

The City of Peace

When the reconstruction of Hiroshima began in 1945, locals believed that no trees or plants would grow in the devastated area for 75 years. Today, it's clear that not only trees and plants but the entire city has blossomed. The reconstruction of Hiroshima was based on creating a living memorial to peace and a reminder of the horrible effects of using nuclear weapons. To that end, the city promotes the sharing of the experiences of those affected by the atomic bomb and hosts events promoting world peace for visitors from every nation.

Also Try...

Bitchū Kokubun-ji, Kibiji Cycling Route

YUSHENG HSU/SHUTTERSTOCK

Kibiji Cycling Route

DURATION	DIFFICULTY	DISTANCE
2–3hrs	Easy	25km

This route links JR Okayama Station and JR Sōja Station via the Kibi Plain (吉備路), once the centre of the Kibi Kingdom, which existed until the 6th century. Many of the resulting sites can still be seen today, creating a ride rich in history. You'll pass Kibitsu-jinja (吉備津神社), an important shrine renowned for its almost 400m-long passageway and double hip-and-gable roof, and the 5th-century green oasis of Tsukuriyama-kofun (造山古墳), Japan's largest keyhole burial ground. Climb to the top for a panorama of the surrounding rice fields. Further along, you'll see the five-storey temple pagoda of Bitchū Kokubun-ji (備中国分寺) while passing lotus flowers in spring and sunflowers in summer. Shops near Okayama and Sōja stations rent bicycles, allowing you to ride in either direction.

Kurayoshi & Lake Tōgō

DURATION	DIFFICULTY	DISTANCE
2–3hrs	Easy	26km

This loop traverses historic, scenic Kurayoshi (倉吉) from Kurayoshi Shirakabe Dozogun Tourist Information Centre (rental bikes available). Start from the central district, a picturesque townscape of *machiya* (wooden townhouses) and carp-filled waterways crisscrossed by small stone bridges, stopping by the 400-year-old white plaster Shirakabe Warehouses once used to store soy sauce or sake. From here, head north to join Rte 161 and follow the Ogamo and Tenjin Rivers through quiet countryside to the coast. Moving inland, you'll reach Lake Tōgō (東郷池), where natural hot springs are piped ashore to be utilised in the lakeside Hawai Onsen, which offers mineral-rich soaks. The goal is Encho-en, a vast Chinese-style garden created as a symbol of friendship between Tottori Prefecture and Hebei Province, northern China.

DREAMNIKON/SHUTTERSTOCK

Akiyoshi-dō cave, Green Karst Highway

Green Karst Highway

DURATION	DIFFICULTY	DISTANCE
5–6hrs	Difficult	38km

The environment is the showpiece of this hilly ride from Shin-Yamaguchi Station (bicycles can be rented) into Akiyoshi-dai Quasi-National Park (秋吉台国定公園). The vast plateau dotted with limestone pinnacles has the highest concentration of karst in Japan and was formed 350 million years ago from a coral reef dissolved gradually by rain. The climb to Akiyoshidai Observatory will reward you with unspoilt views of the landscape, from green in spring and summer to reddish yellow in autumn. A couple of museums en route introduce the plateau's ecology and natural history, while Akiyoshi-dō (秋芳洞) cave reveals the beauty underground: terraces of limestone pools, waterfalls and streams of cobalt-blue water. Akiyoshido Refresh Park, at the end of the ride, offers refreshments and a hot spring.

Shiomachi Kaidō

DURATION	DIFFICULTY	DISTANCE
2–3hrs	Easy	30km

Departing Fukuyama Station (福山駅), where rental bicycles are available, with the city's historic castle as your backdrop, you'll ride 3km to join the scenic path along Ashida-gawa towards the coast. Much of this route is along the edge of Numakuma Peninsula, providing views of the Inland Sea and its many islands in all directions. You can even see Shikoku on a clear day. On reaching Tomonoura (鞆の浦), a laid-back fishing port, take a break at Jōyatō Lighthouse on the waterfront to explore the old town, a preserved district. Four kilometres further and the route reveals Bandai-ji, a temple on the rocky tip of Abuto Cape established to pray for voyages, before winding along more picturesque coastline to reach Tosaki Port.

0 50 km
0 25 miles
Tsugaru Peninsula
Mutsu-wan
Nonai
Noheji
Aomori
Goshogawara
Ogawara-ko
Shimo-hareyama
18
Towada-Hachimantai National Park
Hirosaki
Hachinohe
Sea of Japan
Towada-ko
Ōdate
Noshiro
Kuji
Towada-Hachimantai National Park
Oga Peninsula
Oga
Monzen
Iwate-san
Akita
Tazawa-ko
Semboku
Morioka
Miyako
Kakunodate
20
Hanamaki
Honjō
Kitakami
Tōno
Yokote
Kitakami-gawa
Kamaishi
Chōkai-san
Ōfunato
Sanriku Fukko National Park
Sakata
21
Ichinoseki
Kesennuma
Shinjō
Tsuruoka
Awa-shima
Gas-san
19
Ishinomaki
Matsushima
Bandai-Asahi National Park
Oshika Peninsula
Murakami
Yamagata
Sendai
Zaō-san
Sendai-wan
PACIFIC OCEAN
Shibata
Yonezawa

SANGA PARK/SHUTTERSTOCK

Fukuurajima (p134)

Northern Honshū (Tōhoku)

18 Hirosaki

Head to northern Tōhoku for a ride that takes in Aomori Prefecture's famed orchards, contemporary art and the historic sights of Hirosaki City. **p128**

19 Matsushima Circuit

Visit Miyagi Prefecture for a loop ride that starts and ends in one of Japan's most scenic bays, and also visits a historic temple and reminders of the 2011 earthquake and tsunami. **p132**

20 Tōno

Go well off the beaten path to explore a part of rural Iwate Prefecture infused with folklore. **p138**

21 Sakata Art Ride

Pedal between galleries, museums and more on this short, but arty ride in Yamagata Prefecture. **p142**

Explore

Northern Honshū (Tōhoku)

In an ideal world, you could spend weeks slowly exploring less-trodden Tōhoku (東北), to the north of Tokyo and the Kantō region. In the six prefectures here, you can cycle far off the beaten path, with rides around the bucolic Tōno countryside or a jaunt between art museums in the harbour town of Sakata. In Matsushima, rides come with views of one of Japan's most attractive bays, while in Hirosaki you could visit in spring to coincide with stunning cherry blossoms. Add a loop around Lake Inawashiro or the jagged coastline of the Oga Peninsula, and you'd still only have scratched Tōhoku's surface.

Sendai

Ninety minutes north of Tokyo by bullet train, Tōhoku's largest city, Sendai (仙台) makes a great base for exploring the region. The Matsushima and Hamakaidō rides are on the city's doorstep, while the bullet train also connects to Hachinohe (70 minutes) for the Tanesashi Coast ride, Kōriyama (35 minutes) near the Lake Inawashiro ride, and Shin Hanamaki (55 minutes), where you could change to a local line for the Tōno ride. In Sendai, you'll also find a great range of places to stay, eat and drink, plus a cluster of historic sights connected to the city's legendary founder, samurai Date Masamune.

Aomori

North of Morioka and Sendai on the Tōhoku Shinkansen route, the eponymously named capital city of Aomori Prefecture is a good middle ground for anyone planning rides in Hachinohe (八戸) to the east (25 minutes) or Hirosaki to the southwest (30 minutes) – although both of those cities are worth an overnight stay in their own right. If you do stop in Aomori (青森), there are more hotel and dining options around Aomori Station, rather than Shin-Aomori Station where the bullet train stops. By day, you could check out the incredible prehistoric remains at Sannai Maruyama, make your own seafood breakfast at Gyosai Centre market, and take in the contemporary art collection at Aomori Museum of Art.

WHEN TO GO

Like many parts of Japan, spring and autumn are the best times for cycling in Tōhoku. In winter, much of the region is cold and snowy, and bike rentals are unavailable. In summer, Tōhoku isn't as consistently hot and humid as more southerly parts of the country, so cycling isn't impossible, but you will need to take precautions against heatstroke.

Akita

With easy connections to Tokyo, Sendai and Morioka on the Akita Shinkansen route, the city of Akita (秋田) is a decent base for the Oga Peninsula ride, an hour to the northwest by local JR line. It's also a couple of hours by local JR from the Sakata ride, although you could alternatively reach Sakata via express train from Niigata City. Being Akita Prefecture's biggest city, you'll find plenty of hotels and things to do at night.

Morioka

Like Sendai, the city of Morioka (盛岡) is well connected to other parts of Tōhoku thanks to the bullet train, with Hachinohe in particular just 27 minutes north and Sendai 38 minutes south. Morioka, however, is a smaller and mellower place to stay than Sendai. While that means fewer hotels to choose from, Iwate Prefecture's main city still has plenty to see and do, whether that's chilling out in the green surrounds of Iwate Park, taking on the local *wanko soba* noodle-eating challenge, or heading outside of town for the pastures of nearby Koiwai Farm and Morioka Handicrafts Village.

TRANSPORT

Bullet trains (shinkansen) connect Tokyo to major cities in Tōhoku, including Akita, Aomori, Fukushima, Morioka, Sendai and Yamagata. From here, the regional rail network will take you to all the rides in this chapter. If you're visiting multiple parts of Tōhoku, consider the JR East Pass Tōhoku. It gives five consecutive days of travel on bullet trains and other trains in the region for ¥30,000.

WHAT'S ON

Aomori Nebuta

From 2 to 7 August, colourful floats measuring as much as 5m in height are paraded around Aomori City accompanied by musicians and revellers.

Sōma-Nomaoi

The highlight of this event in Fukushima Prefecture, on the last weekend in May, is a display of samurai equestrianism featuring several hundred riders in traditional armour.

WHERE TO STAY

Tōhoku's cities all have business hotels around their main stations, while Sendai also offers a good selection of midrange Western-style hotels. As you leave the urban areas behind, you are likely to find mid- to high-end ryokan (traditional Japanese inns) in hot-spring towns and lower-cost *minshuku* (family-run guesthouses) in the countryside. There are also opportunities for farm stays. It always pays to book ahead, but especially when travelling in spring and autumn. Don't be surprised to pay a premium during Japanese holidays such as Golden Week (29 April to 5 May) or when the cherry blossoms are in full bloom in April.

Resources

Aomori Cycling *(aomori-cycling.com)* Aomori Tourism's official cycling website outlines multiple rides, plus general travel information.

Miyagi Cycle Platform *(japancycling.jp/en)* Details more than a dozen rides in Miyagi Prefecture.

Tōno Tourism *(tonojikan.jp)* Tōno's official website has details on bike rentals, accommodation and the town's main attractions.

18

Best for

SPRING BLOSSOMS

IRIN SOMSUPPAMONGKOL/GETTY IMAGES

Hirosaki Apple Park

Hirosaki

DURATION	DIFFICULTY	DISTANCE	START/END
1.5hrs	Easy	12km	Hirosaki Station
TERRAIN	Flat and paved		

On the west side of Aomori Prefecture, in Tōhoku's far north, the city of Hirosaki (弘前) is known for its 17th-century castle and the thousands of cherry trees that bloom around it every spring. This ride around Hirosaki visits the castle, but also takes in Zen temples, the traditionally landscaped Fujita Memorial Japanese Garden and a vibrant contemporary art scene. With this part of Aomori being Japan's premier producer of apples, you'll also stop by orchards and have opportunities to try the numerous local versions of apple pie.

Bike Hire

From April to November, the tourist information centre at Hirosaki Station rents push bikes and e-bikes for ¥500 and ¥1000 per day, respectively. There are no rentals in bad weather.

Starting Point

Hirosaki Station on the JR Ou Main Line, 35 minutes from Shin-Aomori Station in Aomori City. Shin-Aomori is on the Tōhoku Shinkansen line.

01 From Hirosaki Station's west side (Central Exit), take the road that leads past the Toyoko Inn hotel. In 500m you'll be at a large intersection, where you need to turn left onto Rte 3 (which soon changes name to Rte 127).

02 In another 600m, you'll be at the first stop: Hirosaki Museum of Contemporary Art (弘前れんが倉庫美術館). The museum is easy to spot. It's a large red-brick building, built in the Meiji era (1868–1912) as a brewery, though now it

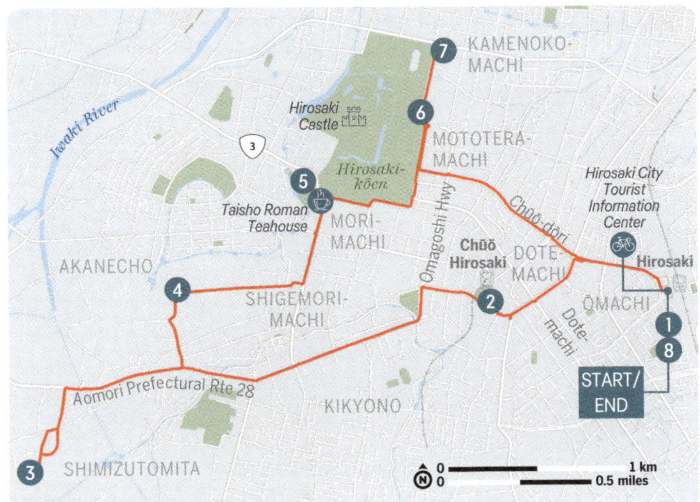

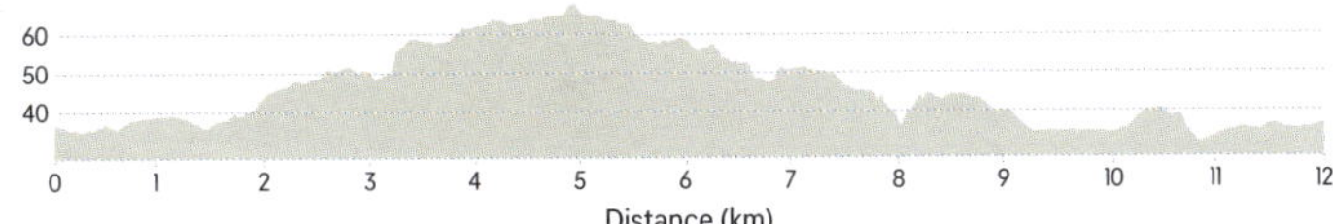

displays work by local and international artists. That includes Hirosaki-born Yoshitomo Nara, whose highly acclaimed paintings and sculptures mix Japanese cuteness with a tinge of dark humour.

03 After the museum, take Rte 127 over a small river and in 300m turn left onto Rte 28 at the traffic lights. By now, you'll already be in Hirosaki's outer sprawl, which feels more like a small town than a city. Cycle 2km west on this road and you should see a sign in Japanese – or more like a red monument – marked '弘前市りんご公園' (Hirosaki Apple Park). Follow the arrow left, on a road that initially feels like it's leading you nowhere, and in a few hundred metres you'll be at the park. You could spend 15 minutes or an hour at the park, depending on how interested you are in apples and whether there are any hands-on experiences – like apple-picking in August to mid-November – running in the park's orchards. At the very least, the orchards are lovely for a stroll and come complete with views of Iwaki-san in the distance. You could also visit a reconstructed farmhouse, learn about apple cultivation and pick up all sorts of apple-related products.

04 Once you are done here, backtrack 650m east on Rte 28, then turn left at the set of traffic lights next to a distinctive traditional-style house. Following this quiet backstreet for 400m (with a right at the fork halfway) will

Hirosaki's Pink Wave

From mid-April to early May, as spring begins to usurp the long Tōhoku winter, something special happens in Hirosaki. The 2600 flowering cherry trees on the grounds of Hirosaki Castle Park burst into a fluffy palette of delicate pinks, creating just about the perfect setting for *hanami* (cherry-blossom-viewing) picnics. This is considered one of Tōhoku's – and Japan's – top cherry-blossom sites, attracting roughly two million visitors every spring. So, if you are planning on staying in Hirosaki for the blossoms, make sure to book a room well in advance.

bring you to the peaceful Zen Temple Area (禅林街). It was here that a local lord had 33 Zen temples relocated in the 1600s, placed on the southwest side of the castle area (deemed an unlucky direction) to give spiritual protection to the castle and his clan. The temples here today are a mix of historic and new, with the most interesting being the first you'll see, Chōshō-ji at the western end of the street, which was built in the 1620s as the clan's family temple.

05 From the gates of Chōshō-ji, cycle down the tree-lined street of temples until you arrive at a T-junction. Go left here for 500m and you'll reach trees marking the southern boundary of the castle grounds. Just on your left is the Fujita Memorial Japanese Garden (藤田記念庭園), well worth 30 minutes for a stroll of its traditionally landscaped garden, waterfalls and ponds, which incorporate Iwaki-san in the distance as *shakkei* (borrowed scenery). The garden also has a Western-style tearoom with a great selection of local apple pies.

06 After the garden, follow the road east then north around the outer moat of Hirosaki Castle (弘前城) for the Sannomaru East Gate, where you can start exploring the castle grounds. As well as the three-storey main keep, which was initially built in the 1600s but then rebuilt two centuries later, you'll also find turrets, castle gateways, a system of moats and a small shrine spread over the 49 hectares that now make up Hirosaki Castle Park. You'll also see thousands of cherry trees, which become an incredible sea of pink in spring.

07 To finish, you could pop to Tsugaru-han Neputa Village (津軽藩ねぷた村) by the northeast corner of the park, to see the giant floats used in Hirosaki's summer festival and catch a performance of the *Tsugaru-jamisen* three-stringed instrument used during the event.

08 From here, it's easy to get back to the station: follow the road south, passing the Sannomaru East Gate, then take a left onto the broad Rte 31, which reaches the station in 1.5km.

Take a Break

At the tourist information centre, you can pick up an English copy of the Hirosaki Apple Pie Guide Map, which details more than 40 places making and serving apple pies in the city, from versions that resemble flans to cinnamon-rich creations wrapped in puff pastry. On this ride, you'll find half a dozen pies to choose from at the TAISHO ROMAN TEAHOUSE in the Fujita Memorial Japanese Garden, where you can get a pie and drink set for ¥850 in an old-fashioned tearoom that could've come from an Agatha Christie story.

SEAN PAVONE/SHUTTERSTOCK

Fujita Memorial Japanese Garden

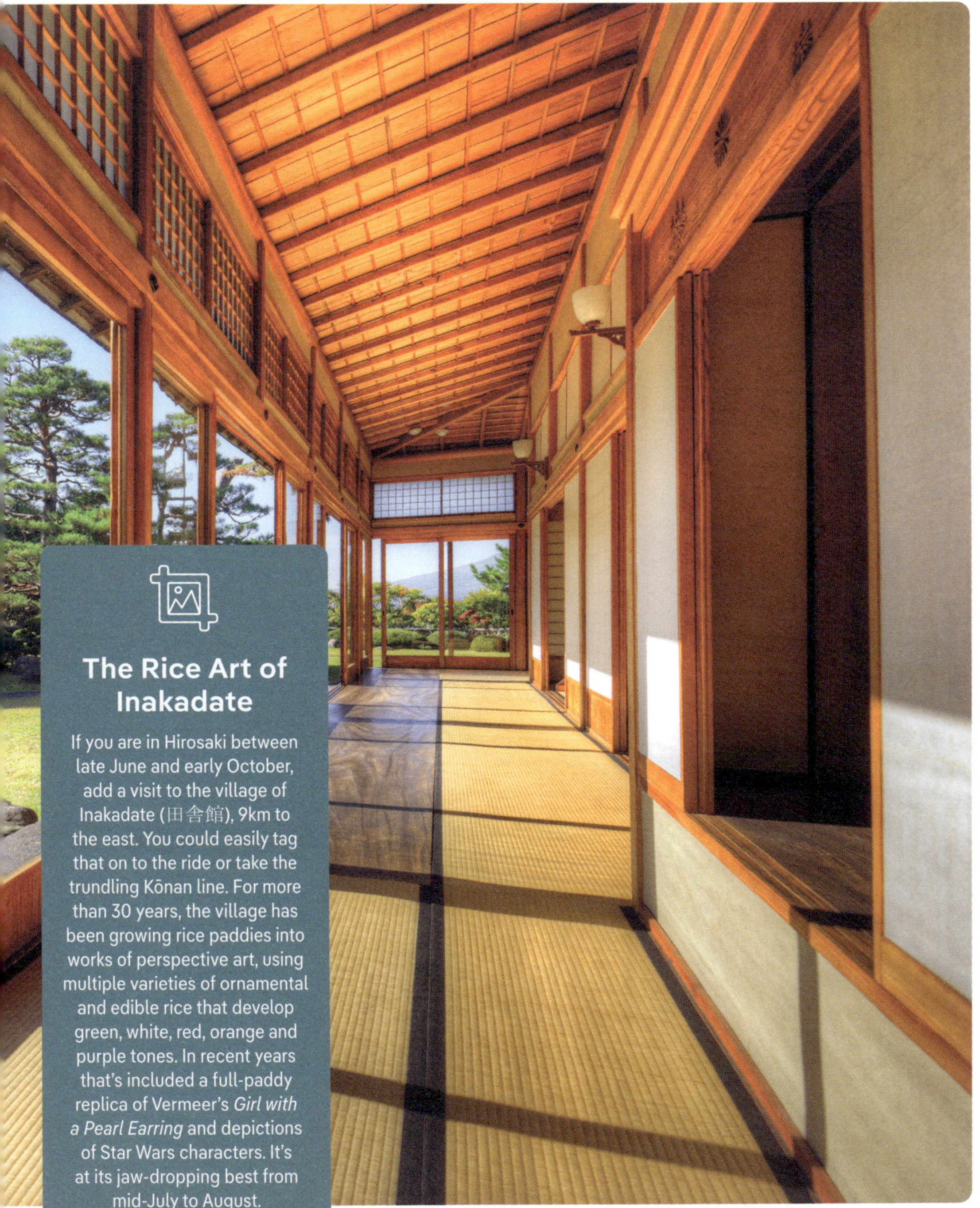

The Rice Art of Inakadate

If you are in Hirosaki between late June and early October, add a visit to the village of Inakadate (田舎館), 9km to the east. You could easily tag that on to the ride or take the trundling Kōnan line. For more than 30 years, the village has been growing rice paddies into works of perspective art, using multiple varieties of ornamental and edible rice that develop green, white, red, orange and purple tones. In recent years that's included a full-paddy replica of Vermeer's *Girl with a Pearl Earring* and depictions of Star Wars characters. It's at its jaw-dropping best from mid-July to August.

19

Best for

COASTAL SCENERY

Matsushima Circuit

DURATION	DIFFICULTY	DISTANCE	START/END
3hrs	Intermediate	32km	Matsushima Kaigan Station
TERRAIN	Paved and mostly flat		

B-HIDE THE SCENE/SHUTTERSTOCK

Buddhist statue, Zuigan-ji (p137)

For centuries, Matsushima (松島) has held a place in the Japanese psyche as one of the country's most beautiful spots. How accurate that is could be up for debate, but Matsushima Bay and its hundreds of pine-tufted islets are certainly photogenic. This slightly shortened version of the Matsushima Circuit starts and ends near the sightseeing boats that ply the bay, winds through rice fields, visits one of the region's finest temples, and offers a chance to learn about the 2011 earthquake and tsunami, which devastated parts of Tōhoku.

Bike Hire

Aihara, in the side street on the left as you leave Matsushima Kaigan Station, rents three-geared shopping bikes from ¥500 for two hours and with a returnable ¥1000 deposit. No reservations accepted.

Starting Point

Matsushima Kaigan Station, which is 40 minutes from Sendai on the JR Senseki line. From Tokyo Station, you can catch a bullet train to Sendai in 90 minutes to two hours, depending on the service.

01 Once you've got your bike, take a left onto the main road (Rte 45) just in front of Matsushima Kaigan Station (松島海岸駅). Initially, this will take you through the sightseeing centre of Matsushima, passing souvenir shops, restaurants cooking up the famed local oysters, and the sightseeing boats plying the islet-studded bay. Because the pavement is very narrow, you'll be riding on the two-lane main road here, where traffic can be heavy, so care is needed.

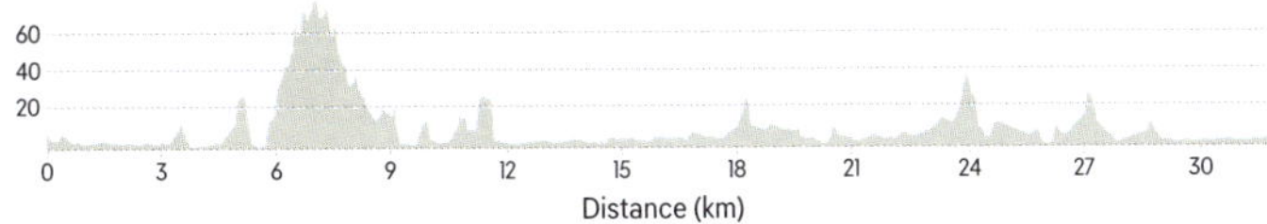

02 After passing the sightseeing boat pier – and getting your first glimpse of the bay's pine-tufted islets – the road will head north for 1km through the largely residential outskirts of Matsushima, eventually following the Taki River and passing under the elevated tracks of the Senseki line. At the next right, turn onto Rte 27 and cross the river. From here, the pavement is wide enough to ride on if you want to get off the main road, although traffic might also begin to thin out.

03 Continuing on Rte 27, the route briefly touches the coast, then goes inland through patches of farmland and the occasional bunch of houses. After 4km, shortly after a major intersection, you'll see a wooden sign on your left saying 'Tomiyama 1.4km'. Otherwise known as Mt Tomi (富山), that's the next stop. To get here, just follow the path uphill through the woods to a set of stone steps. You can park by the bottom of the steps. At the top of these steps, you'll find a small temple called Daigyō-ji (大仰寺). There are a few modest temple buildings and a quiet garden here, but the main attraction is the superb view over Matsushima Bay. Called the *reikan* (elegant view), it's one of the four classic bay views, collectively known as the *shitaikan*. The others aren't on today's cycling route, but if you want to seek them out another day, they are the *ikan* (grand view) from 55m Mt Tamon, *yukan* (spiritual view) from the Ogidani highland, and *sokan* (magnificent view) from 106m Mt Ōtakamori.

TOP TIP:

Pack Snacks

Apart from vending machines and the occasional convenience store, there aren't all that many places to get drinks or snacks once this ride leaves central Matsushima, so it's worth packing a few supplies for the journey.

The Bashō Connection

Some of the sightseeing boats in Matsushima call their bay trips the Bashō Cruise in honour of the wandering haikuist Matsuo Bashō. Why? Well, in his seminal work – the haiku-studded *Narrow Road to the Deep North* – Bashō documents his several-month walk around northern Japan in 1689. The book has become a Japanese classic. In it, the poet was so struck by the bay's beauty, he was at a loss for a suitable haiku. Instead, he simply wrote: 'Much praise has already been lavished upon the islands of Matsushima. Yet if further praise is possible, I'd like to say that here is the most beautiful spot in the whole of Japan.'

Take a Break

A few minutes from the boat pier, MATSUSHIMA FISH MARKET (松島さかな市場) has several options for a good feed. There's ramen on the 2nd floor, or on the 1st floor you could try seafood *donburi* (fresh cuts of sashimi served on a bowl of rice). Next door, the YAKIGAKI HOUSE annexe pulls in crowds for its 45-minute all-you-can-eat oyster deal. Expect queues, especially from November to March, when the oysters are at their best. For more details, visit sakana-ichiba.co.jp/en.

04 Next, head back down to Rte 27 and continue east. Along the coast anywhere in Japan, you will see signs telling you how many metres you are above sea level and pointing to tsunami evacuation zones. Riding along Tōhoku's east coast, these are all too often accompanied by reminders of the Great East Japan Earthquake. That includes the 3.11 Disaster Recovery Memorial Museum (震災復興伝承館), 5km after rejoining Rte 27. This small facility documents the events that unfolded here after a 9.0 magnitude earthquake struck offshore, triggering a tsunami that approached at speeds of 700km/h and reached land at up to 40m in height. On the afternoon of 11 March 2011, this small stretch of coast alone lost 500 people, while the tsunami claimed 20,000 lives across the Tōhoku region, with hundreds of thousands displaced.

05 After the museum, keep following the road east. Soon, it will bend and become Rte 60, a two-lane road (with no pavement in places), with a swathe of rice paddies on one side and a broad river on the other. Keep on this flat road for roughly 5km, then shortly after passing the arched Naruse Oku Matsushima Bridge (on your right), the road will turn west (left) and fork: take the road on the left, marked Rte 45.

06 Cycle along Rte 45, as before with rice paddies dominating the scenery. After roughly 3.5km, watch out for a Cosmo petrol station and take the left at the set of traffic lights about 100m before it. This quiet road cuts south for 2km through woods and more farmland, before reaching the same busy intersection you rode through earlier. Here, turn right onto Rte 27 and retrace your steps 5km back into central Matsushima to explore a cluster of nearby sights. For the first of those, look left by the area where sightseeing boats depart and you'll see a 250m-long red footbridge connecting to an island called Fukuurajima (福浦島). Pedal a minute or two over there and you can pay ¥200 to walk over the bridge, then stroll the island's nature trails for waterside views of the bay.

07 On a little outlook between the bridge and the boats, you could then check out the Godaidō (五大堂), a petite temple building that in its current form dates to the 1600s and is best known for its carvings of the 12 animals of the lunar calendar.

08 Then there's the fleet of multi-decked boats themselves, which make multiple 50-minute cruises around the bay every day – it's why most people come to Matsushima. The

LISSETTE SHOOTS/SHUTTERSTOCK

Matsushima Bay

The Three Views of Japan

In 1643 a scholar called Hayashi Gahō put Matsushima Bay on his list of Japan's most beautiful views – the *Nihon Sankei* (Three Views of Japan) – and the branding has stuck with Matsushima ever since. Along with the pine-clad sandbar of Amanohashidate in Kyoto and the 'floating' Itsukushima-jinja shrine in Hiroshima, these three are still widely considered classic viewpoints. But they aren't the only list in town. Travelling around Japan, you might notice that Japan is very fond of its 'best ofs', from the Three Great Gardens to the 100 Famous Mountains, 100 Night Views of Japan and more.

VASSAMON ANANSUKKASEM/SHUTTERSTOCK

Karantei teahouse

audio guide blasting through the tannoy might make you wish you'd brought earplugs at times, but the up-close views of Matsushima's 260 islets are fantastic. Formed millions of years ago by volcanic ash, sandstone and siltstone, some are small white rocks topped by windswept pines, while others seem to take on familiar-looking shapes, which have earned them names like Kabutojima (samurai helmet island). Some others, so the audio guide goes, were used for moon-viewing parties in the time of samurai.

09 Looking inland from the centre of the pier, you'll also see a side street leading to a temple gateway. This is Zuigan-ji (瑞巌寺), the family temple for daimyō (local lord) Date Masamune, who founded Sendai in the early 1600s and left an indelible legacy on the region. Known as the 'one-eyed dragon' for a combination of his ferocity in battle and an eye lost to smallpox as a child, Masamune built a grand castle in Sendai and created a powerful domain that would be led by generations of the Date clan. He was also known as a patron of arts, which shows in the intricate details at Zuigan-ji. When he came to power, Masamune oversaw a five-year restoration of the temple (then already 800 years old), bringing in more than 100 artisans from Kyoto and Wakayama to essentially rebuild it, in the process decorating Zuigan-ji's main hall with a wonderful collection of sliding doors featuring birds and blossoms on black lacquer and gold-leaf backdrops. You can see more art and Date-clan artefacts at Zuigan-ji's museum.

10 Next to Zuigan-ji, Entsū-in (円通院) is a temple with a sadder backstory. It was built by Masamune's son, Tadamune, as a mausoleum for his own son Mitsumune, who died aged just 19. There's a Japanese-style garden and Western-style rose garden on the grounds, and in autumn the temple's fiery foliage makes this a popular *kōyō* (autumn leaves) spot. Look closely inside the main mausoleum and you'll also see Western motifs, such as crosses, diamonds and clubs, which are unusual for this period in Japan. That's a reflection of the Date clan's interest in international relations. Before Japan banned Christianity in 1614 and introduced a policy of near self-isolation, Date Masamune was open to Christian missionaries and even funded a mission to Rome to establish relations with the pope.

11 From here, you can return to the main road and follow it for a minute or two back to Matsushima Kaigan Station, where trains leave for Sendai several times an hour.

Take a Break

Fancy taking tea in a 400-year-old teahouse? Stop by the KANRANTEI (観瀾亭) between Matsushima Kaigan Station and the sightseeing boat pier. Originally built in Kyoto, the building was moved here in the 1600s to provide comfort and views of the bay for visiting dignitaries. It costs ¥200 to look at the tatami-mat tearooms and their ornately decorated *fusuma* (sliding doors), but for an extra ¥600 to ¥800 you can enjoy matcha tea with a choice of Japanese sweets.

20

Tōno

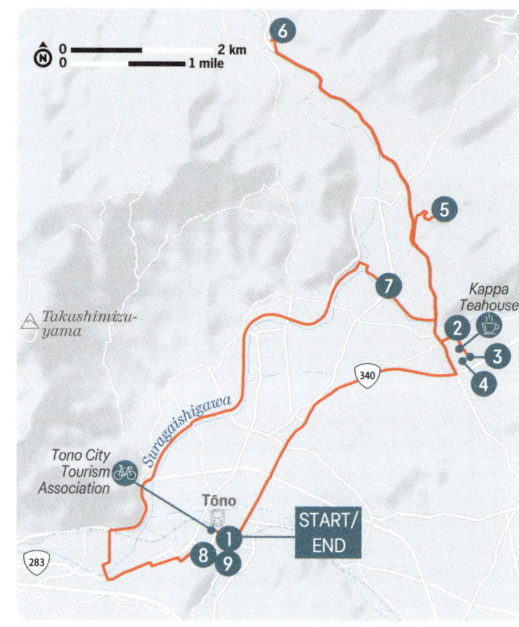

SUZUKI KAKU/ALAMY

DURATION	DIFFICULTY	DISTANCE	START/END
3hrs	Intermediate	28km	JR Tōno Station

TERRAIN	Mostly flat with some hills between Denshōen and Tōno Furusato Village

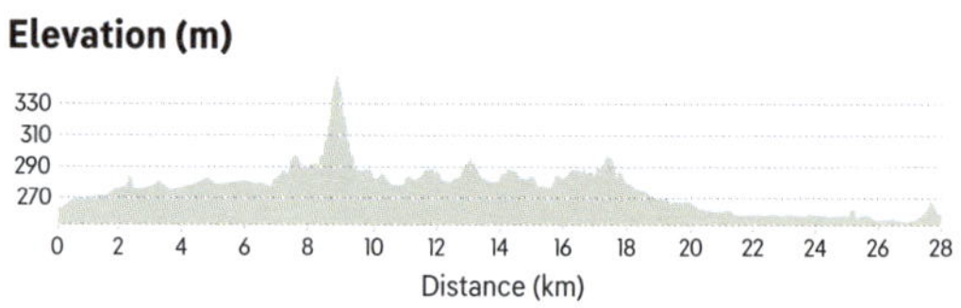

Deep in the countryside of Iwate Prefecture, a ride around the Tōno (遠野) valley is an invitation to slow down and experience rural Japan at its unhurried best. You'll cycle by swathes of rice paddies and riverbanks alive with the hum of insects. You'll come across preserved farmhouses that offer insights into the region's traditions. And there'll be multiple opportunities to discover that Tōno wears its fascinating folklore with justified pride. For a complete contrast to modern, urban Japan, this is the perfect place to linger.

Bike Hire

The tourist information centre by Tōno Station rents push bikes and multi-gear e-bikes from April to November. Four hours costs ¥720/1100, respectively, or you could rent for a full day for ¥1120/1500.

Starting Point

Tōno Station is on the JR Kamaishi line. If you are coming from the Tōhoku Shinkansen, transfer to the Kamaishi line at Shin Hanamaki, which is 45 minutes from Tōno.

From the tourist information centre by Tōno Station (遠野駅), start by cycling three blocks east to Rte 340, where heading north (left) for a couple of kilometres will take you through the outskirts of town and into an expanse of countryside.

After 4km, take a left off Rte 340 onto Rte 160 and follow it for about 500m to a crossroads. Turning right here takes you to the first stop, Denshōen (伝承園), home to preserved thatched farmhouses that give insights into traditional life in Tōno, as well as highlighting some of

Wishes on Oshira-sama dolls, Denshōen

Best for

FOLKLORE

The Legends of Tōno

Compiled by folklorist Kunio Yanigata in the early 1900s, *Tōno Monogatari* (The Legends of Tōno) offers fascinating glimpses into the folklore and traditions of rural Japan. The 119 tales Yanigata documented on his Tōno travels feature mythical beings like the green-skinned *kappa* and oddities such as the farmer's daughter who eloped to the stars with her equine beau. Today, storytellers still pass down the tales, often beginning their stories with an enticing *mukashi mukashi* (once upon a time), and you'll frequently encounter folklore while cycling around Tōno – including anime-like *kappa* on road signs. If you want to read the tales, you can buy an English version at the tourist information centre.

the local folklore. In one L-shaped farmhouse, in particular, you'll come across a room decorated with a thousand Oshira-sama dolls on which are hung wishes written on yellow, blue and red pieces of cloth. That all relates to one of the more unusual Tōno tales, about a farmer's daughter who fell in love with and secretly married her horse, sending her father into such a rage that he killed the horse and hung it from a mulberry tree. There was more to come. As the daughter wept over the horse's body, the farmer grabbed his axe and beheaded it, at which point horse and daughter are said to have magically eloped to the stars. Carved from a pair of mulberry sticks – one with the head of a horse, one with the head of a girl – the Oshira-sama dolls pay homage to their story.

03 After Denshōen, there are a couple of other sights within a couple of hundred metres, so you could leave your bike in Denshōen's car park and go for a brief stroll. Just across the road, after passing a hop field, start with Jōken-ji (常堅寺), where among the highlights are two carved statues of *Niō* guarding the temple's roofed gateway.

04 Just behind the temple you'll also find the Kappabuchi Pond (カッパ淵), where a mythical *kappa* – a green-skinned creature with a love of cucumbers and drowning people – lives. Just in case the legend comes to life and a *kappa* emerges from the water, fear not, for *kappa* have one weakness: politeness. If you bow, they will bow in return, causing the life-giving water to spill from their basin-shaped head and sending them scurrying away for a refill.

05 Get back on your bike and take Rte 160 north, heading over the Kogarase River and then pedalling a couple of kilometres to Fukusen-ji (福泉寺), which is worth a stop to see the temple's 25-tonne statue of Buddha. It's also a lovely spot for cherry blossoms in spring, and red and gold foliage in autumn.

06 From here, follow Rte 160 another 4km north to Tōno Furusato Village (遠野ふるさと村), to see a collection of Edo-era farmhouses that recreate a traditional hamlet, complete with rice paddies and horses in pasture. Sometimes, you can also catch a traditional storyteller here recounting the Tōno tales.

07 Now it's time for a little backtracking. First, cycle 6km back to the Kogarase River, where you'll turn right on to the Tōno-Towa Cycling Road. You'll follow this for about 7km – through rice paddies and idyllic countryside, with buzzards very possibly hovering overhead – as it shadows the river west before

Take a Break

Once you are out of central Tōno, you won't find many places to buy food or drinks other than the occasional vending machine, so make sure you pack some snacks and water. One option early in the ride is KAPPA TEAHOUSE (closed Tuesday and Wednesday) next to Jōken-ji. The menu here includes soft-serve ice cream, coffee and simple soba (buckwheat noodles) served cold with a dipping sauce or in a warming broth.

ZIGGY_MARS/SHUTTERSTOCK

Tōno Furusato Village

looping back into central Tōno and connecting to Rte 238.

08 Once you are on Rte 238, you'll see signs for the Tōno Folktale Museum (遠野物語の館), several blocks south of the station. The museum does a great job of documenting Tōno's folklore and the work of folklorist Kunio Yanagita, with *kiri-e* (paper-cutting art), video installations and regular performances (in Japanese) by traditional storytellers.

09 To end the ride, head a few hundred metres north up the main street to Tōno Station and tourist info centre.

Make a Night of It

If you want to experience an evening in small-town Japan and add more rural rides, Tōno is ideal. The staff at the tourist information centre can provide cycling maps for a second day of riding, and despite being a quiet town there are good accommodation options. That includes Tōno's main Western-style hotel, Aeria Tōno, which has communal hot-spring baths. Or there are *minshuku* like Kuranoya, a couple of kilometres from the station, which has friendly English-speaking owners and offers station pickups. For dinner, Tōno's main street is home to several *izakaya* (casual Japanese pub or bar), or you could stop by the local craft brewer, Tōno Brewing, for an IPA or two.

21

Sakata Art Ride

MIAIKA/SHUTTERSTOCK

DURATION	DIFFICULTY	DISTANCE	START/END
1.5hrs	Easy	15km	Sakata Station

TERRAIN	Flat and paved; no designated cycling paths

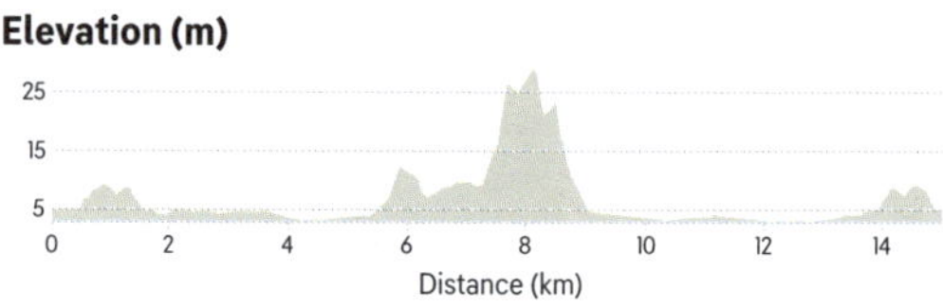

Not many overseas travellers make it to this part of Yamagata Prefecture on the Japan Sea coast. Those who do, however, can enjoy an easy ride that shines a light on everyday urban Japan beyond the main cities, while taking in Sakata's (酒田) collection of art and photography museums, a lively fish market, a beautiful garden and villa, and other sites that offer glimpses of this harbour town's halcyon days. Time your trip for mid-May and you could also catch Sakata's lively annual festival.

Bike Hire

Near Sakata Station in the Miraini complex, the tourist info centre offers free push bikes and rental e-bikes from late March to November. E-bikes are ¥500 for one hour, ¥1500 for four hours or ¥3000 for eight hours.

Starting Point

Sakata Station, which isn't the easiest place to reach. The nearest bullet-train stations are Niigata Station, two hours south on the Inaho express train, and Akita Station, two hours north on the JR Uetsu line.

01 From Sakata Station (酒田駅), take the road that leads by Hotel Alpha One. After 200m, go left at the Family Mart convenience store.

02 You'll now be in front of the first stop, the Homma Museum of Art (本間美術館), although the art on display is just one of several reasons to pay the ¥1100 admission. In the gallery itself, you'll find two rooms of art from the Homma family's eclectic collection, which depending on when you visit could be Japanese prints depicting scenes from daily life in 19th-century Tōhoku or 16th-century tea bowls.

Sankyo Sokō (p144)

Best for

ART

The Sakata Matsuri

Every year from 19 to 21 May, Sakata breaks out its party gear. Held since the early 1600s, its annual festival features parades of floats shaped like giant lion heads, which seek out children and pretend to bite their heads. There are traditional street musicians and portable shrines too. While all that's happening, there's also a bazaar with several hundred vendors selling street food, drinks and local crafts. If you aren't visiting during the festival, you'll still see the lion heads on this ride – or statues of them – on the road about halfway between the Homma Museum of Art and Sankyo Sōko.

Make sure to visit the neighbouring garden and villa (covered by the same ticket), which was built by the Hommas – once Japan's richest family – in the 1800s. Not only is the garden a wonderful example of traditional landscaping, with stone pathways winding around its central pond, but you can take in garden views over matcha and sweets in the tearoom.

03 From the museum, take the main road (Rte 42) south. You'll soon pass a small shrine and the road will then run through a low-rise part of town that, like many regional cities and towns around Japan, is accented by occasional boarded-up shops and derelict buildings. This is as much modern-day Japan as neon-lit images of central Tokyo. After 1.5km, you'll come to a bridge. Take a right here and follow the road 800m to Sakata Seafood Market (酒田海鮮市場). As well as stalls selling seafood, the several buildings here offer plenty of places to grab a bite to eat, with seafood *donburi* a local favourite.

04 Head back to the bridge. On the other side is the next stop, the photogenic Sankyo Sōko (山居倉庫), a row of wooden rice storehouses built in the late 1800s, when Sakata was an important merchant town. Of the dozen storehouses, some are still in use and others are undergoing restoration, but a few are grouped together as a shop selling local produce and crafts – from artisanal sake and craft beer to *sashiko* quilting, indigo silks, painted candles and paper crafts.

05 Now you get to cycle for a few kilometres. From the Sankyo Sōko, keep going southwest down the main road and in about 600m you'll cross the wide Mogami-gawa. About 1km later, at the first major intersection after the bridge, take a left onto Rte 355 and follow it 500m to the Ken Domon Museum of Photography (土門拳記念館). Sakata-born Domon was one of Japan's leading photographers, known for photojournalistic work documenting post-war Japan but also later images of temples, shrines and religious artworks, such as Buddhist statues. Before he died in 1990, he left some 70,000 photographs to Sakata.

06 Leaving the museum, go straight (west) then take the next right (north) and you'll be at the Sakata Museum of Art (酒田市美術館), worth a visit for its permanent collection of Japanese artists, ranging from the oil paintings of Shigeru Morita and Sakata-native Chozo Saito to pieces by sculptor Go Takahashi.

07 From here, take the road north and turn right onto the main road that leads back to the Mogami-gawa and all

JOHN S LANDER/LIGHTROCKET VIA GETTY IMAGES

Garden of the Homma Museum of Art

Take a Break

When you get to SAKATA SEAFOOD MARKET (酒田海鮮市場), head to the 2nd floor of the main building for Tobishima. This lively food hall, on the right at the top of the stairs, serves up the day's catches in several ways, from set meals of sashimi or grilled fish with rice, miso soup and pickles to *donburi* topped with super-fresh cuts of sashimi. Ordering is easy: there are large photos of all the options hanging above the counter.

the way on to the Homma Museum of Art, where a right will get you to the Sakata Station area. If you fancy a detour, however, take a right as soon as you have crossed the river and follow the road 500m south to the Oranda Senbei Factory (オランダせんべい). Here they make *senbei* (rice crackers), an incredibly popular snack in Japan, and for a small fee you can take a tour of the production line, from dough-making to baking, roasting and packing. For an extra fee, you could even get hands-on and try grilling and flavouring a few *senbei*.

Head north back to the main road, turn right and go back to Sakata Station.

Stay for a Hike

Given Sakata isn't the easiest of places to get to, staying a night can make for a much more laid-back experience. There are several simple, but reliable hotels by the station, including Alpha One and Tsuki no Hotel. Twenty minutes away on the Inaho express, you could then add a visit to Tsuruoka, the gateway (via bus) to the sacred mountains of Dewa Sanzan. These three peaks offer a variety of trails and historic sights, as well as opportunities to stay in pilgrim lodges and take part in mindful hikes and waterfall meditation sessions with *yamabushi* ascetics. For more, see hagurokanko.jp/en.

Also Try...

Inawashiro-ko with views of Bandai-san, Fukushima

MUSASHI2001/SHUTTERSTOCK

Hachinohe & the Tanesashi Coast, Aomori

DURATION	DIFFICULTY	DISTANCE
4hrs	Intermediate	44km

This loop ride in Aomori Prefecture traces part of the Michinoku Coastal Trail before heading inland for a hill climb. On the way, you can fill up on fresh seafood at Mutsu Minato Morning Market, take in the gull-covered Kabushima Shrine, and enjoy varied scenery – from the natural Tanesashi lawn to Shirahama swimming beach. If you need a rental bike, plan to start and end the ride by Tanesashi Kaigan Station, which has a rental shop and a good information centre. It's 40 minutes from Hachinohe (a bullet train stop) on the Hachinohe line. And don't worry if the seagulls at Kabushima poop on you – that's considered good luck. The shrine will even give you a commemorative plaque.

Lake Inawashiro, Fukushima

DURATION	DIFFICULTY	DISTANCE
5hrs	Intermediate	58km

Known as the Inaichi, this ride loops around Inawashiro-ko (猪苗代湖; Lake Inawashiro) in Bandai-Asahi National Park, Fukushima Prefecture, passing farmland and lakeside beaches, and delivering winning views of the lake with Bandai-san in the distance. The ride is best between May and November, but it's possible to rent fat-tyre bikes and wrap up warm for a winter ride – just be aware that some places around the lake are closed for winter. Bikes and e-bikes can be rented from several places, including the tourist information centre by Inawashiro Station on the lake's northern side. You can get there from Kōriyama (a bullet train stop) on the JR Banetsu West line (40 minutes).

JAPAN EXPLORERS/SHUTTERSTOCK

Oga Peninsula

Hamakaidō, Miyagi

DURATION	DIFFICULTY	DISTANCE
9hrs	Difficult	114km

If you are travelling with your own long-distance bike, the Hamakaidō ride is a great way to explore Miyagi Prefecture over one or two days – starting and ending at Sendai Airport on a route that mixes urban and rural scenery, visits local markets, and also includes the option for a soak in natural hot-spring baths. Of course, you don't have to do the full route or start at the airport. Miyagi Prefecture's official cycling website *(japancycling.jp/en)* details more than a dozen shorter routes that could be done with a rental bike, from a 22km trip following a pilgrimage trail to a 36km coastal ride. The website also lists places to eat, stay and stop for bike repairs.

Oga Peninsula, Akita

DURATION	DIFFICULTY	DISTANCE
5hrs	Difficult	60km

Do an image search for 'windswept' and you might find a picture of the Oga Peninsula (男鹿半島) on Tōhoku's west coast. A ride here is all about rugged coastal scenery and pedalling for hours in fresh air, and there are a variety of up-and-down loops listed – in Japanese, but with downloadable GPS data – on the local tourism bureau's website *(oganavi.com/cycling)*. That includes a full 60km ride around the peninsula, starting from Oga Station and, among other things, visiting a rock formation that is said to resemble Godzilla. You can rent e-bikes and road bikes from spring through to autumn at Oga Jitensha *(ogajitensha.studio.site)* by Oga Station.

0 50 km
0 25 miles
Sea of Japan
Sea of Okhotsk
PACIFIC OCEAN
Teshio-gawa
Nayoro
Monbetsu
Haboro
Shibetsu
Saroma-ko
Abashiri
Engaru
Notoro-ko
Shari
26
Rumoi
Kitami
Bihiro
Kamikawa
Numata
Asahikawa
Rubeshibe
Kushiro-shitsugen National Park
Asahi-dake
Biei
Kussharo-ko
Takikawa
Ishikari-gawa
25
Daisetsuzan National Park
Teshikaga
Tokachi-dake
Ishikari-wan
Shibecha
Bibai
Furano
Shakotan Peninsula
Furubira
Mikasa
Ashoro
Ishikari
Yoichi
Otaru
Akan-Mashū National Park
Ebetsu
Sapporo
Shimizu
23
22
Shiranuka
Kushiro
Iwanai
Obihiro
Eniwa
Kutchan
Chitose
Niseko
Yōtei-zan
Shikotsu-ko
Poroshiri-dake
Shikotsu-Tōya National Park
24
Tomakomai
Tōya-ko
Toyoura
Mukawa
Sobetsu
Shiraoi
Date
Noboribetsu
Uchiura-wan
Muroran
Shinhidaka
Hiro
Yakumo
Urakawa

THE ASAHI SHIMBUN/GETTY IMAGES

Flower field, Biei (p166)

Hokkaidō

22 Sapporo Explorer

There's lots to see on two wheels in the prefectural capital, the fifth-largest city in Japan. **p152**

23 Niseko Yōtei-zan Loop Trail

A loop trail featuring hot springs, cafes, fresh spring water and spectacular views of Yōtei-zan. **p158**

24 Biking Around Tōya-ko

Ride around the almost perfectly circular caldera lake and seek out 58 sculptures. **p162**

25 Biei's Patchwork Road

Rolling countryside with farm fields and paddocks that resemble a patchwork quilt. **p166**

26 Abashiri on Two Wheels

Museums, history and scenery galore in eastern Hokkaidō, on the Sea of Okhotsk coast. **p170**

Explore

Hokkaidō

It's like a different world up here, or at least it feels like it, with 20% of Japan's land area but only 5% of its population. The Japanese identify this northern land with its wildlife and mountains, greenery and agriculture, snowy winters, temperate summers and straight roads disappearing into the horizon. But there's more to Hokkaidō (北海道) than just the scenery. The realm of its indigenous people, the Ainu, there's a culture here that's unlike other parts of Japan; a 'Wild West' feel as the new frontier that was only really colonised by the Japanese from the 1870s onwards – an island perfect for exploration by bicycle.

Sapporo

The prefectural capital and fifth-largest city in Japan, Sapporo (札幌; population two million) is a dynamic and cosmopolitan urban centre that pulses with energy. Designed by European and American architects in the late 19th century, Sapporo is shaped by its wide grid of tree-lined streets and ample parks, giving it a high level of liveability. It boasts a thriving food scene, stylish cafes, neon-lit nightlife and shopping galore. The population literally doubles during the legendary Snow Festival in February, while Sapporo Beer and Sapporo Ramen are household names throughout Japan. There's excellent cycling around the city with a well-run bicycle-share system known as Porocle.

Niseko

While Niseko (ニセコ) doesn't technically mean 'snow', it may as well do, as this is what the resort town is known for throughout Japan and the winter sports world. Once the snows have melted, Niseko becomes an appealing green resort, trying to attract a year-round clientele with a burgeoning set of summer activities that include some excellent bike rides. Facilities are good and with plenty of accommodation and empty rooms outside of winter, there are bargains to be had.

Abashiri

This east-coast city is famous for the *ryūhyō* (drift ice) in the frozen Sea of Okhotsk, which can be explored on ice-breakers in the colder months. Once things

WHEN TO GO

Winter brings snow and great skiing, though not much biking. For cherry blossoms, visit in late April. *Tsuyu* (the rainy season) famously doesn't affect Hokkaidō, though some swear that's changing, along with the climate. Few typhoons make it this far north; summers are relatively cool and dry. For hills alive with autumn foliage, late September is ideal.

warm up though, Abashiri (網走) is a great jumping-off point for Shiretoko and Akan Mashū national parks, and a good spot to rent a bike. To the Japanese, Abashiri is as synonymous with the word 'prison' as Alcatraz is to Americans. Just mention the city's name and the Japanese will shiver; winters are as harsh as it gets and so is the prison's reputation, thanks in part to the 1965 cult classic film *Abashiri Bangaichi* (Abashiri Prison).

Wakkanai

It's hard to get more remote than Wakkanai (稚内), Japan's northernmost city, but if you're going to the islands of Rishiri-tō or Rebun-tō, you'll have to come here as this is where the ferries leave from. There's a sense of this place still being a pioneering outpost, with frigidly cold winters, and in the warmer months it's not unusual for Ezo-shika (Hokkaidō deer) to come down out of the hills around town and wander the streets at night. Cape Sōya, 31km to the northeast, is the Japanese mainland's northernmost point, and the Russian island of Sakhalin can be seen to the north on a good day.

TRANSPORT

These days, a number of airports across Hokkaidō receive flights from Japan's major cities. The biggest, New Chitose Airport, 45km southeast of Sapporo, is considered the gateway airport, with domestic connections and a growing number of international flights. Catching a ferry is a good option for getting to Hokkaidō, as is the train via the 54km Seikan Tunnel from the top of Honshū.

WHAT'S ON

Sapporo Summer Festival

For a month in summer, Ōdori-kōen in Sapporo becomes a massive playground of eating, drinking, singing and dancing.

Belly-Button Festival

Held in Furano (because it's in the middle!) in July; expect face-painting on people's torsos and a huge parade.

Ainu Cultural Performances

Held daily at Upopoy: National Ainu Museum & Park, and at Ikor Theatre in Akanko Onsen's Ainu village.

WHERE TO STAY

Hokkaidō has the full range of sleeping options, from campsites to business hotels, unusual lodgings run by eccentric characters, all the way up to luxury ryokan (traditional Japanese inns). Ski towns have lots of accommodation places with empty rooms out of the ski season; expect bargains in the warmer months. There are also deals to be had in onsen (hot springs) towns outside of weekends and holiday periods. Your best bet is to look at what's available online at travel.rakuten.com and trivago.com. Want a room in Sapporo during the Snow Festival? You'll need to book way in advance.

Resources

Hokkaidō Love *(visit-hokkaido.jp)* The prefecture's official tourism site.

Welcome to Sapporo *(sapporo.travel)* The capital's website.

Porocle *(porocle.jp/en)* Sapporo's cycle-share system.

Hokkaidō Cycle Tourism Promotion Association *(hkd.mlit.go.jp)* Useful cycling information.

Hokkaido Wilds *(hokkaidowilds.org)* Info on Hokkaidō cycle touring.

22

Sapporo Explorer

DURATION	DIFFICULTY	DISTANCE	START/END
4–5hrs	Easy	42km	Sapporo TV Tower
TERRAIN	Flat and paved		

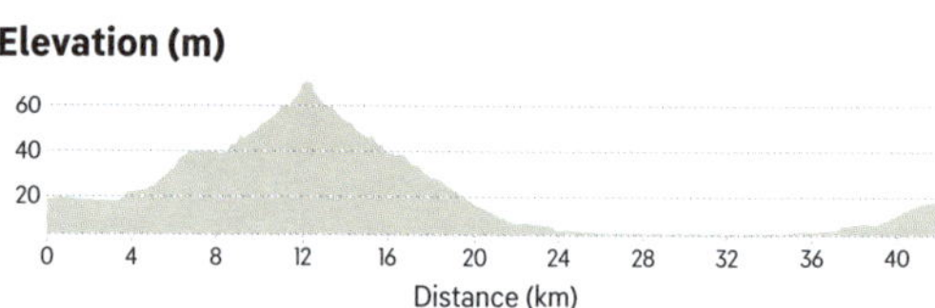

There's no better way to explore Hokkaidō's capital, the fifth-largest city in Japan, than on two wheels. Sapporo has an excellent and efficient bike-share system, Porocle, that offers e-bikes outside of the snowy season, from early April to mid-November. Make the most of this and saddle up, cycling around the city to check out a slew of intriguing attractions, many of which are associated with the parks, Ōdōri-kōen, Maruyama-kōen, Makomanai-kōen and Moerenuma-kōen. The Toyohira-gawa cycling path, down by the river, below the floodbanks, provides an excellent link through this extremely likeable and bikeable city.

Bike Hire

Porocle *(porocle.jp)* is Sapporo's bike-share system, with e-bikes and 60 ports around the city. Pick up and drop off at any port.

Starting Point

The 147m-high Sapporo TV Tower, at the eastern end of Ōdōri-kōen, is a central, highly visible landmark with a Porocle bike port nearby.

01 Before you start your ride, take the lift up to Sapporo TV Tower's (さっぽろテレビ塔) observation deck at 90m. The 147m-high tower, built in 1957, got in there ahead of Tokyo Tower, which went up in 1958. The views are excellent; in particular, look west, directly down the 1.5km-long, one-block-wide Ōdōri-kōen (大通公園), as this will be the first part of your ride.

RICHIE CHAN/SHUTTERSTOCK

Best for

CITY HIGHLIGHTS

Sapporo Shiryokan

02 Back on the ground, on your bike, ride the length of the park – you're not allowed to ride through Ōdōri-kōen, so ride down the road and get off and push when you spot something interesting and want to go into the park and take a look. Originally designed in 1869 as a firebreak to separate the city into a government area to the north, and a commercial and residential area to the south, this marvellous 13-block stretch went on to become a lovely city park, with beautifully manicured gardens, green lawns, overhanging trees and plentiful artwork, fountains, statues, and benches to relax on. Ōdōri-kōen also hosts a number of the city's major events and festivals, such as the Sapporo Snow Festival in February, and four blocks become a massive beer garden in the summer.

03 At the end of the park, opposite the lovely sunken garden is the impressive 1926-built Sapporo Shiryōkan (Former Sapporo Court of Appeals). While the grounds and garden seem like an extension of the park, head inside for free-admission exhibitions such as a courtroom and a memorial hall dedicated to Sapporo-born manga artist and painter Hiroshi Ōba.

04 Carry on riding west along Ōdōri Ave for 2km to the entrance to leafy Maruyama-kōen (円山公園). This extensive parkland is home to the designated natural treasure, Maruyama Wild Forest, numerous sports facilities, Sapporo City Maruyama Zoo, and Hokkaidō-jingū, built in 1869 as Sapporo's main Shintō shrine. If you've been checking out Shintō shrines around Japan and are surprised at the 'newness' of Hokkaidō-jingū, remember that the Japanese really only colonised Hokkaidō from the 1870s. The park is known for its plum and cherry blossoms in early May, seen later here at these higher latitudes than in the main cities of Honshū.

Take a Break

Sapporo is renowned Japan-wide for its tasty ramen noodles and the signature dish here is a hearty *miso-rāmen.* While you'll find ramen shops all over the city, hop on your bike and ride south of Ōdōri-kōen to the entertainment district Susukino to find the infamous GANSO RAMEN YOKOCHŌ, the 'original ramen alley', open since the early 1950s, with 17 tiny, atmospheric ramen shops to choose from. Wander this narrow, often-crowded 150m-long alley before making your pick.

05 Back at the park entrance, turn right on Kanjō-dōri and bike 3.4km to the Moiwa-yama Ropeway (藻岩山) entrance. Park and ride the scenic ropeway and cable-car system to the observation deck and restaurant at the top of Moiwa-yama (531m) for magnificent views over Sapporo city. You may be surprised to see the Moiwa-yama Ski Area up here too.

06 Back on your bike at the bottom, continue riding southeast on Kanjō-dōri to the next main intersection, where you'll see the Sapporo tram tracks; turn left and follow the tracks east across the city. The tram system, known as *shiden,* operates cute little trams on a loop route south from Susukino and first started up in 1909. At the corner where the trams head back north – 2km from the Moiwa-yama Ropeway entrance – continue for 200m to the Toyohira-gawa (豊平川) and make your way down from the floodbank to the riverside cycling path. Turn right, upriver towards the mountains.

07 The area between the river itself and the floodbank is wide, green and home to various sports facilities. On the 1km ride to the Toyohira River Water Garden, a park with a nice playground for kids and families, you'll pass five baseball fields and a pair of tennis courts. Stay on the Toyohira-gawa cycle path, pass under the beautiful cable-stayed Munich Bridge – Munich and Sapporo share an interest in beer, and have been sister cities for over 50 years – then cross the Toyohira-gawa on the Moiwakamino Bridge.

08 On the eastern side of the river now, it's only a short ride to the Sapporo Salmon Museum at the northern end of Makomanai-kōen. Following WWII, infrastructure struggled to keep pace with a huge increase in Sapporo's population, and deteriorating water conditions in the Toyohira-gawa meant that wild salmon failed to return to the river to spawn. Conditions improved in the 1970s, and in 1978 the Come Back Salmon Movement began as a programme to educate the public on the issue. The river was stacked with juvenile salmon and in recent years some 1000 salmon have returned to the river to spawn each year. This museum tells the story with exhibitions and an outdoor pond where you can feed the fish.

09 Makomanai-kōen (真駒内公園), previously a dairy factory and farm, became the main area for the

DOCTOREGG/GETTY IMAGES

View from the Sapporo TV Tower (p152)

A Planned City

While there wasn't much in Sapporo before it was named Hokkaidō's capital in 1868 by the new Meiji government, things soon got moving. European and American architects helped develop a city with a wide grid of streets at right-angles to form city blocks, and plenty of public parks. Thirteen-block-long Ōdōri-kōen split the city north and south, while the man-made canal, Sōsei-gawa, split it west and east. Sapporo city addresses are still given using a quadrant system; for example, Sapporo Clock Tower is at North 1, West 2. As a recently developed city, you won't find old temples, shrines and castles as you do in mainland Japanese cities.

Toyohira River

From the Jōzankei valley, deep in the mountains south of Sapporo, the Toyohira-gawa flows north through the city and into the Ishikari-gawa. Levees were first built to protect the new city from the Toyohira-gawa in the 1890s, but following a series of floods, bigger floodbanks were constructed. The Hōheikyō Dam (1972) and Jōzankei Dam (1989) were subsequently built to control the Toyohira-gawa's water flow, generate power and as a water supply for Sapporo. High floodbanks on both sides of the river mean there are a lot of sports facilities, including bike trails down beside the river, as the Toyohira-gawa flows through Sapporo.

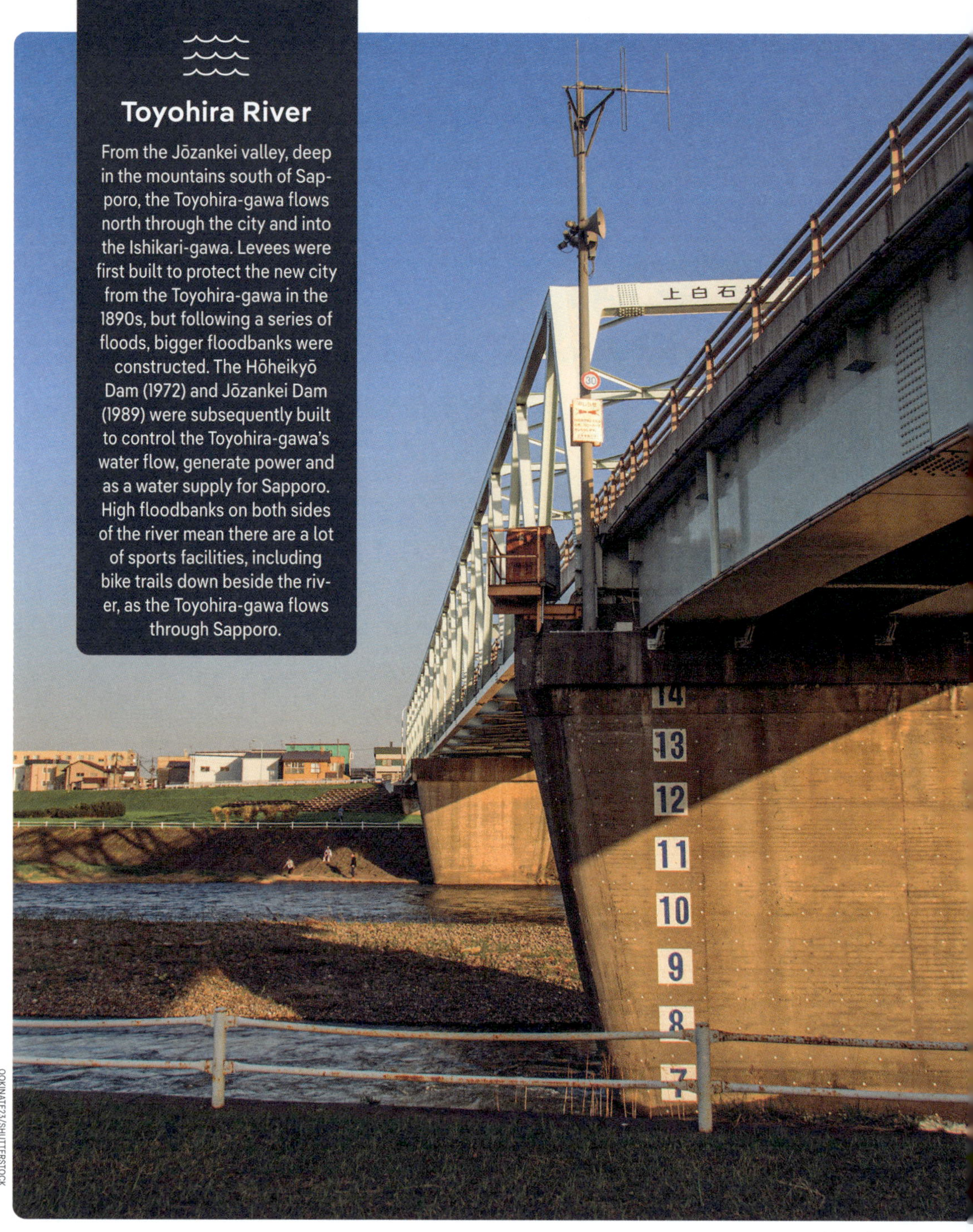

OOKINATE23/SHUTTERSTOCK

Toyohira River

1972 Sapporo Winter Olympics. The opening ceremony was held here at Makomanai Open Stadium, which also hosted the speed skating events. After the Olympics, the site was transformed into a huge park and opened to the public in 1975. These days, Makomanai-kōen has over 10km of walking paths, used in winter as cross-country skiing trails. The Makomanai-gawa flows into the Toyohira-gawa at the park's northern end, just north of the Sapporo Salmon Museum.

10 Return to the Toyohira cycling path and pedal back north, downriver this time, on the same route you came on. After 6.5km you'll get to the Toyohira Bridge; if you've had enough riding for the day, pop back up onto the floodbank, then turn west and ride until you hit the Sosei-gawa canal. Turn right and you'll soon spot the Sapporo TV Tower, where you started.

11 At the Toyohira Bridge, if you'd like to carry on riding out to Moerenuma-kōen (モエレ沼公園; allow two to three hours for the return journey and exploring time), stay on the Toyohira cycle path by the river and continue for 10km. After a couple of major road bridges cross the river above you, you'll notice that the Toyohira-gawa has changed from a winding, curling river to something more akin to a canal – in the 1930s, a new channel was constructed to move the Toyohira's confluence with the Ishikari-gawa permanently downstream to the west. When the small Karikishin-gawa joins the Toyohira-gawa from your left, ride up onto the floodbank and follow the small stream northwest and inland 2km to the Moerenuma-kōen East Gate.

12 Huge Moerenuma-kōen, about 12km northeast of the city centre, is a reclaimed green belt from what was formerly a waste-treatment plant. The task of designing the 160-hectare park was presented to renowned American Japanese artist Isamu Noguchi, who designed it before his death in 1988. His work was completed, and opened to the public in 2005 as a sculpture and art park. When you visit, rather than thinking of yourself being in a massive public park, it's probably more accurate to see yourself as immersed in a huge sculpture piece. You can explore the park by the bike you came on. Kids love this place – there are 126 pieces of playground equipment scattered about, designed by Noguchi, that are both play structures and works of art.

TOP TIP:

Take Your Time

This ride can be cycled in one big day, or you could split it up and do three shorter rides over two or even three days – to each of Maruyama-kōen, Makomanai-kōen and Moerenuma-kōen.

The crowning glory though is the massive glass pyramid *Hidamari,* meaning 'sunny spot', the symbol of Moerenuma-kōen. Don't miss climbing one of five routes to the top of the 61m-high Moere-yama, designed to give a perfectly triangular silhouette.

13 When you've had enough of exploring, return to the Toyohira-gawa, turn south (right) and ride back alongside the river for 10km into central Sapporo. Get yourself onto Ōdōri Ave and you'll soon see Sapporo TV Tower, where you started your ride.

Take a Break

Sapporo is synonymous with beer and there's no better place to try the local brew than at the legendary SAPPORO BEER MUSEUM, an easy 2km ride northeast of Sapporo TV Tower. There's good English signage throughout and you can try beers in the Star Hall tasting room for ¥200 to ¥300 each. Sapporo Beer, first brewed here in 1876, was meant to be enjoyed with the local grilled-mutton speciality *jingisukan* (Genghis Khan); there are three on-site restaurants where you can partake.

23

Best for

HOT SPRINGS & MOUNTAIN VIEWS

Niseko Yōtei-zan Loop Trail

DURATION	DIFFICULTY	DISTANCE	START/END
5hrs	Intermediate	62km	Kutchan Town

TERRAIN	Paved roads, mild uphill and downhill

TKYSZK/SHUTTERSTOCK

Niseko Ostrich Farm

Niseko is known as Asia's premier luxury ski destination, but between June and September it transforms into an excellent cycling and green-season getaway. Yōtei-zan, often called the 'Fuji of the North', is Niseko's iconic peak. This majestic volcano is surrounded by picturesque farmland and dense forests. The Yōtei-zan Loop Trail offers stunning views of the mountain from every angle. Along the route, you can visit serene hot springs, shop for local produce, enjoy a break at a cafe, and cycle alongside the scenic Shiribetsu-gawa.

Bike Hire

Rhythm Niseko Hirafu offers road bikes, e-bikes and mountain bikes – their e-cross bike is popular for the loop trail. It also features a climbing wall, cafe, skate park and shop; English spoken.

Starting Point

We recommend starting this loop trail in Kutchan Town (倶知安), the main hub of the Niseko region, where most accommodation, rental shops, restaurants and cafes are located.

01 Cycle along Rte 5 and follow the signs towards Niseko (ニセコ町). Turn right onto Rte 343 to head into the Hirafu area. In winter Hirafu is a bustling ski town, while in summer it offers plenty of dining options, shops and studios. For other green-season activities, check out Niseko Adventure Park, which features a challenging treetop course. Spanning almost a hectare, the course sits 5m to 13m above the ground and includes over 130 challenges or 'elements'. It offers six difficulty levels, including a child-friendly course. Further up the mountain, you'll find mountain-bike trails.

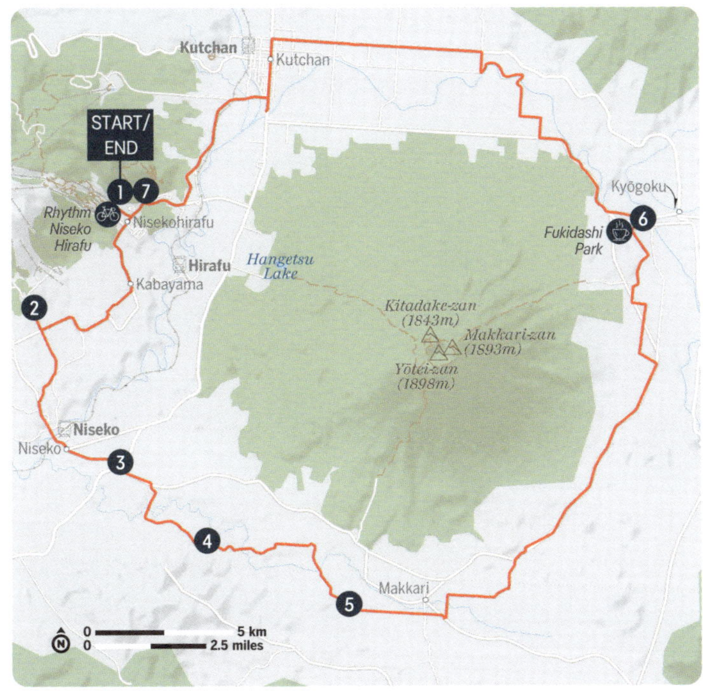

Elevation (m)

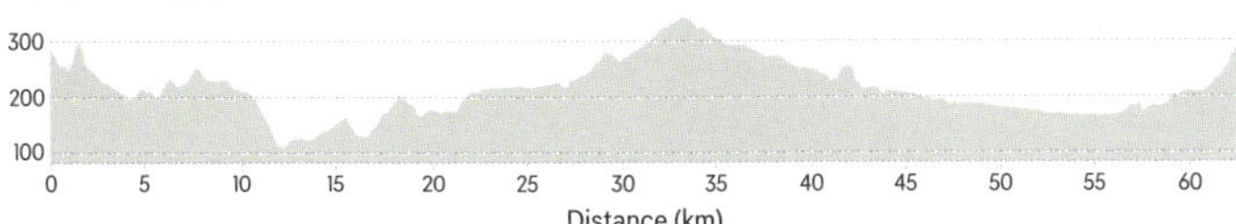

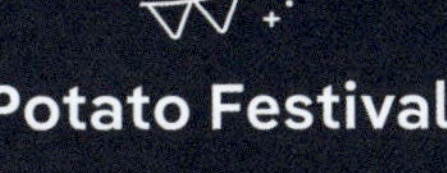

Potato Festival

While Niseko has undergone a major rebranding as a luxury destination and Asia's adventure capital, it was once primarily a farming region – you can still see that today, as much of the area is covered by vast stretches of potato farms. From late June to mid-July, these fields are dotted with white potato flowers, making for great photographs with Yōtei-zan in the background. Every year, on the first weekend of August, the Kutchan Jagamatsuri (Potato Festival) features food stalls, games, activities for kids, dances and *taiko* drumming, all celebrating the area's rich agricultural heritage. Kutchan's mascot, Jagata-kun (a potato wearing a beanie), might make an appearance!

02 Continue along Rte 343 for 6km, then turn right at the Niseko Village sign. Niseko Takahashi Dairy Farm (ニセコ高橋牧場) is just 500m up the road and offers an uninterrupted view of Yōtei-zan. Enjoy fresh ice cream, cheese, sweets and other dairy products made with milk straight from their farm. The farm also has an on-site chocolate shop and restaurants. Further up the road is Niseko Village, a resort with hotels, a family-friendly adventure park, small shopping centre and ski resort.

03 Return to Rte 343 and turn left onto the Niseko Panorama Line (ニセコパノラマライン), also known as Rte 66, enjoying a breezy downhill ride towards Niseko Town. You'll cross the yellow Niseko Bridge over the Shiribetsu-gawa (尻別川). Continue until you reach the intersection with Rte 5, where you'll find the Niseko View Plaza Rest Area. The rest area offers fresh vegetables and produce, local sake and other products, plus a tourist information centre, gelato shop and restrooms. Just across from here is the Pow Bar Cafe, where you can stop for organic energy bars; it also serves delicious coffee and hearty vegan baked goods and meals. Once you enter Niseko Town, the Niseko Panorama Line is called Prefecture Rd Iwanai-Tōya Line (岩内洞爺線).

04 Continue along Prefecture Rd Iwanai-Tōya Line and turn right onto Rte 230, travelling for about 3km. At Niseko Ostrich Farm (ニセコ 第二有島だちょう牧場), you'll see over 60 free-range ostriches (and cattle) with Yōtei-zan looming in the background. You can feed them a pack of ostrich snacks for ¥100, and there's a cafe and shop selling products made with ostrich eggs, such as ostrich *dorayaki* (red bean pancakes) and pudding. The farm takes pride in its ostrich eggs, produced without antibiotics.

05 Continue on Rte 230 for 5km then turn left following the sign to Central Makkari (真狩). A favourite among locals, Makkari Onsen (真狩温泉) boasts mineral-rich natural hot springs with a view of Yōtei-zan from its *rotemburo* (open-air bath). There's also a sauna and an indoor bath. The nearby Makkari Flower Center (道の駅 真狩フラワーセンター) covers 40,000 sq metres and showcases a variety of potted flowers and vegetables, including lily roots, a regional speciality. The centre also features a cafeteria, cafe, farmers market and restrooms.

06 Turn left onto Rte 97, following the signs to Niseko and Kyōgoku (京極), then turn right to continue on Rte 97 towards Kimobetsu (喜茂別町) and Kyōgoku for about 13km. Turn left onto Rte 478 (Kyōgoku Kutchan Line) to reach Fukidashi Park (ふきだし公園), a popular spot for a break where you can refill your bottle with fresh spring water from Yōtei-zan. The park also has an on-site restaurant, and the nearby Kyōgoku Onsen (京極温泉) is worth a visit – for ¥600, enjoy an outdoor bath with a view of Yōtei-zan, sauna and bubbling Jacuzzis.

07 This portion follows part of the Shiribetsu-gawa, one of the cleanest rivers in Japan. The river features 7km of whitewater rapids and is a popular rafting destination, with several rafting companies nearby. Continue on Rte 478 for 4km, then turn right onto a narrower (yet still paved) road. After crossing Kanbetsu Bridge (寒別橋), turn left and continue along the road until you reach River Park, where you can watch the Shiribetsu-gawa flow by. This is a designated cycling and walking path. Central Kutchan Town is just five to 10 minutes from River Park.

Take a Break

Refresh and refill your water bottle at FUKIDASHI PARK, known for its natural spring water sourced from Yōtei-zan's snowmelt. This water is filtered and purified over several decades, becoming rich in minerals. Approximately 80,000 tonnes of water flows out each day, maintaining a consistent temperature of around 6.5°C year-round. The pristine park features clear streams, walking paths, a playground, restaurant and picnic areas. Just a few minutes away is KYŌGOKU ONSEN, a spacious hot spring with waters that are said to ease joint pain.

Fukidashi Park

Mountain Biking

Niseko has a rapidly growing mountain-biking scene, with over 20km of trails developed in just a few years. Grand Hirafu Resort operates lifts in the summer, giving mountain bikers access to trails, including a 3km downhill trail for intermediate and advanced riders, and the Flow Trail, named for its winding shape. The Flow Trail uses the ski slopes and allows bikers to ride naturally through the banks and waves, making them feel as though they are skiing or snowboarding. Twin Peaks Bike Park offers free public access with trails for all skill levels. Additionally, mountain-bike tours and lessons are available from various vendors around town.

24

Best for

ART & SCENERY

Biking Around Tōya-ko

DURATION	DIFFICULTY	DISTANCE	START/END
3–4hrs	Easy	36km	Tōyako Onsen

TERRAIN	Mostly flat and paved

KUROKAWA MOKU/SHUTTERSTOCK

Ukimidō Park (p164)

Riding around this beautiful caldera lake just seems like the natural thing to do here. While paddle steamers run popular cruises, get on your bike for some exercise and stunning views to the north – of Nakajima, the island in the middle of Tōya-ko, all the way to Yōtei-zan, nicknamed Ezo-Fuji, the Mt Fuji of Hokkaidō. The ride is mostly flat and you can't get lost – just stick as close as you can to the lake. The views are always changing, and there are 58 intriguing sculptures to search out and admire. This is a good ride for families.

Bike Hire

Takayanagi Shōkai is just over the road from Tōya-ko Tourist Information Center, two blocks up from the lake. Regular, power-assisted and kids' bikes; friendly elderly owners.

Starting Point

From the bike-rental place, coast down the side road directly to the lake; this will bring you to the Tōyako-kisen ferry terminal and the waterfront trail.

01 Head east from the ferry terminal in Tōyako Onsen (洞爺湖温泉) and after 100m, on your right, you'll see Tōron-no-yu, an attractive little foot bath with superb views out over the lake and of Yōtei-zan (1898m), the Mt Fuji lookalike far in the distance. You're going to ride around the lake anticlockwise and there's plenty going on here at the start, including some excellent sculptures. Inland from the lake, on your right, is a line-up of big hotels with onsen you can try later in the day. Enjoy the outdoor artwork as you head east along the waterfront. *At the Lakeside* by Akihiko Kurokawa features

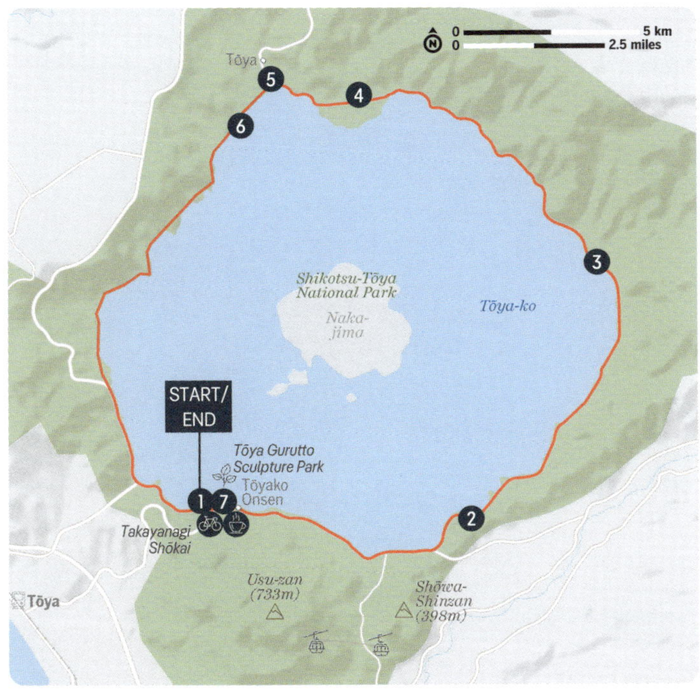

Active Volcanic Area

Tōya-ko is a classic volcanic caldera lake, almost perfectly circular in shape, that formed from an eruption about 110,000 years ago. The big volcano on its southern shores, Usu-zan (733m), has erupted four times since 1900, most recently in 2000, when it showered the region in ash, creating world news. You can ride up the volcano on the Usuzan Ropeway for glorious views. Next door, to the east, Shōwa-Shinzan (398m) caused a stir in 1943 by popping up out of a wheat field – its name means 'the new mountain of the Shōwa period' and it's regularly smoking.

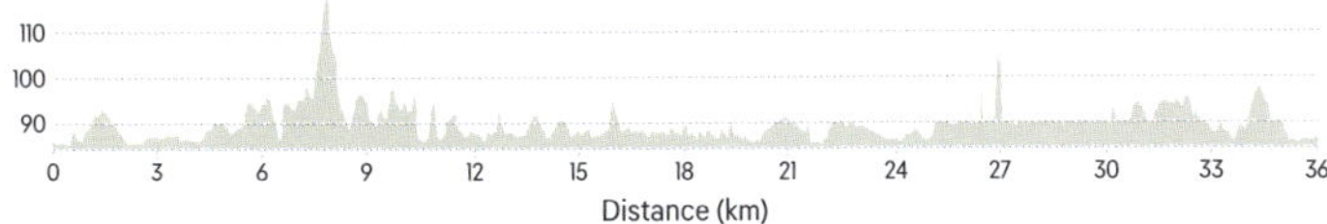

a large man in bronze, sitting on a bench playing the alto sax, with a pigeon perched on his head. Tourists love to take photos with him, with Tōya-ko and Yōtei-zan in the background.

02 After a kilometre or so, the waterfront ride will come out onto Rte 2 and you'll have to pedal alongside the busy road as it curls around the lake's southern shore. The volcanoes Usu-zan and Shōwa Shinzan tower above to your right. At the junction with Rte 132, which carries on around the lake, turn left onto the quiet country road; busy Rte 2 turns south and takes most of the traffic with it.

03 The eastern side of the lake makes a pleasant ride, lakeside through forest, with a few ups and downs plus an occasional small Shintō shrine and roadside Buddhist temple building. As Hokkaidō was only colonised by the Japanese from the 1870s onwards, there are no really old shrines and temples here as on Honshū, though. There are four more sculptures at Nakatōya campsite (仲洞爺キャンプ場), where there's also a nice little onsen open to the public (¥450) and the chance to buy drinks. It's a good spot for a break down by the lake.

04 Carry on next to the lake, as it gradually curls around the northern shore. You'll know you're about halfway through the ride when Nakajima, the island in the middle of the lake, hides the view of Tōyako Onsen, on the southern shore. The road stays straight and inland for a kilometre or so after crossing the Sōbetsu-gawa, then leads into Tōya township (洞爺町) on the northern shore, the second-largest town on the lake.

05 Tōya town has plenty of interest going on, including more statues, a popular pastry shop, bakery and Tōya Mizu-no-eki (Water Station) at the boat jetty. This complex has a small market, an udon restaurant, cafe and seating overlooking the lake, and is a pleasant place for a break. Kusaemon Orihara's *Playing in the Waves* statue next to the jetty is beautiful, with Nakajima island viewed through the space in its middle.

06 By now you'll have caught sight again of Tōyako Onsen on the southern side of the lake. At the southwestern end of Tōya township, at Ukimidō Park, at the end of a small point poking out into the lake, Ukimi-dō is a small Buddhist building in which an image of Prince Shōtoku (574–622 CE), a Buddhist scholar who made significant contributions to Japan, is enshrined. A festival is held here each July.

07 Carry on down the western shore, past more sculptures, remaining lakeside until the road runs into Rte 230, then stay beside the lake, heading onto Rte 2. Chinko-jima is a small island that is connected by a narrow bit of land to the shore. The views are magnificent and Tōyako Onsen appears close at hand. The huge bronze statue of a face, *Tusuki-no-hikari* (Moonlight), by Polish artist Igor Mitoraj sits beside the lake in Usu-zan Eruption Memorial Park, then the wide waterfront path heads east past Fountain Square and back into Tōyako Onsen. Soon you'll be back where you started, at the ferry terminal on the waterfront. It takes only a few minutes to ride back up the hill and return your bike.

Take a Break

Tōyako Onsen on the lake's southern shore is a popular resort town, all set for after your ride. There are a dozen free *ashi-yu* (foot baths) and hand baths scattered about town, mostly along the waterfront, plus impressive high-rise hotels such as Tōya Kohan Tei with 'panorama baths' that you can visit as a day guest. For over 40 years, Tōyako Onsen has been running nightly 20-minute fireworks displays at 8.45pm, from late April to late October. Consider staying overnight in this lively onsen town.

CHATNARA/SHUTTERSTOCK

Shōwa Shinzan (p163)

Sculpture Park

A highlight at Tōya-ko is the Tōya Gurutto Sculpture Park, with a total of 58 impressive statues of stone, bronze, stainless steel and other materials that have been carefully placed around the shores of the lake. Information on each of the pieces, by well-known Japanese and foreign sculptors, can be found in English on the Tōya-ko town website *(town.toyako.hokkaido.jp)*. Based on the theme 'Anthem of Life', the contemporary pieces have turned Tōya-ko into a huge open-air art gallery. The pieces are not spaced evenly around the lake; 34 are clustered around Tōyako Onsen and the lake's southern shores.

25

Biei's Patchwork Road

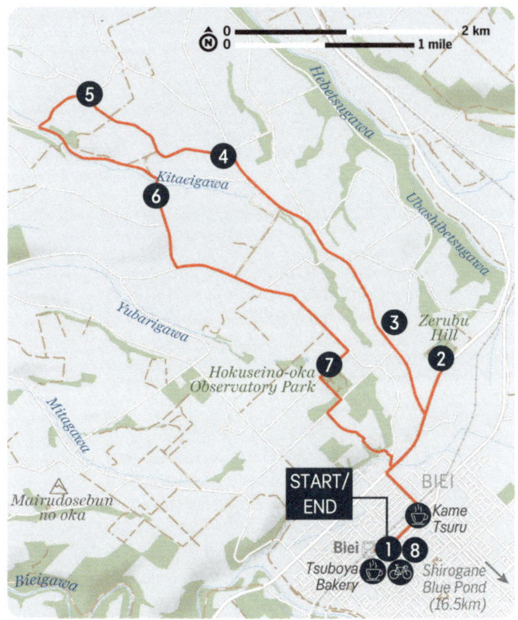

DURATION	DIFFICULTY	DISTANCE	START/END
2–3hrs	Easy	18km	JR Biei Station

TERRAIN	Rolling hills and paved roads

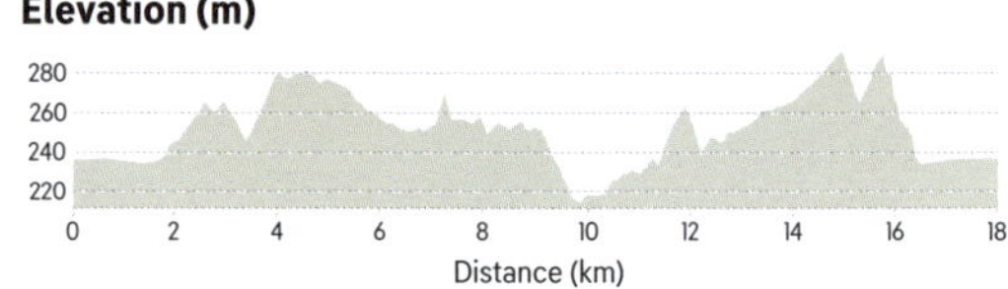

Easy with an e-bike, the Patchwork Road course to the northwest of Biei township is a popular ride in a region renowned as a fun, scenic cycling destination. The cycling routes around Biei and Furano, to the south, are designed for romantics coming to explore the countryside, pick up local produce from farm stands and visit a cute little cottage cafe. Local scenery, with the Daisetsuzan National Park mountains as a backdrop, is famous, and many Japanese people come to see where their favourite television advertisements were filmed.

Bike Hire

There are a number of bike-hire operators in the area around JR Biei Station; get yourself an e-bike for this ride in the hills around Biei.

Starting Point

Begin your ride at attractive little JR Biei Station after visiting the Biei Tourist Centre, only 100m away; pick up a map of the route here.

01 There's something very appealing about Biei (美瑛) and a good way to start your ride is to potter around in town a bit, getting used to your bike. The streets are wide, the air is fresh and there's a sense of being in a cutting-edge place ripe with alternative lifestylers. When you're ready, head northeast on the main street (Rte 213) outside the station, then left at the first set of traffic lights and onto Rte 966. Cross the rail line, then at the next major road, turn right onto Rte 237; this is the main road that connects Furano and Asahikawa, Hokkaidō's second-largest city, 30km north of Biei.

Flower fields

Best for

COLOURFUL COUNTRYSIDE

Spectacular Flower Fields

The valley's flower fields, with a latitude similar to that of the south of France, have changed focus since the 1950s, when lavender was simply a profitable agricultural product. Cheaper imported lavender in the 1970s made growers put their thinking caps on, to come up with a yearly flower extravaganza that thrills visitors. Sprawling flower fields up and down the valley are carefully organised, with staggered blooming seasons, to produce a rainbow of colours. Expect poppies, lupins and rape blossoms in June, lavender and lilies from July, and cosmos, salvias and sunflowers in August and September. It's a raging summer spectacle of colour.

02 It won't take you long to start congratulating yourself on choosing an e-bike for this ride. The road climbs steadily; pass the road coming in from the left, but take note, as you'll be coming back down the hill to take that road later. At the top of the hill is Zerubu-no-oka (Zerubu Hill), ostensibly a flower farm, but more of a visitor attraction; you'll have ridden a little over 2km from Biei Station by this point. It's free to wander around the glorious flower fields, but if biking up the hill was all too much, you can rent an ATV (all-terrain vehicle) or pay for a golf-buggy ride. A lavender-flavoured soft-serve ice cream at the cafe may well hit the spot.

03 Head back down the hill and follow the signage to turn right; 2.5km of riding from Zerubu-no-oka will bring you to the Ken & Mary Tree. This lone poplar became famous in a 1972 Japanese television advertisement and, surrounded by rolling farm country, has been a popular photo stop ever since. The Patchwork Road got its name from the colourful pattern of crops and flowers that resemble a patchwork quilt over the countryside, constantly changing in colour with the seasons. It's worth noting that tourists in rental cars also follow the Patchwork Road and you're unlikely to be out here by yourself. You may also have to share the road with large agricultural vehicles, especially at busy farming times, so if you stop to take photos, get well off the road.

04 Follow signage and continue along the rural farm road for 2.2km to Hokuei Komugi-no-oka (Hokuei Wheat Hill). Here you'll find Restaurant bi.ble, overlooking wheat fields. Biei wheat is high in protein, with excellent baking qualities and at Restaurant bi.ble there's a boulangerie with croissants and pastries to die for. This French-style place is in the converted buildings of the former Hokuei Elementary School, with a 40-seat restaurant and hotel rooms.

05 Next up is a 1.5km ride through attractive patchwork farmland to the Seven Stars Tree, a standalone oak on top of the hill that became famous throughout Japan for being on the packaging of Seven Stars cigarettes. You'll be getting into the swing of things by now; the highlights are not so much the stopping points on this ride as much as the rural countryside that you're riding through.

06 Follow signage to the Parents & Child Tree, a 1.3km ride away, best viewed from a spot around the corner and below the trees themselves. The three oaks appear nestled together; with two bigger oaks representing the parents, and a smaller oak in-between being the child.

Take a Break

Stock up with goodies for your ride at TSUBOYA BAKERY on the corner opposite JR Biei Station. This little place has it all in terms of tasty breads, pastries and cakes that will have you drooling – and possibly dropping back in after your ride. If you're after a restaurant that locals swear by, head to KAME TSURU. A 10-minute walk from the station, it has great lunch and dinner options with English on the menu – try the Biei pork rib bowl.

WATCHARIT PRAIHIRUN/GETTY IMAGES

Shirogane Blue Pond

07 Last stop is Hokusei-no-oka Observatory Park 2km on, with seasonal lavender and sunflower fields. A large pyramid-shaped observatory offers excellent views of the surrounding Patchwork Road area, Biei township and the valley to Daisetsuzan National Park and the Tokachi mountains. To the east you can see Asahi-dake (2291m), the highest mountain in Hokkaidō; it's easy to see why the national park is nicknamed 'the rooftop of Hokkaidō'.

08 It's a 2.5km ride back to Biei station to return your bike and partake in refreshments.

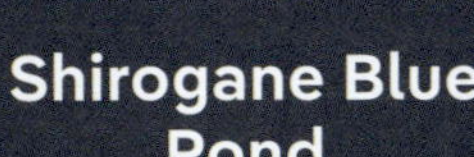

Shirogane Blue Pond

Seen on computer screens worldwide after it was used at the unveiling of the Apple MacBook Pro in 2012 and then as a Mac Wallpaper, Shirogane Blue Pond helped put Biei on visitor bucket lists. The image of the startlingly azure pond with bare trees sticking up out of the water was a big hit, prompting Biei to construct an 18km off-road riverside bicycle trail known as the Refresh Line Course out to the pond. The bike trail continues 3km from there to a couple of attractive waterfalls and Shirogane Onsen. Following the river, it's fairly flat, but an e-bike is a good idea.

26

Best for

HISTORY & CULTURE

Abashiri on Two Wheels

DURATION	DIFFICULTY	DISTANCE	START/END
3–5hrs	Easy	18km	Michi-no-eki Abashiri

TERRAIN	Paved roads; hilly

VARIOUS IMAGES/SHUTTERSTOCK

Museum of Northern Peoples (p172)

To the Japanese, Abashiri is as synonymous with the word 'prison' as Alcatraz is to Americans. Winters here are as harsh as it gets and the city is also known for 'drift ice' cruises in ice-breakers out into the Sea of Okhotsk. Come the warmer months though, and Abashiri is a great place to explore on two wheels. Visit a slew of intriguing museums, including Abashiri Prison Museum, Okhotsk Ryūhyō (Drift Ice) Museum and the Museum of Northern Peoples, plus take in spectacular views of the region from atop 208m-high Tento-zan.

Bike Hire

Michi-no-Eki Rent-a-cycle *(visit-abashiri.jp)* has e-bikes, cross bikes and regular bikes for hire, with three-hour and one-day rates. Get an e-bike for this ride.

Starting Point

Start at Michi-no-Eki Abashiri, the large roadside stopping and information area beside the river where you can rent an e-bike; there's lots of parking here.

01 Make sure you've got an e-bike (there's a hill to climb) before riding out of Michi-no-eki Abashiri and heading inland, upstream, alongside the Abashiri-gawa for about 3km to the small bridge over the river.

02 Turn right and cross the bridge to visit the Abashiri Prison (網走刑務所), which was opened in 1984 and holds inmates with sentences of less than 10 years. Older parts of the prison were relocated to the other side of the river in 1983 to become Abashiri Prison Museum, the

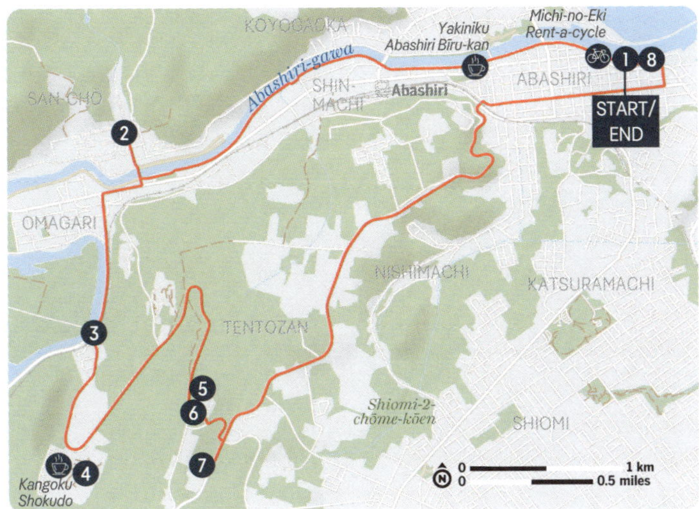

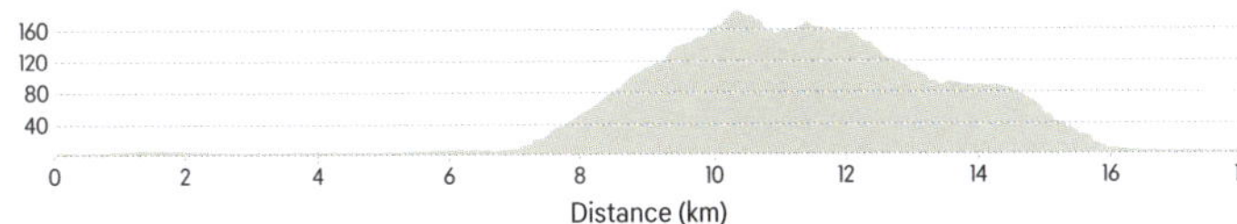

only prison museum in Japan. The reason you've come to the 'new' prison is to check out the imposing, old red-brick prison gate and to drop in to the prison shop, selling products made by prisoners such as ceramics, leather goods, sushi boards and clothing that make good souvenirs.

03 Return across the river and turn right, back onto Rte 240. After about 300m, follow signage and turn left onto Rte 39. Riding approximately 1km further, turn left for Abashiri Prison Museum (博物館 網走監獄). It's at around this stage that you'll be happy you picked up an e-bike for this ride as the road starts to climb.

04 Abashiri Prison has a fearsome reputation in Japanese history. Over 1000 political prisoners were sent here in 1890, including many ex-samurai from the Tokugawa period who were convicted of rebellion against the Meiji Restoration. Conditions were harsh and many died while constructing infrastructure such as their own prison and roads to connect the frozen eastern Hokkaidō outpost of Abashiri with Asahikawa. The prison's reputation was only enhanced by the roaring success of the 1965 film, *Abashiri Bangaichi* (Abashiri Prison), which was so popular that it spawned a series of 18 *Abashiri Bangaichi* movies and made Ken Takakura into the Clint Eastwood of Japan. The films captured the imagination of the Japanese just as much as

Sea of Okhotsk

If the name Okhotsk doesn't sound very Japanese to you, you're dead right. The Japanese never had a name for the sea that borders the eastern coast of Hokkaidō, north of the Shiretoko Peninsula and Kuril Islands, so they adopted (and adapted) the Russian name. The name Okhotsk may even make you shiver, given it's 80% covered in drift ice in winter and was the scene of countless Cold War operations. Strange then that the Japanese call this part of Japan, one of nine sub-prefectures of Hokkaidō, the Okhotsk Region (Ohōtsuku-chihō), using a very un-Japanese name.

Escape from Alcatraz did in the US. The sprawling open-air museum is oddly pleasant considering its gruesome history, and you could easily spend an hour or two here.

05 It's really time to congratulate yourself on getting an e-bike as the road climbs steadily up the hill to 208m-high Tento-zan (天都山), where there are sweeping views of the surrounding landscape, out over the Sea of Okhotsk and right down to World Heritage–listed Shiretoko National Park on a good day.

06 Here you'll also find the Okhotsk Ryūhyō (Drift Ice) Museum (オホーツク流氷館). While ice-breakers head out from late-January to late-March on one-hour cruises into the Sea of Okhotsk from exactly where you picked up your e-bike in Abashiri, outside of those months, this is your best chance to learn more about the 'drifting sea ice' phenomena that brings visitors to Abashiri in winter. There's a great rooftop viewing platform, interesting 'drift ice' displays and the tiny *kurione* (clione; sea angel), a funky translucent relative of the sea slug that has become an Abashiri mascot.

07 Hop back on your bike and ride down to the Museum of Northern Peoples (北方民族博物館; Hoppō Minzoku Hakubutsukan) only a few hundred metres away. This excellent museum focuses on the culture and traditions of people inhabiting northern, subarctic regions of the planet, including the Ainu, the First Nations people of northern Canada, the Inuit, the Sami and Siberian peoples. Exhibits illustrate the differences and similarities among the various northern peoples, and good information in English is available.

08 It's a 5km ride on Rte 483 down and back into Abashiri. Keep an eye out for the temple Eisen-ji (永専寺), which has Abashiri Prison's 1912-built gate and red-brick walls as the temple's main gate; it was moved there in 1924 as thanks to the temple priest who worked many years on prisoner rehabilitation. Before you take your bike back to the Michi-no-eki, ride a couple of blocks towards the sea to check out Ryūhyō Glass Museum (流氷硝子館), a gallery producing exquisite glassware and artwork from recycled fluorescent lamps.

Take a Break

Ready to try prison food? At Abashiri Prison Museum cafeteria, KANGOKU SHOKUDO, try a meal that is provided to prison inmates at the current Abashiri Prison. The two options are surprisingly tasty. One to save for after your ride is an Abashiri Prison Stout, produced by local craft brewery, Abashiri Beer. Try it at their restaurant YAKINIKU ABASHIRI BĪRU-KAN, along with colourful beers such as Shiretoko Draft, representing the national park with an emphatic green, and Ryūhyō (Drift Ice) Draft in a startling blue.

PAULWONG/SHUTTERSTOCK

Abashiri Prison Museum (p171)

Okhotsk Cycling Road

For a wonderful longer ride from Abashiri, pick up a bike and take on this 40km (one way) cycle path that was constructed on the old Japan National Railways Yumō line once it was closed down in 1987. Gradients are fairly gentle and it's a good course for just about everyone. The trail initially heads west, along the Abashiri-gawa, then along the foreshore of Abashiri-ko, before turning north and along the shores of Notoro-ko. It continues west along the Sea of Okhotsk coast to Saroma-ko. If 80km return is too much, just turn around at any point.

Also Try...

Rishiri-tō

RUJIN/SHUTTERSTOCK

Wakkanai to Cape Sōya

DURATION	DIFFICULTY	DISTANCE
4–5hrs	Intermediate	62km

Pick up a rental bike from the Wakkanai Tourist Information Center at JR Wakkanai Station, then head east, out of town, on Rte 238 to the northernmost point on mainland Japan, Sōya-misaki (宗谷岬; Cape Sōya). It's a 31km ride each way, easy to turn around and turn it into a shorter ride should you wish. The road, with a wide footpath, passes Wakkanai Airport, then fishing villages, before getting to the cape, where a windswept monument marks the goal of length-of-Japan walkers and bikers. On a good day, you can see Sakhalin, Russia, 43km north across the La Pérouse Strait. Bikes available from late April to late October.

Rishiri Island Circuit

DURATION	DIFFICULTY	DISTANCE
5–7hrs	Intermediate	60km

While Rishiri-tō (利尻島), about 40km west of Wakkanai at the northern tip of Hokkaidō, is a lovely spot, winters are harsh and you're unlikely to be visiting before May or after October. The island is basically a big circle of land around the 1721m-high volcano Rishiri-zan, a popular peak for hikers. There's a 25km 'cycling road' around the north of the island connecting the two ports of Oshidomari, where the ferry from Wakkanai arrives, and Kutsugata on the west coast. A circumnavigation of the island is a 60km ride, best done clockwise to be in the sun in the morning and in the afternoon. Book a bike before you go with Rishiri Greenhill Inn *(rishiri-greenhill.net)*.

EQROY/SHUTTERSTOCK

Furano wine

Fun in Furano

DURATION	DIFFICULTY	DISTANCE
4–5hrs	Easy	20km

With a nickname of *heso-no-machi* (belly-button town) as it's in the middle of Hokkaidō, Furano (富良野) is a ski destination in winter, and all-round great place the rest of the year. Similar in latitude to the south of France, there's a decidedly French thing going on here. Pick up an e-bike outside JR Furano Station to ride to Furano Winery, Furano Cheese Factory and, if you're feeling frisky, further afield to Farm Tomita, to the lavender and flower fields. Wander around Furano Marché in town and consider visiting Ningle Terrace, an art and craft bonanza of 15 tiny log-cabin galleries up by the New Furano Prince Hotel at the base of the ski resort.

Ride Around Ōnuma

DURATION	DIFFICULTY	DISTANCE
1.5–2hrs	Easy	14km

Lovely Ōnuma (大沼; big pond), about 20km north of Hakodate, is the starting point for explorations in Ōnuma Quasi-National Park, a popular destination for Japanese and international visitors since the Emperor Meiji turned up for a look in 1881. Ōnuma sits below the impressive volcano, Komaga-take (1131m), and is known for the walking trails that use 18 bridges to connect islands in the lake. With bicycle rentals around the station, there are excellent cycling options, including riding anticlockwise around the lake for views of Komaga-take, waterbirds and reflections. This is an enjoyable, leisurely ride that won't strain your calf muscles. For afterwards, craft brewery Ōnuma Beer awaits near the station.

Hiroshima
Fukuyama
Mihara
Onomichi
Shōdoshima
29
Miyajima
Kure
Eta-jima
Ikuchi-jima
Inno-shima
Ōmi-shima
Hakata-jima
Takamatsu
Shido
Sea of Harima-nada
Inland Sea
Marugame
Iwakuni
Seto-nai-kai National Park
Ō-shima
28
Kotohira
Naruto Channel
Awaji-shima
Sea of Aki
Inland Sea
Imabari
Kanonji
Sea of Hiuchi
Naruto
Kii Channel
Yanai
30
Tokushima
Mima
Yashiro-shima
Niihama
Iyomishima
Komatsushima
Saijō
Matsuyama
Anan
Iyo
Ishizuchi-san
Tsurugi-san
Sea of Iyo
Ōtoyo
Yuki
Hiwasa
Ōzu
Kōchi
Nankoku
Kainan
Yawatahama
Sakawa
Tosa
Aki
Tōyō
Yusuhara
Tosa-wan
Susaki
Uwajima
Kubokawa (Shimanto-chō)
Muroto
Muroto-misaki
27
Kuroshio-machi
Shimanto City (Nakamura)
Sukumo
PACIFIC OCEAN
Tosa-Shimizu
Ashizuri-misaki
0 50 km
0 25 miles

GNOHZ/SHUTTERSTOCK

Angel Road (p190)

Shikoku

27 Shimanto-gawa Trail

Follow the bends of Shimanto-gawa, one of Japan's last free-flowing rivers, over its distinctive, rail-less submersible bridges. **p180**

28 Yumeshima Kaidō

Accessible only by boat, this picturesque seaside route connects four Inland Sea islands beyond the typical tourist trail. **p184**

29 Shōdoshima

Japan's birthplace of olives, explore the island's culinary industries old and new, coupled with some unconventional fun. **p190**

30 Tokushima & Around

Cross the mighty Yoshino-gawa to Tokushima's outskirts for an immersive tour of the city's artisanal and cultural highlights. **p194**

Explore

Shikoku

Between its larger neighbours of Honshū and Kyūshū in the country's southwest, Shikoku (四国) is the smallest and least populated of Japan's four main islands. Meaning 'four provinces', the relative solitude of its modern-day prefectures of Kagawa, Tokushima, Kōchi and Ehime has seen the region emerge as one of Japan's cycling capitals. Abundant in nature, Shikoku's lengthy coastline, island-dotted sea, dramatic capes and meandering rivers provide the perfect backdrop for laid-back pedalling. Ehime, in particular, has built a reputation as a cycling hub, with many of the region's most famed routes emanating from its northern coastal city of Imabari.

Imabari

Shikoku's cycling capital and gateway to the Shimanami Kaidō (p24), Imabari (今治) is a destination a cyclist will quickly become familiar with. Whether you plan on island-hopping the Inland Sea or cruising the mainland's coastline, you'll likely find yourself directed here at least once. Plentiful hotels and restaurants make it a convenient cycling base with a few attractions of its own, including Imabari-jō (Imabari Castle) and the Towel Museum, dedicated to the city's famously high-quality towels. From Matsuyama Station, it's around 40 minutes on a limited express train or up to 1½ hours on a local service.

Takamatsu

Kagawa's prefectural capital of Takamatsu (高松), with the only rail link from outside Shikoku, is a popular entry point to the region. Find a good concentration of the prefecture's 540 restaurants dedicated to *sanuki-udon* (a delightfully chewy noodle and Kagawa's speciality) here. Vibrant dining and shopping precincts aside, the city's magnificent Ritsurin-kōen, awarded the maximum three stars in the Michelin Green Guide for attractions 'worth a special journey', is a beautiful place to wander. From Takamatsu Port, it's a quick boat ride to some of Shikoku's most renowned art islands, including 'olive island' Shōdoshima.

Tokushima

Capital city of the prefecture of the same name, Tokushima's (徳島) downtown occupies an easily walkable island sandbar

WHEN TO GO

As a general guide, April to July and September to November provide moderate temperatures and good conditions for bike riders. Try to avoid the rainy season around June and keep an eye on typhoon updates around September. From December to March, winter snowfall brings icy road conditions to some interior locations; the warmer Inland Sea islands are a good alternative in cooler months.

surrounded by the Suketō and Shinmachi Rivers. A great cultural wealth has developed out of this water-rich city, from the country's indigo-dyeing trade to the summer dance, Awa-odori. Two wheels can transport you to the wider city limits, where opportunities to connect with traditional artisans and regional residents multiply. A special place for pilgrims embarking on the Shikoku 88 Temple Pilgrimage, Tokushima is home to Ryōzen-ji – Temple 1 on the 1140km circuit – which takes several weeks by bike.

Kōchi

Another city that shares its prefectural name, Kōchi's (高知) palm-tree-lined streets couldn't be a better visual representation of its relaxed persona. Food and drink underpin its welcoming *okyaku* culture, in which spontaneously inviting strangers to eat and have a tipple together is second nature. Dine at lively Hirome Market, visit its impressive castle Kōchi-jō and stroll Makino Botanical Garden, an eight-hectare green space with a multi-level conservatory of towering palms and streaming waterfalls. Beyond the downtown highlights, it's a launching point into the prefecture's stunning natural scenery, from its winding rivers to lofty mountain passes.

TRANSPORT

Each of Shikoku's four prefectural capitals has an airport for easy domestic connections from major Japanese cities. Numerous ferries link Shikoku with ports in Honshū and Kyūshū, while three major bridges allow you to drive to the island on your own schedule. The only rail link from outside Shikoku is from Okayama to Kagawa via the Great Seto Bridge.

WHAT'S ON

Cycling Shimanami

(cycling-shimanami.jp) A biennial cycling event giving the rare opportunity to ride the Shimanami Kaidō while closed to traffic. General entry is by lottery.

Setouchi Triennale

One of Japan's largest contemporary art festivals; held every three years over approximately 100 days on 12 islands in the Inland Sea.

Inno-shima Suigun Festival

A late summer festival commemorating the Inland Sea's pirate past with boat races and fiery historical re-enactments.

WHERE TO STAY

In Shikoku's major hubs, you'll have options at just about any price point, from high-end hotels and ryokan (traditional inns) to hostels and holiday rentals. Along the region's established cycling routes, you'll also find guesthouses largely directed at a cycling clientele. These accommodation options are typically simple, often at convenient midway or start/end points, and they focus on providing access to a clean bed and amenities of priority to riders, such as laundry and bike tools. Some double as 'Cycling Oases', designated locations with various support services for cyclists, and may offer use of showers and change rooms to nonguests for a small fee.

Resources

Visit Shimanami *(visitshimanami.com)* A useful English-language website to prepare for Inland Sea cycling on the Shimanami and Yumeshima Kaidōs.

Shikoku Circuit *(cycling-island-shikoku.com/en)* A 1000km stamp-collecting cycling challenge around Shikoku, with convenient day-by-day breakdowns for those wanting to attempt smaller sections.

27

Shimanto-gawa Trail

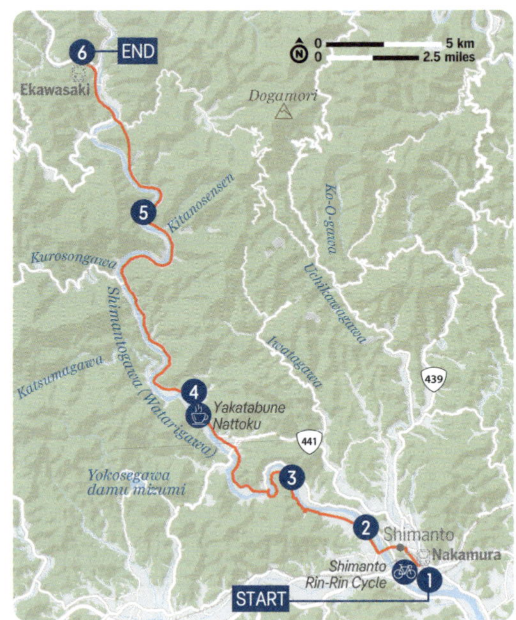

DURATION	DIFFICULTY	DISTANCE	START/END
2–3 hrs	Easy	40km	Nakamura Station/ Ekawasaki Station

TERRAIN	Flat, paved roads

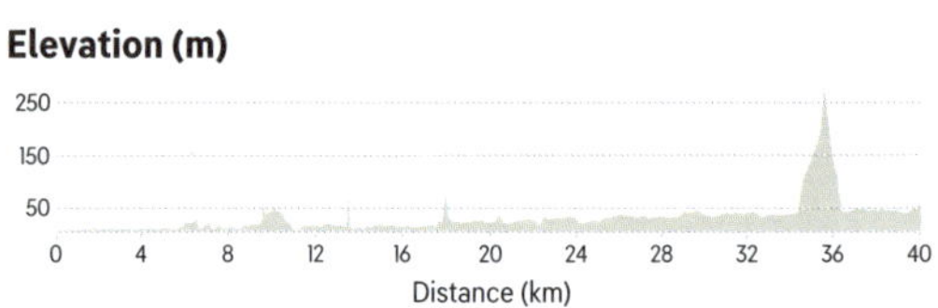

Kōchi Prefecture on the island of Shikoku seems to have it all: stunning coastline, lush mountains, rich cultural heritage and delicious, abundant seafood. This leisurely half-day course takes you along the 196km Shimanto-gawa, often referred to as 'Japan's last clear river' thanks to the rich forests that are the river's source, and its lack of dams. Renowned for its *chinkabashi* bridges and outdoor activities such as kayaking and fishing, it meanders through the pristine landscapes, offering a tranquil escape into untouched nature.

Bike Hire

Shimanto Rin-Rin Cycle is located at the Shimanto City Tourism Association office at Nakamura Station. Rent or return bikes at seven terminals along the 40km between Nakamura and JR Ekawasaki stations.

Starting Point

Start at Nakamura Station in Shimanto City. Shimanto City is the main town in the area with plenty of accommodation options, supermarkets and good *izakaya* (casual Japanese pub or bar).

01 From Nakamura Station (中村駅), head towards Nakamura Daiichi Hotel then turn right on Rte 439 following the sign towards Ekawasaki. Turn left at the Family Mart convenience store then continue for about five minutes. You'll reach the red iron Shimantogawa Bridge (四万十川橋 赤鉄橋), which goes over Shimanto-gawa. Cross the bridge and turn right following the river for about 10 minutes.

02 The river bank will narrow entering Irida Yanagi Forest (入田ヤナギ林), a natural willow forest. The Nanohana Festival is held here at

***Chinkabashi* bridge, Shimanto-gawa**

Best for

RIVERSIDE VIEWS

Sinking Bridges

Chinkabashi (sinking bridges) are a unique feature of the Shimanto-gawa. They are designed to submerge during floods, preventing damage from strong currents. These low-water bridges are an example of traditional engineering that allows for the smooth flow of the river while safeguarding the surrounding environment and keeping costs relatively low. Kōchi is one of the few places where you can find these iconic landmarks dotted along crystal-clear rivers. When crossing, be sure to dismount and walk your bike safely as the bridges are narrow with no side rails, and cars also sometimes use them.

the end of February to March, as around 10 million *nanohana* (rape blossoms) bloom, painting the area a bright yellow. The festival has local products and food stalls. The surrounding area also features walking paths and free campsites that are open year-round. Continue for another 10 minutes and you'll reach Shimanto River Sakurazutsumi Park (四万十川桜づつみ公園). The cherry blossoms here bloom late March to early April and are beautiful with Shimanto-gawa as their backdrop.

03 After cycling for 2km, you'll reach Sada Observatory (佐田展望所), a wooden lookout point. Just five minutes away is Imanari Sada Chinkabashi (佐田沈下橋). The *chinkabashi* (sinking bridges) were first built in Kyūshū and were mainly found around western Japan. Although most *chinkabashi* have been replaced by modern bridges with side rails, they remain in the Shimanto region as the Shimanto-gawa is prone to flooding and water rising after a typhoon. Sada is the first *chinkabashi* you'll see on this course and the longest of its kind. These bridges have appeared in promotional posters and Japanese TV dramas, making them a popular destination for Japanese people, yet because of their location, the region retains its quiet uncrowded charm.

04 Cross Sada Bridge to the right side of the river facing the mountain and turn left following the river upstream onto Rte 340, passing Misato Chinkabashi (三里沈下橋) along the way. Continue on Rte 340 until you get to the intersection with Rte 441, then go left. You'll find Nattoku – a *yakatabune* (traditional roofed wooden boat) station – where travellers can hop on a cruise and enjoy lunch on the Shimanto-gawa. *Yakatabune* are usually found on Japan's iconic rivers, and Shimanto-gawa being the longest river on Shikoku is definitely one of these. Nearby is Kawarakko, an autocamp site that also offers bungalow stays and guided kayaking, stand-up paddleboarding (SUP) and canoe tours on a gentle part of the river. Shimanto-gawa is recommended for beginners as it is mellow year-round with few rapids. Kawarakko is also a bike-rental terminal.

05 Continue on Rte 441 for 13km (about 20 minutes) passing Soga Shrine and Jinmo Shrine to Shimanto Gakusha (四万十楽舎). This unique guesthouse is a former elementary school and offers fishing, canoe tours and a wooden rafting experience. You can also try *sawanobori* (stream-climbing). There are three courses and you can walk against the current while observing shrimp and fish. There are courses with

Take a Break

While cycling or walking along the Shimanto-gawa, you'll notice *yakatabune* leisurely cruising by. *Yakatabune* are traditional roofed wooden boats that ride low on the water. Travellers can not only enjoy the scenery, but also tuck into *bentō* boxes featuring locally caught *ayu* (sweetfish) or eel for lunch (must be booked in advance). Rather than chairs, tatami mats cover the floor on the inside of the boats bringing passengers even closer to the river's surface. There are several *yakatabune* cruises along the picturesque river, including Yakatabune Shimanto-no-Ao and Nattoku.

FLYINGV3/SHUTTERSTOCK

Katsuo-no-tataki

deep pools and waterfalls with a drop of four metres. Back on the cycling route, about 4km up the road, you'll come across a fork in the road, one leading to a tunnel (still on Rte 441). Veer to the left road to continue along the river. Ride for around 2km then cross the red Tsu Bridge. Turn right on Kōchi Prefectural Rte 8 and carry on for 1.5km until the road intersects with Rte 441 again.

06 Continue on Rte 441 for about 2km (five to ten minutes) towards JR Ekawasaki Station (江川崎駅). There are more dining options by the station. Around 900m from here is Road Station Yotte Nishitosa (道の駅よって西土佐), which sells local produce and has a riverside BBQ to reward your hard work. Road Station Yotte Nishitosa, Ekawasaki Station and the nearby Shimanto River Station Canoe House are all bike-rental terminals. You can also do this course in reverse, starting at Ekawasaki Station and heading towards Nakamura Station.

Seared Bonito

The must-try *katsuo-no-tataki* (seared bonito) is a signature dish from Kōchi Prefecture, made by searing this tuna-like fish over a bed of straw to impart a distinct smoky flavour. The bonito is lightly grilled on the outside, leaving the inside raw, and sliced into thin pieces. After grilling, the fish is usually served with garlic, green onions and grated daikon radish, often paired with soy sauce or ponzu (soy sauce with *yuzu*, a Japanese citrus) for dipping. Bonito is the prefectural fish of Kōchi and this dish was originally a fisherman's meal eaten on board a boat, which was was later introduced to the public.

28

Best for

SEA VIEWS

Yumeshima Kaidō

DURATION	DIFFICULTY	DISTANCE	START/END
5hrs	Intermediate	50km (end to end)	Yuge Port/ Iwagi Port
TERRAIN	Paved; road cycling		

KAMIJIMA TOWN TOURISM PHOTO SERVICE/FLICKR/PDM 1.0

Yumeshima Kaidō

The Yumeshima Kaidō (ゆめしま海道; Dream Island Road) is a 50km cycling route across four islands, of 25 that make up the town of Kamijima in Ehime. Located around the halfway point of the Shimanami Kaidō, it's a convenient add-on or alternative to the region's more well-worn cycling paths. You won't find a single traffic light on Yuge-jima, Sa-shima, Ikina-jima or Iwagi-jima, the island chain accessible from outside only by boat. Bridges between the four islands make a short half-day cycle possible, but an unhurried approach to explore the full route and welcome unexpected interactions is the way to go.

Bike Hire

Setouchi Exchange Center (Yuge-jima), Tateishi Port Office (Ikina-jima) or Iwagi Tourist Center (Iwagi-jima). Book for weekends and holidays *(kamijima.info/cycling/bicycle_rental)*. Return at a different terminal for a fee.

Starting Point

Yuge Port (Yuge-jima) and Tateishi Port (Ikina-jima) are most popular, having the double benefit of bicycle rental and convenient ferry connections from Innoshima and Imabari on the Shimanami Kaidō.

01 The most populated of the four islands, Yuge-jima (弓削島) is home to around 40% of the 5900 residents along the Yumeshima Kaidō. A main hub, find a concentration of accommodation and restaurants by the island's two ferry terminals – Yuge in the island's central-west and Kami-Yuge in the northwest.

Start at Yuge Sea Station Flat *(yugeseastation.com)*, around 300m from Yuge Port. This 'Cycling Oasis' (a location with facilities to assist cyclists) has wi-fi,

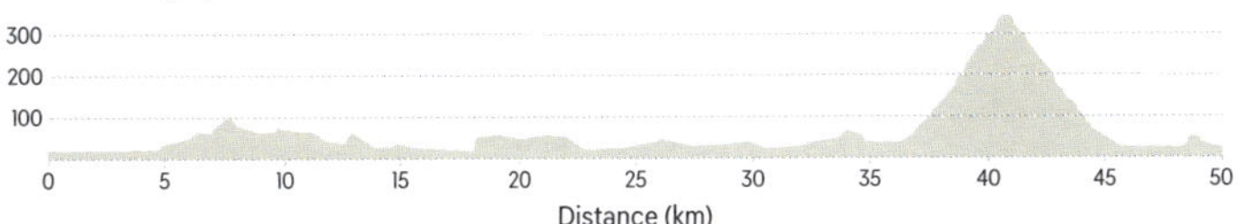

maps and English-speaking staff, along with toilets, showers, a laundry and bike pumps.

From Yuge Port, begin a clockwise 13km circumnavigation of the top section of the island; the 'blue line' painted on the road leads the way. In around 2.5km, you'll reach the Kami-Yuge Port area and some easy take-away options to fuel you for the road. Grab a hand-kneaded bagel and in-house-roasted coffee from Kitchen 313 Kamiyuge (11am to 3.30pm Tuesday, Thursday and Saturday) or *Kamirin-yaki* (a pancake-like treat with filling in the shape of Kamijima's sea deity mascot) from Oyatsu Time (11am to 3pm Wednesday, Saturday and Sunday).

As you proceed across the island's northern rim, stop at Takahama Hachiman-jinja and Ōmori-jinja, both shrines featuring seaside *torii* gates. Just 50m from Ōmori Shine is the first of three 'Breakwater Art' murals on the Yumeshima Kaidō, featuring the winning entries to the 'Setouchi Kamijima Art Project 2019'. The Yuge-jima piece, titled *Heavenly Flowers* by painter Hizuki Miwa, is made up of colourful florals designed to evoke the hopefulness of a rainbow. If time allows, proceed towards the dead-end at Umatate-no-Hana to reach the northernmost corner of the island and a sandy beach.

Back at Ōmori Shrine, either do a U-turn and return to Yuge (the flatter, easier option), or head south and then east, following Rte 172 down the undulating eastern coast. The area known

TOP TIP:

If you rented a bike outside the Yumeshima Kaidō islands, have the ferry bicycle fee waived with a 'cycle free ticket' *(kamijima.info/pdf/cyclefree_eng.pdf).* Bikes cannot be taken on some 'Geiyo Kisen' services from Habu Port (Inno-shima) and Imabari.

Island Temple Pilgrimage

On Yuge-jima, find a mini version of Shikoku's famed '88 Temple Pilgrimage' *(kamijima.info/yuge88).* This more accessible route over a much smaller footprint reduces the time required by bike from weeks to just a day. While most of the temples could be described as roadside altars and therefore don't offer commemorative stamps, their close proximity (sometimes within mere metres) requires less mental fortitude. Incredibly, neighbouring Sa-shima also has its own full set of 88 temples, but the route has mostly been overgrown and is no longer recommended. Brush up on your Japanese numbers, as the temples are only marked in kanji.

Take a Break

Yuge-jima has the most choice for dining and relaxation. Convenient to Yuge Port, SHIMA DE CAFE (9.30am to 5pm, closed Tuesday) is a cyclist-friendly eatery with lemon pork dishes and homemade sweets, and TRATTORIA ARU (11am to 2pm Friday to Monday), is a favourite for Japanese curry. If a relaxing bath beckons, the Inland Sea Resort FESPA by Matsubara Swimming Beach and mixed-gender saltwater spa Shio-no-yu (swimsuit and cap required) are good for achy muscles.

as Yuge-Ōtani has particularly picturesque and expansive Inland Sea views. Once back in Yuge town, continue through to the 980m-long Yuge Ōhashi bridge to Sa-shima.

02 The smallest of the islands on the route, Sa-shima (佐島) has a population of just 400 residents. The most built-up section is in the northwest, just below the Ikina Bridge, where you'll find the island's only eatery, Book Cafe Okappa (11.30am to 5pm Friday to Sunday), and two accommodation options. The closest you'll find to a convenience store or supermarket here is Sa-shima Island Plaza (佐島しまのひろば; 9am to 5pm), an unstaffed community space selling local fruits and vegetables via honesty boxes. Although there is an on-site vending machine, it's best to plan ahead with drinks and snacks.

As there is no continuous road around Sa-shima's perimeter, an island loop is not possible. Instead, the Yumeshima Kaidō will take you on an 8km out-and-back detour to Sa-shima's southern tip and one of the ride's most photographed attractions. Known as the 'Blue Line U-turn', a large 'u' painted in blue, the guiding colour for cyclists on the Inland Sea's archipelagos, can be found at the culmination of a dead-end path that opens to Nagaiso Beach. Popularly, visitors will place their bike by the marking for a distinctive photo.

On the final 2km to get here, the narrow, dark road is unmaintained and often littered with sand and forest debris. Coupled with plenty of ups and downs, it's one of the most difficult sections of the Yumeshima Kaidō. In spring and summer, look out for rash-inducing *kemushi* (hairy caterpillars) hanging from the surrounding foliage.

Less-adventurous cyclists who wish to bypass this section can stick to the island's 'downtown', visiting Sa-shima Hachiman Shrine, site of October's Autumn Matsuri when the shrine's *omikoshi* (portable shrine) is purified in the sea, and Saihō-ji, a Buddhist temple known for its *Niō* (guardian deity) statues with unusually thick eyebrows.

03 Cross over to Ikina-jima (生名島) by way of the 515m-long Ikina Bridge, landing at Ikina-bashi Memorial Park. A stone monument with 'Yumeshima Kaidō' inscribed in Japanese (also found at Sa-shima Rest Area) is a popular photo spot.

Start a mostly flat, 8km counterclockwise loop, with the main attractions north of Tateishi Port. Visit Sanshū-en, a garden at the

KAMIJIMA TOWN TOURISM PHOTO SERVICE, PUBLIC DOMAIN, VIA WIKIMEDIA COMMONS

Sanshū-en Menhir (p189)

YOSHINORI OKADA/SHUTTERSTOCK

'Lemon-Fed' Cuisine

Citrus is a recurring theme of Kamijima's cuisine. Iwagi-jima, known as 'green lemon island', harvests their lemons before fully ripened, resulting in a fruit with a distinct sourness and aroma when cut. Lemon souvenirs – from cake to jam to liqueurs – are widely available. Leftover pulp and rinds from juice extraction are integrated into feed for pigs. The meat, called 'lemon pork', is tender and richly flavourful with a mild sweetness. Considered the islands' soul food, 'lemon-fed' pork is often served with rice and Yuge-jima *nori* (seaweed). Pig manure becomes fertiliser for the lemon trees, creating a sustainable cycle.

Mt Sekizen Observation

foot of Mt Tateishi founded by Asō Ito (1876–1956), a pioneering female entrepreneur known for dressing in male attire.

The Sanshū-en Menhir, an incredible 7m-tall stone *kyoseki* (megalith) found on the grounds, is believed to have been worshipped since the Yayoi period (c 300 BCE to 300 CE). How a non-endemic stone of this size came to rest here is a topic for eternal debate, with theories ranging from feats of human engineering to the mystical. According to one Japanese folklore story, a giant dropped the large stone while trying to juggle it. From the garden, there's a 30-minute hiking trail through other ritualistic Yayoi remains to Mt Tateishi Observation Deck. A statue of Ito marks the trail entrance.

Continue following the road north and across to the western coast. Once you hit the shoreline, you'll find the second instalment of the Breakwater Art project. Titled *Everyone's Whale* and led by sculptor Takeda Mitsuo, this artwork is the result of many different sketches produced at a community workshop. It features finless porpoises, once abundant in these waters, filled with 'everyone's thoughts' around a map of Kamijima.

Next door, Sound Hakanda Campground offers tent and equipment rental, and BBQ packs featuring local wild boar, making camping possible for cyclists arriving empty-handed (reservations are required: yumeshima.club/camp). From here, it's a 3km cycle down the western coast to Iwagi Bridge.

The Iwagi Bridge, opened in March 2022, established road access to Iwagi-jima (岩城島) and the Yumeshima Kaidō as a cycling route proper. Previously, cyclists would need to backtrack to a port to reach the island by ferry. The 916m bridge is not flat, so expect an uphill ride until you reach the central apex. Oddly, no bicycle lane or pavement was integrated into the design, so be mindful of traffic.

The largest of the islands, a defining feature of Iwagi-jima's landscape is 370m Mt Sekizen in the island's interior, with 3000 cherry trees that explode in colour come spring. The Yumeshima Kaidō will take you on a 16km counter-clockwise circumnavigation of the island following Rte 174, including a detour to Mt Sekizen Observation Deck for panoramic views. There are several options, but the approach from the north is shorter (3.8km) and less winding.

Naturally, you'll encounter inclines here; an e-bike makes less work of them. The closest you can get to the summit by bike is the 'East Parking Area' (東駐車場), from where it's 130m, or three minutes on foot, up a grassed slope to the viewing platform. If you get tired of pedalling, you can dismount at the lower 'West Parking Area' (西駐車場) and walk 600m (12 minutes). Both locations have bicycle racks.

Descend the mountain and take the western coastal route south to the final Breakwater Art piece. Called *Listen to the Sea* by illustrator Kan Mayuki, it features a series of people and animals crouched down listening intently. Visitors are encouraged to take a moment to connect with the sounds of the sea. From here, it's only 2km to Iwagi Port, where you'll find several opportunities to try the island's famed lemon pork and other lemon products. Limone Plaza opposite the port offers meals and a selection of souvenirs.

From Iwagi Port, there's a high-speed ferry to Imabari (50 minutes). Alternatively, complete your cycle at Okogi Port on the island's north to access Ikuchi-jima, or return to Ikina-jima or Yuge-jima for connections to Inno-shima.

Take a Break

When it's time for a caffeine boost, find Kamijima's first house-roasted coffee specialty store upstairs in a deceivingly lacklustre former port office. YUMESHIMA COFFEE ROASTERY (10am to 4pm, closed Sunday and Monday), located by Ikina Port, was opened in July 2024 by teacher-turned-barista Amako Tsukasa. The changing menu, deliberately small and handcrafted, features quality international beans – from Ethiopia and Guatemala to Thailand and Indonesia. Take a counter window seat and watch the boats roll in. Confirm opening times on Instagram *@yumeshima_coffee_roastery*.

29

Best for

FOOD & DRINK

HAYAKATO/SHUTTERSTOCK

Shōdoshima Olive Park (p192)

Shōdoshima

DURATION	DIFFICULTY	DISTANCE	START/END
2.5hrs	Easy	22km (one way)	Tonoshō Port
TERRAIN	Paved; road cycling		

Credited as the birthplace of olive cultivation in Japan, Shōdoshima (小豆島) off mainland Kagawa is olive mad, with the island accounting for more than 90% of the country's total shipping volume of olives. Find everything from olive noodles, ice cream and sake to oil-infused hair and skincare products here. It's also significantly larger (and overall more challenging to ride) than most islands in the Inland Sea. This course covers a feasible day trip along the generally flat southern route, taking in a number of the island's top highlights.

Bike Hire

There are bike-rental points at Tonoshō (most choice), Kusakabe, Ikeda and Sakate ports. All but Sakate have electric options. There's also a 'Hello Cycle' bike-share programme *(hellocycling-shodoshima.com)*.

Starting Point

Start at Tonoshō Port on the island's west. It's a one-hour journey by ferry or 30 minutes by high-speed boat from Takamatsu. There are also connections from Shin-Okayama and Teshima.

01 From Tonoshō Port, take a short 2km ride southeast to one of Shōdoshima's most popular attractions, Angel Road (エンジェルロード). This 500m sandbar appears only during low tide, allowing visitors to walk from mainland Shōdoshima to a series of three offshore islets.

It is said if you walk the road hand-in-hand with a romantic partner, your relationship will strengthen. *Ema* (votive plaques) in the shape of hearts and shells can be purchased from the Angel Road Tourist Information Centre. Write your wish on the plaque, carry it across the sandbar and hang it on an islet

Elevation (m)

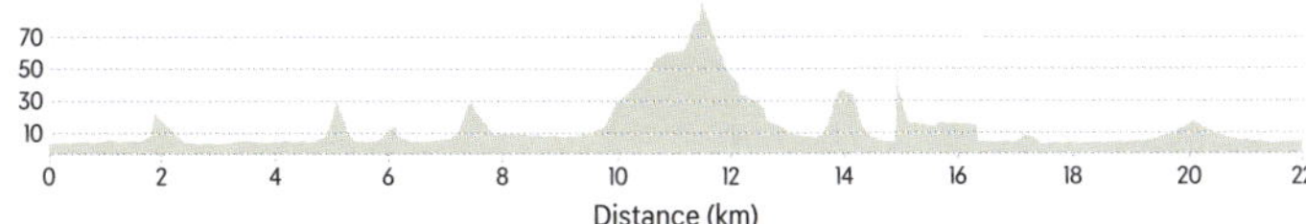

Why Olives?

Attempts to cultivate olives in Japan began in the early 20th century, as the oil could be used to preserve and export fish to Europe. While traditional Japanese cuisine doesn't feature olives at all, the oil could conserve the large amounts of fish being hauled in from the country's expanded northern territory, acquired as a result of the Russo-Japanese War (1904–05). Kagawa was one of three prefectures where olive production was trialled, but it was only in Shōdoshima's Nishimura district where the trees managed to survive. Over 100 years later, the area remains the 'olive capital' of Japan.

tree in the hope it will come true. An elevated view of Angel Road can be had from Promise Hill Observation Deck.

As this stop is completely time-dependent, schedule according to the day's tide timings (posted at ports and tourist information points). In spring and summer, low tide occurs twice a day, with up to a six-hour window each time, while in winter it only occurs briefly once per day.

02 From Angel Road, it's less than 1km through quiet, residential streets via Saikō Temple to central Tonoshō's Maze Town (迷路のまち). Called 'Meiro-no-machi', its haphazard, labyrinthine layout was a design choice to baffle would-be invaders in the warring imperial court period of the 14th century.

A performance-art project has led several of the town's buildings to be repurposed as Yōkai Art Museum (9am to 9pm Friday to Tuesday, to 5pm Thursday). A catch-all term to describe ghosts, demons, monsters and shapeshifting tricksters of the supernatural world, *yōkai* often feature heavily in Japanese folklore. At the museum, you can view over 800 artworks of these curious apparitions and visit Yōkai Bar, playfully billed as a gathering point exclusively for *yōkai* with a small 'human' menu for any mortals that happen to stop by.

03 For a short-lived but quirky 'been there, done that' moment, pause at Dofuchi-kaikyō (土渕海峡), officially the narrowest navigable strait in the world at just 9.93m wide at its narrowest point. A copy of a letter from Guinness World Records can be found on site to prove the title.

Cross the tiny strait by an equally petite bridge, and if you fancy, pop into the nearby Tonoshō Town Hall (8.30am to 5.15pm Monday to Friday), where for a small fee you can obtain a commemorative certificate of your crossing.

04 Bar one sloped stretch around halfway, it's a relatively flat 9km ride east on Rte 436 to Shōdoshima Olive Park (小豆島オリーブ公園) and the precise location of the island's olive success. This terraced park and roadside station, surrounded by olive groves, centres around Olive Memorial Hall (8.30am to 5pm), which houses exhibits on the island's olive history and an olive-focused souvenir store.

Nearby is a Greek windmill famously featured in cult Studio Ghibli classic *Kiki's Delivery Service*. A steady stream of visitors can be seen jumping on broomsticks to recreate a scene from the beloved 1989 animation. Broomsticks can be borrowed for free from the memorial hall.

05 Continue on Rte 436 for 5km, before detouring 500m north to soy sauce brewery Yama-Roku Shōyu (ヤマロク醤油; 9am to 5pm), featured in the Netflix series *Salt, Fat, Acid, Heat* (2018).

Take a free walk-in tour of the 150-year-old brewery to see their enormous cedar fermentation barrels and taste-test various vintages of *shōyu* (soy sauce). Afterwards, enjoy vanilla ice cream drizzled with *shōyu* at the on-site teahouse. More menu items are available on weekends.

06 Cycle 2km south to the island's only sake brewery, Shōdoshima Shuzō (小豆島酒造; 9am to 5pm Saturday to Wednesday), also known as Morikuni Sake Brewery. Try a sake tasting flight, which you can pair with lunch or dessert sets incorporating sake lees, a by-product of sake production. The brewery has developed several products using olive-derived yeast.

Return to Tonoshō Port (with the most frequent ferry departures) or, if timing and rental bike return conditions allow, the closer Ikeda, Kusakabe or Sakate ports, for connections to Takamatsu.

Take a Break

Try the island's hand-stretched *sōmen* at SAKUBEI (作兵衛; 10.30am to 2pm), conveniently located at a midpoint on the ride's main artery, Rte 436. The menu is deliberately simple to honour the flavour and texture of the fresh noodles, chewier than the dried variety thanks to the high water content. Find cold, plain and olive *sōmen*, along with *nyūmen* (*sōmen* noodles served in a warm broth). Experiment with different flavour profiles by adding extra-virgin olive oil, available tableside, to your dishes. Closing days vary; see sakube.co.jp.

THE ASAHI SHIMBUN/GETTY IMAGES

Sōmen **noodle production**

400-Year-Old Industries

Olives are not the only product worth trying on Shōdoshima. Predating olives by several centuries are the island's traditional industries of hand-stretched *sōmen* (thin, wheat-based noodles) and wooden barrel-aged soy sauce. In an era of automation, time-honoured methods take passionate precedence here. As you tour the island, find rows on rows of *sōmen* noodles delicately placed on outdoor racks to dry naturally under the Shōdoshima sun, and gigantic cedar soy-sauce barrels. Over a third of Japan's wooden barrels used for maturing soy sauce can be found here, concentrated around Hishio-no-Sato ('Soy Sauce Village') between Kusakabe and Sakate ports.

30

Best for

ART & CULTURE

Tokushima & Around

DURATION	DIFFICULTY	DISTANCE	START/END
3hrs	Easy	27km	JR Tokushima Station
TERRAIN	Paved; road cycling		

Awa Jūrōbē Yashiki Puppet Theatre and Museum

Tokushima (徳島), Japan's capital of indigo dye, puppetry and the summer dance Awa-odori, has a long history of artistic expression. Instrumental in the development of traditional trades has been the flow of the Yoshino-gawa, just north of central Tokushima City, where the 194km river meets the Kii Channel. This ride will take you up close to this magnificent waterway on a leisurely cycle that provides a first-hand look at some of Tokushima's most loved cultural exports, including live performances and hands-on workshops.

Bike Hire

Rent a city or electric bike from the underground Bicycle Parking Lot in front of Tokushima Station. Alternatively, Yeti&Ltb Rental Cycle Tokushima deliver to transport hubs by reservation.

Starting Point

Start at JR Tokushima Station, just over one hour by limited express train from Kagawa's JR Takamatsu Station. Highway buses connect Kōbe with Tokushima via Awaji Island.

01 From Tokushima Station, start a 6km cycle out of downtown Tokushima. Cross the 1km-long Yoshino-gawa Bridge (Rte 11), where low guardrails give an expansive view over one of the widest points of the Yoshino-gawa. Once you reach the opposing riverbank, take a right and head towards Awa Jūrōbē Yashiki Puppet Theatre and Museum (徳島県立阿波十郎兵衛屋敷).

Here you can watch a compelling 30-minute *ningyō jōruri* performance – a type of traditional theatre involving three performers simultaneously operating each puppet, skilfully synchronising their

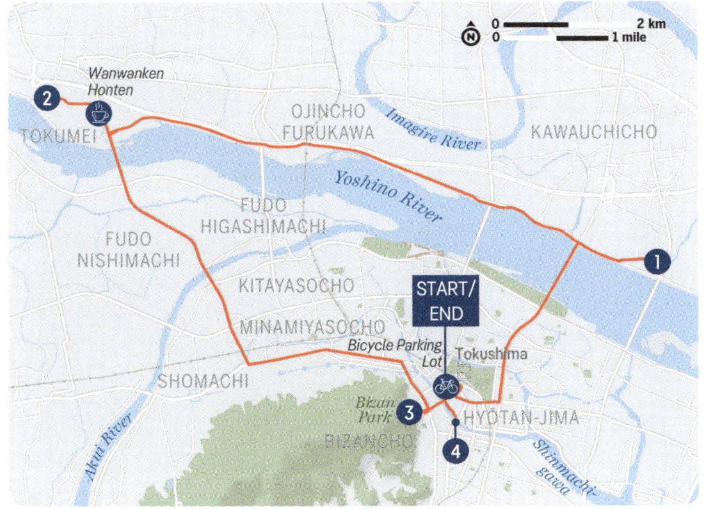

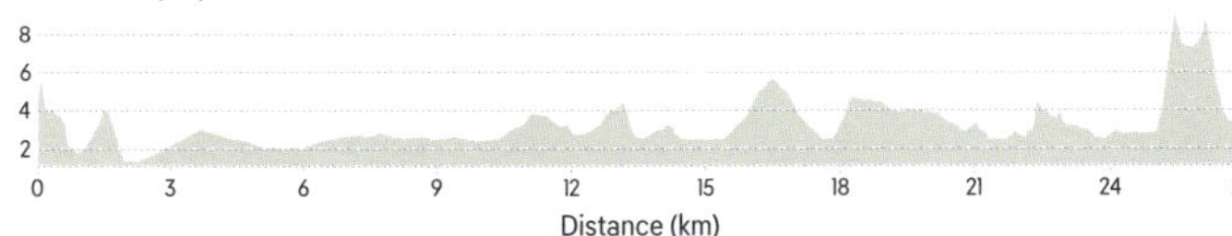

movements while completely cloaked, face included, in black sheaths. English-speakers can follow the lyrical storytelling via electronic subtitles that appear above the stage.

While the theatre is open 9.30am to 5pm (until 6pm in summer), you'll want to time your visit with one of the two daily performances (typically 11am and 2pm). Before or after, check out the small on-site museum with its English explanations (included in the ticket).

02 From the puppet theatre, cycle 11km west along the northern bank of the Yoshino-gawa. The obvious choice, Prefectural Rd 137, is a popular thoroughfare too narrow to accommodate cyclists. Instead, use road-adjacent or riverside paths, or drop a few streets back to take quieter, residential roads.

Your destination is Aizumi-chō Historical Museum (藍住町歴史館 藍の館; Ai-no-Yakata; 9am to 5pm, closed Tuesday), which has excellent multi-lingual exhibits related to *aizome* (indigo dyeing), and preserves the former residence and factory of local indigo merchants, the Okumura family.

Conveniently, visitors can participate in an indigo-dyeing workshop here without a reservation. From a small hanky to large silk scarf, experience first-hand what it's like to dye cloth with indigo and watch as the material, stained green from the natural dye, transforms into signature 'Japan blue' under running water. The 30-minute to one-hour workshops run on a rolling basis; last entry is at 3.30pm.

Legacy of the Yoshino-gawa

Tokushima has been the number-one producer of the dried and fermented natural indigo dye *sukumo* since the Edo period, and it has the Yoshino-gawa to thank. The river's routinely flooded banks made the surrounding farmland unsuitable for rice cultivation but, in turn, abundantly fertile for highly valuable indigo crops. The prosperity that came from the thriving *aizome* (indigo dyeing) industry spilled over into the development of *ningyō jōruri,* a captivating form of lyrical puppet theatre. Tokushima remains Japan's leader in puppetry, with more puppet theatres than anywhere else in the country and a vast network of open-air community stages.

03 With your own custom souvenir in hand, take Rte 1 to loop back over the Yoshino-gawa and towards town via the 800m-long Nada Bridge. Steadily see Mt Bizan come closer into view as you cycle 9.5km to the foot of the mountain and the next stop, Awa Odori Kaikan (阿波おどり会館; 9am to 9pm). While Tokushima's Awa-odori Matsuri is an annual festival, this multi-storey complex allows visitors to experience the famed dance throughout the year at one of its five daily performances. Live shows at the 250-seat capacity Awa Odori Hall (2F) take place at 11am, 2pm, 3pm, 4pm (adult/child ¥1300/700; 40 minutes) and 8pm (adult/child ¥1600/800; 50 minutes). To delve further into the dance's history, head to the Awa Odori Museum (3F; 9am to 5pm; adult/child ¥500/300), where handy QR codes provide thorough English translations. Upstairs, take a 290m cable car from Bizan Ropeway Station (5F) to the summit of Mt Bizan for fine city views (adult/child one-way ¥900/500, return ¥1500/800; 9am to 9pm April to October, to 5.30pm November to March). Set discounted tickets for two or all three attractions are available.

04 It's now only a few hundred metres to Tokushima's downtown, concentrated on Hyōtan-jima, a gourd-shaped sandbar encircled by the Suketō and Shinmachi rivers. Meaning 'gourd island', Hyōtan-jima's extensive river promenades entice residents for relaxed strolls, buskers, weekend markets and river cruises.

You'll find the Hyōtan-jima Cruise terminal (ひょうたん島クルーズ; adult/child ¥600/300; 20 to 30 minutes) by the Ryōgoku Bridge. This is an easy and inexpensive way to tour the city from water level; enjoy zipping under the numerous low bridges that connect the central business district with the rest of the city. Departures are every 40 minutes from 11am to 3.40pm, with additional summer night cruises in July and August (5pm to 7.40pm). It's less than 1km from here to Tokushima Station.

Decide on the number and order of stops based on your desired starting time, performance schedules, cycling speed and time of year. Combo tickets for Awa Odori Kaikan can be used over multiple visits on the same day (entry to each attraction is once only).

Take a Break

Stop at WANWANKEN HONTEN (支那そば 王王軒 本店; 11am to 8pm, closed Thursday) to try a rich bowl of Tokushima ramen. The prefecture has three regional ramen varieties. The one from Tokushima City features a distinctive, brown-coloured soup made from a *shōyu* (soy sauce) and *tonkotsu* (pork bone) broth blend, and topped with pork belly, green onions, fermented bamboo shoots and a raw egg. At Wanwanken, you can select your ramen without pork belly or egg via pre-set options on the vending machine. Expect a queue at opening time.

YASUYOSHI CHIBA/AFP/GETTY IMAGES

Awa-odori Matsuri

Awa-odori

In August, more than one million people flock to Tokushima to experience its sizzling four-day dance festival, the Awa-odori Matsuri. Theories about the origins of the dance abound, including a spontaneous drunken street party after the completion of Tokushima-jō (Tokushima Castle). What is more likely, according to the history books, is that the dance developed much more slowly, evolving from regional summer *bon-odori* folk dances inviting the ancestors back to the human world. Imagery of the dance is built into the very architecture of the city, from bridge railings to toilet-block embellishments, and the year-round performance hall Awa Odori Kaikan.

Also Try...

Dōgo Onsen, Hamakaze Kaidō

MASAYUKI NAKAYA/LONELY PLANET

Hamakaze Kaidō

DURATION	DIFFICULTY	DISTANCE
5hrs	Easy	50km

The Hamakaze Kaidō (はまかぜ海道) is a 50km coastal route from Ehime's cycling hotspot Imabari to prefectural capital Matsuyama. Aptly named 'Sea Breeze Road', it mostly follows Rte 196 along the shoreline with a number of coastal parks and bathhouses for pleasant breaks with a sea view. Stop at Kawara-kan, a museum dedicated to the area's long manufacture of Kikuma roof tiles, used on Matsuyama-jō, Dōgo Onsen Honkan and the Imperial Palaces of Kyoto and Tokyo. It's a good way to connect a Shimanami Kaidō (p24) ride with Matsuyama, but keep in mind Shimanami bike-rental services don't extend here. End your ride with a steaming soak at legendary hot springs Dōgo Onsen.

Gogo-shima

DURATION	DIFFICULTY	DISTANCE
2hrs	Intermediate	12.5km

For a quieter take on Ehime's prefectural capital, hop on a 15-minute ferry from Matsuyama's Takahama Port to nearby island Gogo-shima (興居島). A cycle here is best started at Yura Port and Cotton John Coffee, a seaside coffee shop that doubles as tourist information. A convenient short course will take you north to Iwagami-jinja, a small but atmospheric shrine with stone steps, as well as to the western side of the island for beautiful Inland Sea views from Washigasu Beach and the elevated Yūhigatōge Pass, a popular sunset spot. Adventurous cyclists may enjoy the longer, more undulating southern road. Ports are unstaffed here; register for bike rental and obtain keys from ferry staff en route.

VIEW PHOTOS/A.COLLECTIONRF/GETTY IMAGES

Cape Ashizuri

Sanuki Kaidō

DURATION	DIFFICULTY	DISTANCE
10hrs	Intermediate	85km

The 'Ishizuchi Route' on the Sanuki Kaidō (讃岐街道) extends from Imabari in Ehime to Kanonji City in Kagawa. With the Inland Sea to one side and Ishizuchi-san, the highest peak in western Japan, to the other, the 85km course will connect you with the highlights of western Kagawa via Saijō City. Dubbed the 'spring water capital of Japan', an incredible 90,000 tonnes of natural spring water, originating from nearby Ishizuchi-san, spouts daily from approximately 3000 *uchinuki* (self-priming wells). Given the length of the ride, it's best completed over two days. Saijō, around 30km from Imabari, makes for a good layover. Be mindful of expressways and national highways on this route, utilising less busy roads when needed.

Cape Ashizuri Loop

DURATION	DIFFICULTY	DISTANCE
4hr	Intermediate	30km

A 30km loop of Cape Ashizuri (足摺岬) is an excellent introduction to the dramatic, cragged cliffs of Kōchi's Pacific Ocean–facing coastline. Numerous hotels by the cape's tip have rental bikes, making this once quite isolated peninsula accessible to the casual rider. Don't miss Ryūgū-jinja, a secluded shrine on a rocky outcrop, and, further on, the birthplace of John Manjirō, a 19th-century Japanese historical figure whose shipwrecking, rescue and transportation to the US ultimately contributed to the Meiji Restoration, ending Japan's long period of isolation. The fascinating John Mung Museum nearby tells more. For the thrill of twists and turns on a road not often used by vehicles, return via the central Ashizuri Skyline.

Yukuhashi
Iizuka
Tagawa
Sea of Suo
Hime-jima
Fukuoka
Nakatsu
34
Bungo-Takada
Sea of Iyo
Karatsu
Kunisaki Peninsula
Hirado
Sugihata
Kitsuki
Imari
Taku
Kurume
Hita
Sasebo
Saga
Kusu
Beppu-wan
Beppu
Kashima
Ōita
Oshima Island
Sea of Ariake
Oguni
Ōmura-wan
Ōmuta
Kujū-san
Usuki
Ōmura
31
Isahaya
Taketa
Unzen-Amakusa National Park
Ueki
Aso-Kuju National Park
Saiki
Nagasaki
Shimabara
Tachibana-wan
Kumamoto
Takachiho
Shimabara Peninsula
Shimabara-wan
Hondo
Yatsushiro
Kunimi-dake
Nobeoka
Amakusa Islands
Kami-jima
Shimo-jima
Sea of Yatsushiro
Minamata
Hitoyoshi
Nagashima
Izumi
Takanabe
Ebino
Saito
Kobayashi
Kirishima-Yaku National Park
Satsumasendai
Miyazaki
Koshiki Islands
Kamo
Kirishima
Miyakonojō
32
Kagoshima
Sakurajima
Nichinan
Okinawa
Isena-jima
Shibushi
Kushima
35
Kinkō-wan
Iejima
Satsuma Peninsula
Kanoya
Shibushi-wan
Makurazaki
Nago
Ōsumi Peninsula
Ibusuki
Ikeda-ko
Nejime
Ishikawa
33
Okinawa City
PACIFIC OCEAN
Naha
Itoman
Ōsumi Straits
0 50 km
0 25 miles
0 50 km
0 25 miles

OKIMO/SHUTTERSTOCK

Niya Thiya Cave (p223)

Kyūshū & Okinawa

31 Yūka Family Road

Tranquil riding through Kumamoto's fertile plains and woodland. **p204**

32 Nichinan Coast

Sea views, rock formations carved by the sea and historic sites. **p208**

33 Ibusuki Poké Trail

Embrace wellness while catching Pokémon along the coast. **p212**

34 Maple Yabakei Road

The Yamakuni River is lined with Japanese maple trees that blaze in the autumn. **p218**

35 Iejima

This small island off the coast of Okinawa's Motobu Peninsula is perfect for a spin. **p222**

Explore

Kyūshū & Okinawa

Home to only 10% of Japan's population, Kyūshū is rich in nature, from fertile plains, lush forests and gushing waterfalls to mountainous peaks, active volcanoes and hot-spring areas. Due to its proximity to the rest of Asia, the island has long been a cultural gateway, evidenced today by its historic sites and culinary diversity, particularly in the port cities of Fukuoka and Nagasaki. Expect warm hospitality and a laid-back vibe in both Kyūshū and Okinawa, where the archipelago's long independence as the Ryūkyū kingdom can be seen in the mix of Japanese and Chinese influences on the history and culture.

Fukuoka

Kyūshū's largest, most cosmopolitan city, Fukuoka (福岡) has vibrant energy. *Yatai* (street stalls) are an integral part of the food scene, serving dishes like the city's renowned *Hakata rāmen* (pork-bone-based broth with thin noodles and pork) and *goma-saba* (sesame mackerel). For restaurants and bars, head to the Hakata Station area, or to Tenjin and Canal City Hakata for shopping. The city is rich in history, being the site of Japan's first Zen temple, Shōfuku-ji, which was founded in 1195 and enveloped by nature. Ōhori Park is a popular spot for cycling, and Momochi Seaside Park is only 6km from downtown.

Kumamoto

Kumamoto-jō, in its hilltop position, is a symbol of Kumamoto (熊本). First built in the mid-15th century, the fortification has created a historic and cultural legacy, particularly in the Chūō district, with its samurai-era houses like Kokindenju no Ma and Suizenji Jōjuen Garden. The area is home to several museums related to the city's history and art, as well as *higo-zōgan* (inlay metalwork) artisans, a craft begun by castle gunsmiths in the 17th century. The technique involves hammering gold and silver leaf, and can be experienced at various shops. For shopping and dining, visit the Shimotori and Kamitori arcades.

Kagoshima

Located within Sakurajima-Kinkōwan Geopark, Kagoshima (鹿児島) offers outdoor activities in a subtropical setting.

WHEN TO GO

The region enjoys mild, dry winters. March to May and September to November have temperatures of 16–22°C in Kyūshū, and 23–30°C in Okinawa. Rainy season is early May to late June (Okinawa) and early June to mid-July (Kyūshū). July and August have temperatures of 35°C or above, while typhoon season is June to November (Okinawa) and July to October (Kyūshū).

Sakurajima, an active volcano, is 4km from downtown across Kinkō Bay. Ferries go back and forth 24 hours a day in this area, where you can swim, kayak, windsurf and bathe in hot springs. At Iso Beach, you may even spot dolphins. For dining, try the Tenmonkan district or Kagomma Furusato Yataimura, a collection of eateries selling dishes and drinks from Kagoshima's mainland and islands, such as *kurobuta* (black pork) and *shōchū* (a sweet-potato spirit).

Naha

Okinawa's largest city, Naha (那覇) was once the centre of the Ryūkyū kingdom, which was independent until 1609. It traded extensively in the region, particularly with China, whose influence can be seen in Shuri-jō (Shuri Castle) and Fukushūen Garden, but there are also sites you would expect in Japan such as the shrine Naminoue-gū, overlooking the beach. Naha's hub is Kokusai-dōri, where you'll find shops selling traditional items and souvenirs, as well as bars and eateries serving local favourites like *gōya champuru* (stir-fried tofu, pork and bitter melon). For upscale restaurants, craft beer and shopping malls, try the Omoromachi area.

TRANSPORT

By shinkansen, Fukuoka (Hakata Station) is three hours from Osaka and five hours from Tokyo. From Hakata, the shinkansen runs south to Kagoshima and west to Nagasaki. Fukuoka is served by overnight buses from Honshū and Shikoku. Fukuoka and Okinawa welcome flights from most domestic airports, as well as South Korea, Taiwan, Hong Kong, Thailand and Singapore.

WHAT'S ON

Tamaseseri

Scores of loin-cloth-clad men compete for possession of a wooden ball at Fukuoka's Hakozaki-gū in this traditional form of fortune-telling.

Naha Hārī

Annually from 3–5 May, this lively event involves beautifully decorated dragon boats racing, a way to pray for safe voyages and fruitful fishing.

Himeshima Bon Odori

This mid-August festival brings Hime island alive with music and creative, humorous dances, including one where participants dress as foxes.

WHERE TO STAY

Kyūshū offers diverse accommodation, from hostels and campsites to full-service hotels and *onsen* (hot spring) resorts. Larger cities have more Western luxury hotels, such as The Ritz-Carlton in Fukuoka and the Marriott Hotel in Nagasaki, but there are ample options for mid- and high-end hotels and Japanese ryokan inns across the island. You'll find business hotels like the Toyoko Inn even in small cities, often beside transport hubs, and glamping sites are common in popular destinations, particularly on beachfronts. Okinawa's options range from Western- and Japanese-style resorts, such as Hilton or Hoshinoya, and private condos on the coast to hotels in urban areas.

Resources

Kyūshū Tourism Organization *(visit-kyushu.com/en/)* The Official Kyūshū Travel Guide.

Cycling Island Kyūshū *(cyclingisland-kyushu.com/en)* Destinations, tours and guides.

Welcome Kyūshū *(welcomekyushu.jp/cycle-in-kyushu/en)* Courses, maps and links.

Visit Fukuoka *(crossroadfukuoka.jp/en/articles/cycle)* Routes and cycle stations.

Visit Okinawa Japan *(visitokinawajapan.com)* Okinawa travel site.

31

Yūka Family Road

DURATION	DIFFICULTY	DISTANCE	START/END
4–5hrs	Intermediate	34km (68km return)	Kumamoto City International Center/ Yūka Family Road

TERRAIN	Flat; paved cycle paths

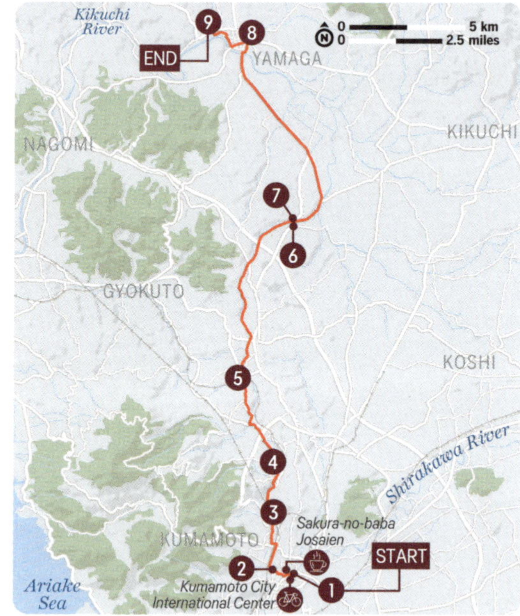

ALON ADIKA/SHUTTERSTOCK

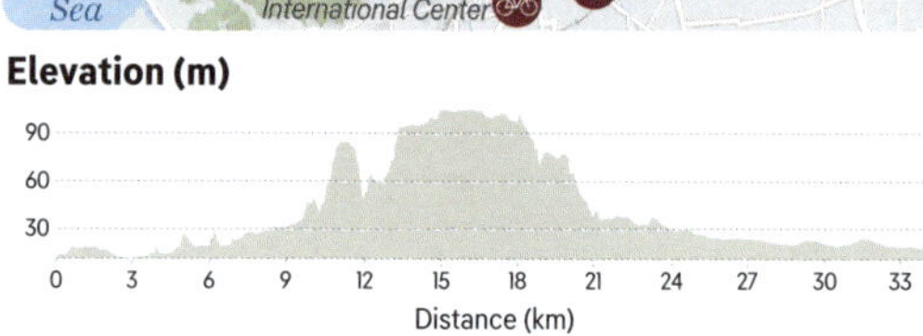

This well-marked ride connects Kumamoto (熊本) and Yamaga (山鹿), two cities that have played an important role in Japan's history. The prefectural capital is home to Kumamoto-jō, the site of one of the samurai's final battles before their demise in the mid-19th century, while Yamaga was a post town on the Buzen Kaidō route that once linked north and south Kyūshū. Delve into this history on the Yūka Family Road, a cycle path that includes part of an old railway track, weaving through quiet woodland and rice paddies of the Kikuchi River Plain.

Bike Hire

Kumamoto City International Center rents bicycles and e-bikes from 9am to 9.30pm for ¥1000 or ¥1500 per day respectively (helmet and insurance included). Identification, such as a passport, is required.

Starting Point

Take the A Line Kumamoto City Tram from JR Kumamoto Station for 18 minutes and get off at Hanabatachō Station, from where it's a few minutes' walk to Kumamoto City International Center.

01 From Kumamoto City International Center, turn left, cross over the Tsuboi-gawa and take the first left. After 300m, turn right and continue towards Kumamoto-jō (熊本城; Kumamoto Castle), following the signage. From the bicycle parking, it's a short walk to reach both Kumamoto Castle Park and the main building of Kumamoto Prefectural Museum of Art.

02 Leaving the parking area, take the first right and then turn right at the crossroads, where there is a convenience store. This is a

Kumamoto-jō

Best for

GETTING AWAY FROM IT ALL

Kumamoto-jō

Renowned as one of the three great castles of Japan, Kumamoto-jō dates from the mid-15th century and comprises 13 structures designated as important cultural properties and 29 castle gates. Though heavily damaged in a 2016 earthquake, the main tower has been restored and offers exhibits on the castle's storied past and a bird's-eye view of the city. The vast grounds are particularly popular in March and April, when 800 cherry trees of three varieties create a sea of pink and white blossoms.

good place to pick up snacks and drinks as there are limited options along the way. After 200m, turn right and then right again at the traffic lights to join the road with the tram line. Continue for 1.2km and turn left at the junction before the tram stop for Kenritsutaiikukan-mae. Continue straight, passing under the train tracks to join Rte 330 (Yūka Family Road). From here, the path hugs the river for 2.2km, passing through Kumamoto's suburbs before moving inland. You'll then go under some roads and rejoin the river as the landscape opens up to reveal lush agricultural land, one of Kyūshū's vital breadbaskets, on both sides.

03 When the path joins Rte 300, cross over the railway tracks and turn left onto Rte 31. Continue for 1km, where a sign will indicate you to turn left. Head over the river and the level crossing to reach another sign to turn right. Take the second left, so the river is on your right side.

04 Moving into a more rural area, the ride becomes increasingly tranquil. You'll pass fields of rice and greenhouses packed with vegetables and fruits including the area's popular kumquats. Look out for watermelon, too, as Kumamoto is Japan's top producer of this fruit. Lightly forested areas may reveal bird species as diverse as wagtails, sparrows, finches and thrushes. After about 4km, you'll need to climb up and down steps while pushing your bike.

05 Approaching Ueki Station, watch for the dedicated signage as the route does a hairpin bend to head northeast. On the next stretch you can enjoy the sound of tall, lean bamboo swaying in the breeze as you pass through some bamboo grooves. After crossing under Rte 3, follow the route for 1.2km to reach a convenience store at Ueki Tarumizu, a good place to take a break and stock up for the rest of the ride.

06 After about 800m, this residential area leads to beautiful countryside. The route runs by trees and fields alongside the Toyoda-gawa for the next 6km, the only break in the peace and quiet being the crossing under the Kyūshū Expressway. Now deep in nature, shady parts provide opportunities for having an alfresco lunch or rest stop.

07 Crossing under Rte 3, you'll travel alongside Rte 53 before passing into the countryside again to traverse a patchwork of fields of various shades and tranquil forest as you continue to head north.

Take a Break

There are few eateries as the route is almost entirely on a dedicated cycle path. SAKURA-NO-BABA JOSAIEN, beside Kumamoto Castle Park, has numerous restaurants offering local favourites such as soba noodles, seafood, and Aso-reared beef, popular for its leaner composition and high-quality fat. About halfway along the route, IZAKAYA SAKABA-SHOKUDO MICHIBATA is open for lunch and dinner, serving snacks and light meals. Alternatively, pick up food and drinks before leaving Kumamoto and enjoy a shady alfresco break in one of the forested areas along the way.

VARTS/SHUTTERSTOCK

Rice fields, Kumamoto

08 After 13km, the Kikuchi-gawa will come into view. Turn right onto Rte 3 and then left on to Rte 325. In 300m, turn left to reach Yamaga Lantern Art Museum, which introduces the history and culture of the craft of paper-lantern-making that has been carried out in the local area since ancient times. Legend is that villagers here first used lanterns to safely guide the visiting 12th emperor of Japan, who reigned in the 1st century, during heavy fog. Today, lanterns are made from *washi* (Japanese handmade paper) and glue, often in the shape of shrines, castles and temples, and make for interesting exhibits.

09 Leaving the museum, turn right onto Rte 325 and rejoin the Yūka Family Road before reaching the Kikuchi-gawa. Passing through the Kikuchi River Plain, where wild plants flower along the path and cherry blossom trees bloom during March/April, you'll reach the end point, marked by a gate.

Kumamoto Art

Located in the northwest corner of the castle grounds, the Kumamoto Prefectural Museum of Art houses collections related to three categories: ancient Japanese art connected with Kumamoto; Japanese modern art, often by artists with links to Kumamoto; and western art. In addition to paintings and drawings, you'll find *ukiyo-e* (woodblock prints), tea utensils, objets d'art, masks from traditional theatre art *nō*, suits of armour and decorated *kofun* (megalithic tombs dating from 200–600 CE). Some 200 of Japan's 700 decorated tombs have been found in Kumamoto. Exhibitions are rotated regularly throughout the year. A cafe and terrace overlook the castle grounds, providing a scenic view.

32

Nichinan Coast

JESSE33/SHUTTERSTOCK

DURATION	DIFFICULTY	DISTANCE	START/END
3–4hrs	Intermediate	18km (36km return)	Nichinan Tourist Information Centre/Sun Messe

TERRAIN	Mostly paved cycle paths or pavement

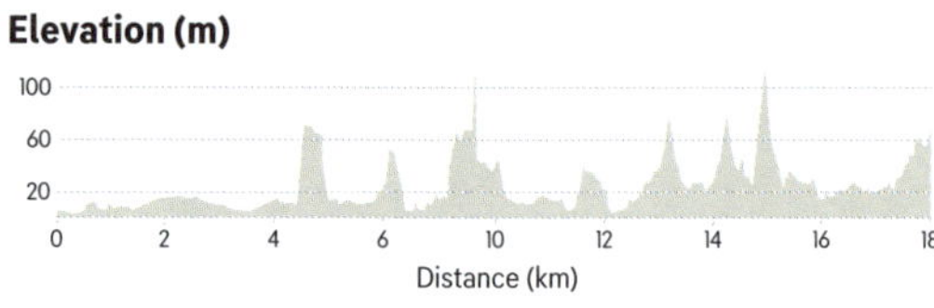

The rugged 90km strip of the Nichinan-kaigan (日南海岸) coastline runs south of the prefectural capital, Miyazaki (宮崎), to Cape Toi (都井岬) for a ride that rivals any in Japan for ocean views, salty air and a laid-back atmosphere. The trail hugs the coast, unveiling the palm-fringed shores and unusual volcanic formations of the Nichinan-Kaigan Quasi-National Park and provides easy access to some of the prefecture's most famous sites: the cliffside shrine Udo-jingū (鵜戸神宮) and Sun Messe (サンメッセ日南), a park featuring *moai* statues.

Bike Hire

Nichinan Tourist Info Centre has four bicycles for rent from 9am to 5pm. Reservations are not possible. The cost is ¥500 per day (insurance and helmet included). ID such as a passport is required.

Starting Point

Catch the train to JR Aburatsu Station (油津駅), which is served by the Nichinan Line for Miyazaki in the north and Shibushi (志布志) in the west. Then walk 10 minutes to reach Nichinan Tourist Information Centre.

01 From the car park of Nichinan Tourist Information Centre, turn left and cross the bridge over Horikawa Canal, the waterway connecting the mouth of the Hiroto-gawa to Aburatsu Port. Built in the late 17th century, and once used to transport local cedar, this picturesque canal is now used as a shooting location for films. Turn left at the Lawson convenience store onto Rte 220. As the last general shop on the ride, it's a good place to stock up on drinks or snacks.

Udo-jingū

Best for

SEA VIEWS & CULTURAL SITES

Udo-jingū

Situated deep in a cave and facing a rugged coastline, Udo-jingū is the most important shrine in the complex. Its dramatic, contrasting colours and peaceful atmosphere are sure to impress. The path through the main gate and down the sloping hill and winding steps to reach the structure has a subtropical feel and opens up to a terrace overlooking the ocean. Make a wish and throw an *undama* (lucky ball) into the loop of rope sitting on top of the turtle-shaped rock below to attain harmony in marriage. Udo Inari Shrine, marked by rows of red *torii* gates leading to its hilltop location, is another popular site on the grounds.

02 The trail begins on a wide pavement that follows the road for almost 4km. After winding through the residential outskirts of Nichinan, cross the bridge over Hiroto-gawa. As you progress, palm trees line the road and pops of colour emanating from the path's edges reveal wildflowers and native butterflies. The road moves briefly inland before turning towards the Hyūga Sea.

03 When the road opens up, take the dedicated walking/cycling path that separates you from traffic for most of the next 6km. Sandwiched between the road and the coast, this smooth section offers the trail's most expansive ocean views. Look ahead and below to take in the Devil's Washboard, a natural phenomenon of striated basalt carved over the centuries by waves and tides. The formations create rows of shallow pools in long furrows that disappear at high tide, making morning the best time to ride this part of the route.

04 Before turning inland, look back for views of the southern Miyazaki coastline, famed for its resemblance to Hawaii due to its palm trees, rugged seaboard and sandy beaches. The island is Ōshima, home to Japan's oldest unreinforced concrete lighthouse, which is registered as a tangible cultural asset.

05 The trail begins to climb gently as you head towards Udo-jingū, the first of the route's main attractions. Leave the main road at the signpost for the shrine and pass under the giant vermillion *torii* gate that marks the entrance to holy ground. Here, the road narrows and has some tight corners. It also tends to be busy with visitors so you'll need to take care. Following the road, you'll come upon a row of small shops and restaurants selling local products and firm favourites such as fresh sashimi, sourced from the adjacent working harbour. Look out for fishers taking in their catch and the family of hawks that swoop low over the road to prey on fish.

06 Turning the corner reveals a steep hill with about 100m to climb before reaching the shrine. But it's all downhill after that to the bicycle parking near the entrance. Udo-jingū consists of several shrines, including one in a cave and one with a tunnel of *torii* gates, as well as steep cliff faces of jagged rocks and ocean views.

07 Leaving the bicycle parking, retrace your route back to Rte 220 and turn right. From here, you'll need to climb gently on the pavement or the road before entering the New Udo Tunnel. Though short, there is reduced visibility so you should take care. After exiting the tunnel, you might be lucky enough to see

Take a Break

Udo-jingū has a cafe serving hot and cold beverages, including a wide range of coffees, and sweet treats such as mango parfait and lemon or custard choux buns. For something more substantial, including local favourites like *chikin nanban* (fried chicken with tangy sauce and tartar sauce) and curry with rice, you can dine at Sun Messe. If you'd like to break your journey earlier, try one of the eateries at Udo harbour, where you'll find home-cooked favourites made using fresh fish and seafood sourced in the area.

KOREKORE/GETTY IMAGES

Devil's Washboard

the wild monkeys that live in the next lightly forested section of the trail, which involves slight ascents and descents. Though cute, these Japanese macaques can be dangerous; it's best not to approach them.

08 At the next junction, turn right and follow the road until you see the sign for the end point of your ride, Sun Messe. Located on the left side of the road, this seaside park is characterised by expansive ocean views and seven *moai* statues that have been replicated with permission from Rapa Nui (Easter Island). Climb the very steep, zigzagging route halfway up the hill, pay a fee to enter and explore the rest of the attraction, which also features art, exhibitions, shops and restaurants. If you want to return to the starting point, simply retrace your route. For optimal riding, set off from Sun Messe a couple of hours before sunset to enjoy views of the Miyazaki coastline, framed with the setting sun in the background.

Moai Statues

The centrepiece of Sun Messe Nichinan is the row of seven *moai* statues, replicated with permission from Rapa Nui. Facing the Bell of Thanksgiving, a monument ideated by various religious groups around the globe to usher in world peace, the *moai* have their backs to the ocean, creating an ideal photo spot. The *moai* exhibition tells the story of why the complex sought and secured permission to recreate the statues from Japanese tuff, while the insect exhibition showcases rare butterflies from around the world. You can also explore indoor and outdoor art exhibits dotted throughout the vast green expanse, or dine and shop in the Welcome Plaza.

33

Ibusuki Poké Trail

DURATION	DIFFICULTY	DISTANCE	START/END
1–2hrs	Easy	14km	JR Ibusuki Station/Saraku Sand Bath Hall

TERRAIN	Mostly paved cycle paths or pavement

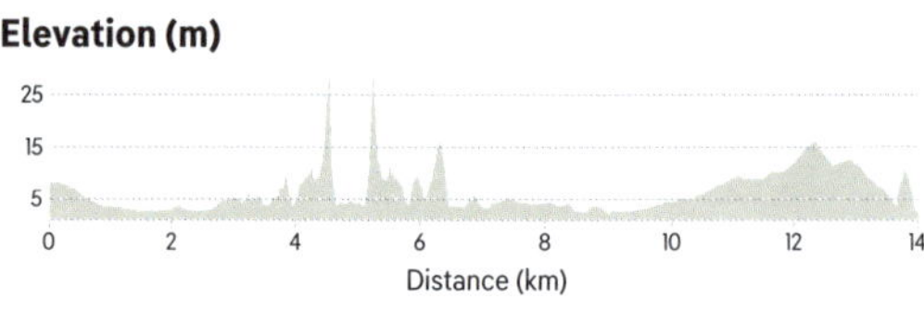

Ibusuki (指宿) has been a popular destination for Japanese travellers for some 300 years, thanks to its picturesque seaside location and abundant onsen (hot springs) including steamy sand baths overlooking Kinkō Bay. Since 2018, the city has been attracting fans of popular culture too, becoming the first place in Japan to introduce colourful manhole covers featuring Pokémon characters. This easy ride encompasses both aspects of Ibusuki, revealing views of the coastline, the elusive island of Chiringashima (知林ヶ島) that appears only at high tide, and some of Japan's famous anime, as well as opportunities for relaxing, rejuvenating soaks.

Bike Hire

The Tourist Information at JR Ibusuki Station has four bicycles for rent from 9am to 5pm. Reservations are not possible. The cost is ¥500 for every two-hour period (insurance and helmet included).

Starting Point

JR Ibusuki Station is accessible from Kagoshima Chūō Station via limited express train (50 minutes) or the Ibusuki no Tamatebako tourist train, whose window-facing seats afford scenic coastal views.

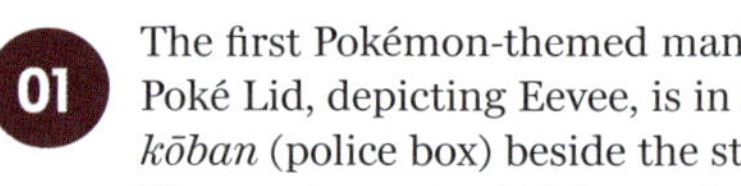

01 The first Pokémon-themed manhole cover, or Poké Lid, depicting Eevee, is in front of the *kōban* (police box) beside the station. Eevee is one of the most popular Pokémon characters due to her ability to evolve into many forms; each subsequent Poké Lid on the ride is one of her forms.

02 Exit the station area, turning left towards the commercial area lined with small shops and family-run eateries. Cross over

Best for

SCENERY & SPOTTING POKÉMON

IJIMINO/SHUTTERSTOCK

Bekko tombo

Rte 240 and follow signs for Rte 238, also known as Hibiscus Road due to the beautiful flowers that line parts of it. En route, you will also see tourist signs indicating the way to Chiringashima, making this an easy-to-follow ride.

03 After 1.4km the road passes over a couple of rivers at their mouth and enters the suburbs. One kilometre further and the right side of the road opens up, revealing wide green spaces. Palm trees, a nod to the area's subtropical climate, line the route and separate the pavement and the road. You'll pass beautiful gardens, lush with all kinds of trees and colourful flowers, and a children's playground.

04 Follow the road around the coastline to be rewarded with views of Kinkō Bay (錦江湾), the vast expanse separating the prefecture's two peninsulas, and leafy vegetation on both sides of the road. Soon, you'll enter Kirishima-Kinkōwan National Park (霧島錦江湾国立公園), part of Kagoshima and Miyazaki that has been shaped by thousands of years of volcanic activity, creating rocky cliffs, sandy beaches, abundant vegetation and diverse kinds of onsen.

05 On the left side, you'll see a car park and a small wooden building, which operates as a wildlife hide. Enter for views out to the biotope and Mt Uomi behind or to take a break at one of the sheltered picnic tables. The pond and its surrounds were built to create the ideal environment for the bekko tombo, a native species of dragonfly that is facing extinction. The dragonfly is most likely spotted between April and June, but the sights and sounds of many creatures can be enjoyed year-round. The biotope is home to Japan's largest white butterfly, which is native to India, southeast Asia, Taiwan and southern

Take a Break

For a tranquil rest stop, opt to bring your own snacks and use one of the picnic tables at the biotope. Thanks to the roof, this is a relaxing setting no matter the weather, where it's possible to listen to birdsong while taking a break. Alternatively, soak up the sea air and the coastal scenery while you rest at Chiringashima, where there is a wide tarmac set of steps to sit and take in the view. The adjacent Ibusuki Eco Campground also has public toilets.

Kyūshū, as well as butterflies such as the heavily patterned Asian swallowtail, the pale blue-green half-transparent chestnut tiger, and the brightly coloured peacock pansy. It's also possible to see birds as varied as the Oriental turtle dove, Japanese bush warbler and black kite.

06 Continue for 500m and turn right into Ibusuki Eco Campground, from where it's possible to access Chiringashima. Follow the road until you reach the far end of the car park, nearest to the beach, taking care as the road narrows and the site can be busy. From here, choose the tree-lined path signposted for Chiringashima or lift your bicycle over a couple of steps to cycle along the raised tarmac path alongside the sea. The end of the path is marked with an information board where you can park your bicycle and explore.

07 Walk to the end of the beach, towards Chiringashima, for optimal views. To the north lies Sakurajima, one of Japan's most active volcanoes, while the east and south offer views of the Ōsumi Peninsula. At low tide, between March and October, Chiringashima is connected to the mainland by an 800m-long sandbar known as the Chiri Ring Road, which takes about 20 minutes to reach on foot. It is not permitted to swim in the area or travel to the island outside this period due to strong currents and the presence of venomous octopi.

08 Retracing your steps, return to your bicycle and move to the main building where you'll find Leafeon on a Poké Lid. Turn left out of the campsite, continue back along Rte 238 towards the park area and turn right at the sign for Fureiai Plaza Nanohanakan. You'll pass a large recreation spot before reaching the facility on the left. Part of its structure resembles a giant rocket on its side, making it stand out, and Pokémon character Jolteon is visible from the road.

09 From here, continue in the same direction and turn left at the crossroads onto Yunosato Street to join Ibusuki's 'Healthy Road', marked with green and orange arrows on the pavement and cycle path. Stay on this path for 2.2km to reach Ibusuki Central Park, an open space of vast lawns suitable for a relaxing break and the home of another Poké Lid, Espeon.

10 Leaving Ibusuki Central Park at the southeast corner, join Rte 240.

Chiringashima

Fragrant Isle of Happiness

Farmers once produced potato, sweet potato and rapeseed on Chiringashima, which has a circumference of only 3km. Today, much of the isle is forested and criss-crossed with walking paths, including to the summit of a 90m hill. Make the climb for spectacular ocean views to the south and west, and ring the bell of happiness. On your return journey, take time to notice the scent of the sea breeze off Chiringashima and the sandbar, which is registered by the Ministry of the Environment as one of Japan's 100 Most Fragrant Landscapes.

JUNKO KIMURA/GETTY IMAGES

Get Buried in Warm Sand

Located on the beach, where the sand is warmed naturally by geothermal currents, Saraku Sand Bath Hall offers sand bathing while listening to the waves lap the shore. Don a *yukata* (cotton kimono) and lie down to be buried neck to toe for 10 minutes. At 50°C, the sand gently stimulates perspiration, improving blood circulation, removing impurities from the body and alleviating stress. After about 10 minutes, return to the facility to rinse off and enjoy a regular bath in the mineral-rich water. The waiting area has vending machines, a noodle stand and shops selling local souvenirs.

Sand bath

After about 350m, turn right and then left in short succession to stay on Rte 240 and cross the train tracks. Turn left after 40m and left again after another 60m, following the narrow road to reach the back of Ibusuki Station. You'll find Pokémon character Umbreon near the parking area.

11 With the Poké Lid behind you, go straight for 30m and turn left. After 60m, turn right and then left after 70m. The library on the right is the next stop to find a Poké Lid, this time Sylveon.

12 From Ibusuki Library, go straight for 500m to reach the Ibusuki Archaeological Museum Cocco Hashimure, where you'll find the Pokémon character Glaceon. This museum features interactive exhibits that introduce finds from the nearby Ibusuki Hashimurega-wa archaeological site, renowned in Japan as the site that enabled the first clarification of the relationship between the Jōmon period (14,000 to 300 BCE), which was characterised by hunter-gathering, and the Yayoi period (300 BCE to 300 CE), that started in the late Neolithic period and continued through the Bronze Age and into the Iron Age. The museum's highlights include a reconstruction of the village that was found, and experiences for visitors include trying on replicas of ancient clothing and making stone charms using traditional methods.

13 From here, go straight for 550m and turn left down a narrow road flanked by car parks. At the end of the road, turn right. At the level crossing, turn left and then take a right at the first crossroads. Continue on this road for 240m and turn left before the traffic lights onto a single-track road – be careful as these residential roads are narrow. After 30m, turn right and follow this road to its end, making a slight right turn half way along. Turn right, followed by a left after 15m. With the river now on your right, follow the road until its end, take a right and continue until the road meets Rte 238. More palm trees will appear as you turn right, with the sea on your left, and go straight for 220m. The onsen accommodation Ginshō will be on your left and is the site of the Pokémon character Vaporeon.

To reach the final spot, simply retrace your route back up Rte 238 for 200m to reach Saraku Sand Bath Hall on the right, home of Pokémon Lid Flareon. This onsen facility offers a sand bath experience right on the beach. With everything provided for visitors, including a *yukata* for the sand bath, as well as towels and amenities for having a bath afterwards, this is ideal for riders interested in soothing weary muscles and absorbing some local culture while enjoying the scenery. On a clear day, the sand bath offers views of the rolling hills of the Ōsumi Peninsula beyond Kinkō Bay.

TOP TIP:

Tide Times

While at the tourist info area at Ibusuki Station, ask for the expected times of low tide so you can safely cross the sandbar at Chiringashima. Ensure you leave the summit of Chiringashima with sufficient time to return to the mainland without the need to rush.

Take a Break

Ibusuki's eateries are concentrated around the station and coastal areas. Noodle-lovers can opt for *sōmen* (wheat noodles) at CHŌJUAN IBUSUKI or ramen at TAKETORA, both within 100m of the station. For heartier fare and a cosy atmosphere, choose AOBA, whose specialties include *shabu-shabu,* a hot pot of vegetables and Kagoshima's signature black pork. On the way to Saraku Sand Bath Hall, try OIMO NO OMOI for coffee and a local sweet-potato snack, or CAFÉ & BAR TETESEN for light meals.

34

Maple Yabakei Road

DURATION	DIFFICULTY	DISTANCE	START/END
Up to 4hrs	Easy	50km/22km	Yabakei Cycling Terminal
TERRAIN	Paved		

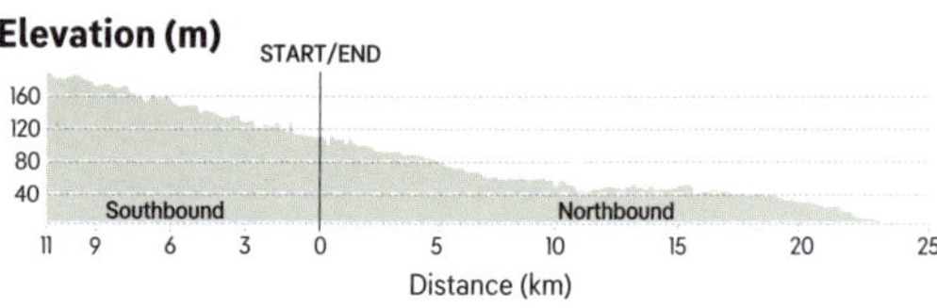

Known as the Maple Yabakei Cycling Road (メイプル耶馬サイクリングロード), this route was repurposed from the Yabakei Railway which closed in 1975. The gentle grades and lack of traffic attract cyclists of all levels to enjoy the breathtaking beauty of rural Ōita Prefecture following the Yamakuni-gawa. The route is dotted with stunning natural landscapes and places of historical significance, perfect for those who want a relaxing ride with plenty of stops to take in the view. The route starts in the middle; the northbound route can be up to 50km return, while the southbound route is 22km.

Bike Hire

Rent a bike at Yabakei Cycling Terminal (耶馬溪サイクリングターミナル). Over 200 bikes are available: adult road, cross, general use, children's, tandem and electric. Open 8.30am to 5pm; closed Wednesday.

Starting Point

Yabakei Cycling Terminal is the hub for the Maple Yabakei Cycling Road. Along with rentals, the facility offers showers and simple lodgings for those who wish to get an early start.

The ride begins at the Yabakei Cycling Terminal, curiously located near the middle of the cycling road rather than at one end. This gives you flexibility in the length of your ride, however, as you can head north or south, or combine them both into one long ride.

Northbound ride

This ride technically ends at Nakatsu Station, although you don't have to go that far. Once you enter Nakatsu city, you'll share the road with motor vehicles; not ideal

Yabakei Gorge

Best for

NATURE

Beautiful & Busy Autumn

It isn't called the Maple Yabakei Cycling Road for nothing. Yabakei Gorge is famous throughout Japan for its incredible autumn foliage, largely due to the abundance of Japanese maple trees that change to fiery reds and oranges in mid- to late November. Expect that the road might be busier with casual cyclists on autumn weekends and arrive early to make sure you can secure a rental bicycle. Most cyclists will be domestic tourists, however, so weekdays should be relatively peaceful.

if you are riding with children. You can ride as far as you are comfortable and there are many restaurants and places to take a break within the city limits.

N2 Your first point of interest in this direction is the Yamakuni River Bridge, a former railway bridge that curves gently over the Yamakuni-gawa. Surrounded on both sides by rugged mountains, it's a great spot for your first selfie along the route.

N3 About 4km further, keep an eye on the river for the Bakeibashi Bridge. A stone bridge with five arches, this is one of the river's – and perhaps Ōita Prefecture's – most beautiful bridges. Bakeibashi, along with Rakanji Bridge 4km further, and Yabakei Bridge 1.5km after that, make up the Three Famous Bridges of Yabakei.

N4 Just past Rakanji Bridge and before Yabakei Bridge, you'll come to an area where sheer rock formations butt up against the edge of the river. In the 18th century, a local monk named Zenkai single-handedly carved a 342m-long tunnel through the rock over 30 years. This tunnel is now known as Ao-no-Dōmon, the 'Blue Tunnel'. Although the cycling road doesn't pass through the tunnel, it's worth taking a short break here to walk through the tunnel and admire Zenkai's handiwork and determination.

N5 About 6km past Yabakei Bridge, the dedicated cycling road ends and you'll be on Nakatsu's city streets until you arrive at Nakatsu Station a further 7km along. As there is less scenery in this section, you might want to grab a bite to eat as you pass a local restaurant or grab a *bentō* (boxed meal) lunch from Shinsen Ichiba Ōsada supermarket and have a picnic at nearby Daihatsu Kyūshū Sports Park.

Southbound Ride

The southbound route is decidedly more rural, with a public onsen marking the turnaround point at the southern end. Restaurants are harder to come by on this part of the route, so don't pass up a chance to eat if you're hungry.

S2 A few hundred metres after leaving Yabakei Cycling Terminal, you'll pass through a long narrow tunnel that was used by the railway. In the humid summer months, you'll prize this refreshingly cool stretch of the route, but it's an interesting way to begin your adventure.

S3 About 3km along, you'll notice an odd bridge crossing the Yamakunigawa. This is the Yōkaichi Bridge, a low, single-lane bridge with no

Take a Break

Northbound riders can enjoy Nakatsu's famous fried chicken at MURAKAMI SHOKUDO, a cosy roadside restaurant close to Ao-no-Dōmon. It isn't just popular because of its proximity to the cycling road; locals who get a craving for it will travel long distances for a taste. Southbound riders can enjoy a meal, hot-springs bath, or both at YASURAGI NO SATO, created by an organisation hoping to revive the local tourism industry in this once popular onsen town.

MH0646/SHUTTERSTOCK

Ao-no-Dōmon

barriers to keep vehicles from going over the sides into the water. This type of bridge is used in areas where the river floods frequently, its sleek profile keeping it from being washed away.

Heading another 6.5km further, you'll arrive at Roadside Station Yamakuni. This facility is typical of Japanese rest areas found along main highways, with clean bathrooms, restaurant facilities and a shop selling locally produced goods. Fried chicken is Nakatsu's famous food, so have your fill here before you continue your ride.

S5 In only another 2.5km, you'll reach the end of the southbound ride: Yamakuni, a town of hot springs and natural beauty. Yasuragi no Sato is a public hot-springs facility that visitors can use before heading back to the Cycling Terminal. There is a restaurant here, but it is closed between 3pm and 5pm.

Stay Overnight in Yamakuni

Another option for the Maple Yabakei Cycling Road is to begin and end your ride in Yamakuni. There is simple accommodation available here with tatami and futon mattresses or western-style bunk beds, and you'll be able to enjoy the hot-springs facilities at different times of the day and night. Keep in mind that bicycle rentals will be much more limited here, and there is a possibility that a bicycle might not be available to rent at the time you need it, which is much less likely if you begin and end your ride at the Cycling Terminal.

35

Best for

LOCAL ISLAND CULTURE

Iejima

DURATION	DIFFICULTY	DISTANCE	START/END
2–3hrs	Easy	21km	Ie Port
TERRAIN	Paved, with mild hills		

OKIMO/SHUTTERSTOCK

GI Beach (p224)

Iejima (伊江島) is a small island off the coast of Okinawa Island. Known for its beautiful beaches, dramatic coastlines and historical significance, it offers picturesque landscapes including Gusuku-yama. Also called Peanut Island for its shape and peanut crop production, in spring it's famous for its lily fields. Iejima was heavily involved during the Battle of Okinawa nearing the end of WWII, and its historical sites add depth to the island's charm. Easily accessible by ferry, Iejima is only 20km in circumference, and is a fun, easy bike ride.

Bike Hire

Rental bicycles are available in front of Ie Port at Tama Car Rentals for ¥400 per hour and ¥1000 per day. Note that these are Mamachari bikes (a city bicycle with a front basket).

Starting Point

From Okinawa's main island, take a 30-minute ferry from Motobu Port to Ie Port, Iejima's main ferry terminal. There are four departures daily and a return ticket costs ¥1390.

01 From Ie Port (伊江港), go towards Gusuku-yama (城山) in the middle of the island, turning right from Ie Port onto Rte 180, and right again after 500m, still on Rte 180. Follow the sign to Gusuku-yama and Ie Village Office, turning left onto Rte 225. Cycle for about 170m and you'll come to a five-way intersection. Take the second road on your left: the Ie Village Hall should be on your immediate right as you go down this path. Cycle for about 500m, passing the Pawn Shop Ruins (公益質屋跡), a structure with a gaping hole on its side. This was the only building that avoided being burnt down

Elevation (m)

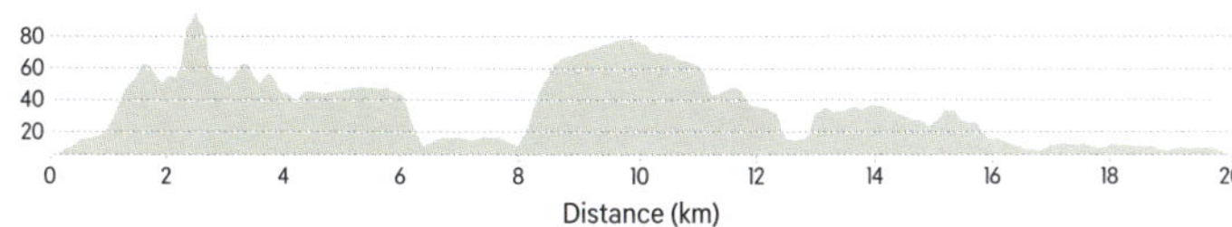

Island Produce

Iejima is known for its arable farmland, with peanut farming and cattle rearing as staple industries. Springy and sweet *jimami tofu,* with a pudding-like texture, is made by mixing and cooking peanut milk with sweet potato starch. The island's Ie beef is highly regarded, rivalling regional wagyu beef. While cycling, you'll also see rows of sugar-cane fields. The island also produces Ie soda, a carbonated drink that uses fresh spring water from Wajee. The black cane cola is particularly popular due to its unique blend of local spring water and *kokuto* (Okinawan brown sugar).

during the Battle of Okinawa near the end of WWII.

02 Continue up the road and turn right, cycle for 350m then head left to Gusuku-yama's east entrance (東登山口) which is a paved uphill climb to a car park and the trailhead. As Iejima is almost completely flat, the 172m-high Gusuku-yama stands out. The mountain is also called Iejima Tacchū, which means 'pointed' in the original Okinawan language. There are steps all the way to the top and while steep, it's not difficult, taking only 15 to 20 minutes. Enjoy 360-degree views of the island from the top.

03 Go back on the road passing the Pawn Shop Ruins for about 300m then turn right, passing Shimamurayakankō Park (島村屋観光公園) and Hōkon Monument (芳魂之塔), which commemorates those who passed away on the island in WWII. After 600m, go right at Iejima Kanjōsen or Road 225 and continue for 2.5km. Turn right onto Rte 181 and continue until you come to an intersection then turn right again towards Niya Thiya Cave (ニャティヤ洞). It will take about 15 to 20 minutes to get here from Gusuku-yama. This large cave is also called Sennin Gama, the Cave of 1000 People, referring to when over 1000

Okinawans hid here and survived during WWII. Nearby is GI Beach, an isolated beach with white powdery sand and clear waters.

04 Backtrack to the intersection and continue north on Rte 181 for another 3km (15 minutes). Turn right and then left to Wajee Viewpoint (湧出展望台) on Rte 225. Wajee boasts arguably the best views of the island with its rugged cliffs and azure waters. This was an important source of mineral-rich spring water and is still used as drinking water today. Look down from the observatory and you can see the point where the spring water comes out.

05 Continue along Rte 225 heading to the east side of the island and following the coast for 2.5km. Go left to Lily Field Park (リリーフィールド公園). As its name suggests, this 86,000 sq metre park hosts the Iejima Lily Festival from late April to Golden Week in early May with over a million Easter lilies and a view of the ocean.

06 Head back on Rte 225 for 15 minutes, following the road to the east side of the island and passing the Iejima Country Club. Next door is the Hibiscus Garden (ハイビスカス園), which is open year-round and features more than 1000 different varieties of hibiscus.

07 Two kilometres down Rte 225 is Ie Island Beach Side Horse Park (ie-horse.wixsite.com/ieuma). Enjoy leisurely horseback rides along sunny Ie Beach and through a forested campsite with courses ranging from 20 minutes to almost two hours. No prior riding experience is required, but beginners must take an introductory lesson for an additional fee. Prices start at ¥6000 for a 20-minute course and ¥18,000 for an hour. Between May and September when the water is warm, you can even ride and swim with your horse in the ocean.

08 Head back to the south part of the island on Rte 225 for 10 minutes and keep going straight, passing the Family Mart convenience store. Cycle for about 450m until you reach an intersection then turn left onto Rte 180 and continue until you are back at Ie Port.

Take a Break

Historically, Okinawa was economically challenged compared to other parts of Japan due to limited water, which made rice cultivation difficult. However, sugarcane has been grown on the islands since 1630. Formerly an *awamori* (Okinawan spirit made from rice and black koji mould) distillery, IEJIMA DISTILLERY *(ierum.ie-mono.com)* produces Santa Maria Rum using local sugarcane. Established in 2011, they aim to use minimal intervention throughout production. Free distillery and sampling tours in Japanese are available with a reservation.

TANK200BAR/SHUTTERSTOCK

Scuba diving, Iejima

Scuba Diving

Iejima is surrounded by diving spots all around and is an all-season diving destination. There are caves, tunnels and drop-offs in the north, while the south features white sandy sea floors with coral reefs. Ohoba Cave in the northeastern part of the island is as large as a school gym and can only be accessed by local Ie island services with their boats. Species such as white-tip reef sharks, red-banded grouper, comet fish and sweeper fish can be found here. There are several diving companies to choose from including Iejima Diving Service *(iejima.com)* and Iejima Mariner *(okinawa-iejima-mariner.com).*

Also Try...

Irabu Bridge, Miyako-jima

RIKACIMINIERI/SHUTTERSTOCK

Hirado Loop

DURATION	DIFFICULTY	DISTANCE
4–5hrs	Difficult	20km

One of Japan's most westerly points, Hirado (平戸) became a centre of Japanese–Dutch relations in the 16th century when trade and Christianity came to the island. This challenging loop is steeped in this history, setting off from the Dutch Trading Post, a museum that details international commerce at that time, to reach Hirado Xavier Memorial Church, a Gothic structure named after missionary Francis Xavier (1506–1552). Steep climbs lie ahead to Kawauchi Pass Observatory and the undulating Kawauchi-toge Pass but you'll be rewarded with azaleas in spring, verdant grasslands in summer, and pampas grass in autumn, as well as views of the East China Sea and islands of Saikai National Park. Bicycles can be rented from Hirado City Tourist Information Centre.

Miyako-jima to Irabu-jima

DURATION	DIFFICULTY	DISTANCE
4–5hrs	Easy	32km

This beachcombing ride begins at Pai Nagama Beach on Miyako-jima (宮古島). There are several bicycle rental shops in town, and many hotels and guesthouses also have rentals available to guests. This ride leaves the western tip of Miyako-jima and crosses the Irabu Bridge, the 3450m-long bridge crossing the open ocean, and the longest toll-free bridge in Japan. Once on Irabu-jima (伊良部島), follow the beach along the southern curve of the island until you get to a smaller bridge where you can hop over to Shimoji-jima, a yet smaller island clinging to Irabu-jima's coast. Ride north along the islands' twin coastlines until you pass the airport and come to 17 End, a white-sand beach where you can swim and watch planes glide over an unbroken expanse of blue before returning to Miyako-jima.

VECTONIVERSE/SHUTTERSTOCK

Yakushima coast

Fukiagehama Cycling Road

DURATION	DIFFICULTY	DISTANCE
3-4hrs	Easy	24km

Connecting the cities of Minamisatsuma and Hioki, this path traverses one of Japan's three largest sand dunes and uses part of the Nansatsu Railroad that operated from 1914 to 1983. You'll bike through Fukiagehama Seaside Park before arriving at Sunset Bridge, where you can look for fiddler crabs and waterfowl in the tidal flats or enjoy panoramas over the East China Sea. Further north you'll reach one of the former stations, which features old photos and covered benches for rest. Ride in early May to take in the Fukiage Sand Festival, which displays 100 huge sand sculptures, or in June to see Shōen Pond covered with a violet carpet of water hyacinth. Bicycles are available from RinRin Cycling Terminal, near the start of the ride.

Yakushima Coast

DURATION	DIFFICULTY	DISTANCE
5-6hrs	Intermediate	40km

Introducing the primeval temperature rainforest, white-sand beaches and dramatic cliffs of Yakushima (屋久島), this ride follows part of Rte 78 around the island's coast. From Yakushima Kankō Center, where it's possible to rent bicycles, explore the adjacent Yakushima Environmental and Culture Village Center to learn about the island and gather information. Leaving Miyanoura, you'll take in impressive sea views, including at the East China Sea Observatory and Sunset Hill Observation Deck, before reaching Nagata Inakahama Beach, a spawning ground for sea turtles in the spring. Be careful of wild monkeys and deer as you pass through Western Forest Road, home to 100-year-old cedars and 80 varieties of indigenous plants, to reach Segiri Observation Deck for ocean views.

Arriving

Most international visitors will arrive in Japan by air, to Haneda (HND) or Narita (NRT) in Tokyo, or Kansai (KIX). The next largest international airports are Nagoya (NGO), Fukuoka (FUK), Sapporo (CTS) and Naha (OKA). All of these airports are accessible by rail.

Travelling with a Bike

If you're bringing your own bike to Japan, there are a few things to be aware of. First, when flying, it will have to be secured in a bike box or bag. A fee for oversized baggage may apply and varies by airline. Oversized items may be placed to the side of the baggage carousel upon arrival rather than circling on the conveyor belt.

Rinkobukuro (special bike bags) are essential if you plan to take your bike on public transport. You'll need to take off a wheel, at least, unless you have a folding bike. There are a few specialty trains that allow you to roll your bike on, such as the B.B.Base train in Chiba, and the Ohmi Railway in Shiga.

Even though bikes in bags are allowed on trains, it's best to avoid rush hour, where there's barely space to breathe, let alone for bulky luggage.

Airport to City Centre

	Narita	Haneda	Kansai
TRAIN	1hr ¥2750	30 mins ¥510	1hr ¥1680
BUS	1¼hr ¥1500	25 mins ¥1000	1hr 10mins ¥1800
TAXI	1hr ¥30,000	30 mins ¥7000	1hr ¥21,000

IMMIGRATION

Japan is visa-free for citizens of more than 70 countries, for periods between 15 and 90 days. Entry is efficient, though all foreign nationals are photographed and fingerprinted.

WI-FI

Free wi-fi has become ubiquitous in recent years, and is available at most hotels, airports and many stations and shops. eSIMs have also become cheap and plentiful, and useful if wi-fi isn't available.

ATMS

ATMs will often offer a better exchange rate than money changers. Look for machines in convenience stores and post offices; bank ATMs often serve only their own customers.

TOUCH & GO

Cashless payments are widely used compared to just ten years ago. Stored-value IC cards like Suica or Pasmo can be used for transport, at convenience stores and many restaurants.

Getting Around

Japan's public transport infrastructure means that the connections between air, rail, road and sea are practically seamless.

IT'S ALL CONNECTED ☆

Public transport modes are generally well connected, and you should be able to switch between buses, trains and boats easily. Frequency declines rapidly the further you get from a city centre. Check Google Maps or Japan Transit Planner at world.jorudan.co.jp/mln/en to map your route in advance. In rural areas, you may need a taxi for the last mile. Go is the top taxi app and has an English interface.

Air

Low-cost carriers (LCCs) offer cheap domestic flights if you book far enough ahead. Different carriers serve different regions; search for AirDo, Skymark, Solaseed, Peach, Vanilla Air, StarFlyer and Jetstar. Flying is often cheaper than the train.

Rail

The train network is extensive, comfortable and fast, and will take you right to the city centre. Stored-value IC cards like Suica work across most transport networks, and rail passes are a good bet for those who want to cover a lot of ground quickly.

Sea

Ferries run between all the main islands and many of the smaller inhabited ones. This isn't the speediest method – for example, Tokyo to Kitakyūshū takes 34 hours. Bicycles are allowed on most ferries for a small fee. For more information, see jlc-ferry.jp/en.

Rental Car

Driving in Japan is possible and even pleasurable outside of big city centres thanks to multilingual navigation systems. International Driving Permits are required. Many rental agencies will not have a bike-rack option.

DRIVING INFO

Drive on the left.

Road closed to all.

Pedestrians and bicycles only

TRAVEL COSTS

Car rental
From ¥7000/ day

Petrol
Approx ¥185/litre

Tokyo-Kyoto shinkansen
¥14,000

Flight Tokyo-Okinawa
From ¥12,000 one way

FROM LEFT: SEAN PAVONE/SHUTTERSTOCK, KUUTANX/SHUTTERSTOCK

Accommodation

CYCLING TERMINALS

Though these have dwindled in recent years, there are still a few Cycling Terminals (CT) that have inexpensive accommodation geared towards cyclists. Originally aimed at young people travelling on a shoestring, expect no-frills rooms in dormitory-style buildings, plenty of bicycle storage and locations near cycling routes. One night starts at around ¥4000 without meals. Enquire at tourist information centres, especially those that have bicycles. Try the Cycling Terminal Sunrise Itoyama in Imabari near Ride 1 (p24), or the Yabakei Cycling Terminal near Ride 34 (p218).

HOW MUCH FOR A NIGHT IN A...

Regional business hotel
From ¥7000

Farm stay with two meals
From ¥12,000

Shukubō with two meals
From ¥10,000/ person

Shukubō

Pilgrims making a visit to a sacred temple to pay their respects would stay at *shukubō* (temple lodging; pictured above). Many temples still offer accommodation, even to the non-devout traveller. *Shōjin ryōri* (Buddhist vegetarian devotional cuisine) is usually included. Expect to sleep on tatami mats and wake up early for prayer. Try this at Kōya-san after Ride 11: Wakayama & the Kinokawa. For more information, visit japan.travel/en/guide/temple-stays/.

Farm Stays

Stay on a working farm, often in a *kominka* (traditional Japanese house). Sleep on a futon, and you may have the opportunity to cook or do simple farm chores with your host. Two meals are generally included. Ride 20: Tōno (p138) is a great place to look for a farm stay. See www.japan.travel/en/guide/homestay-farmstay/ for more.

Onsen Ryokan

The traditional Japanese inn with on-site hot springs and elaborate *kaiseki ryōri* (set meals) is the ultimate relaxation experience in Japan, and can have a price tag to match. An onsen ryokan is a fabulous reward after a hard day of cycling, such as in Ride 6: Izu Peninsula: Numazu to Shuzen-ji Onsen (p52).

Business Hotels

Designed as a port of call on domestic work trips, business hotels are compact and economical but with everything you need. Clean, narrow rooms usually have a desk and wi-fi, en-suite shower and toilet, simple amenities like toothbrushes and combs, plus a basic breakfast included. There's likely no space to keep your bicycle in the room, so enquire ahead about storage.

CAPSULE HOTELS

If you don't suffer from claustrophobia, capsule hotels are fun to experience at least once. Sleeping quarters are in stacked pods about the size of a single bed, with power outlets and a door or curtain. There are common areas for lounging and shared bathing facilities. Limited to medium and large cities, some are men only. Try one in Sapporo after Ride 22: Sapporo Explorer (p152).

Bikes

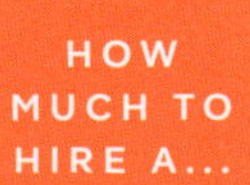

HOW MUCH TO HIRE A...

Standard bike

From ¥1000/day

E-Bike

From ¥2000/day

Half-day tour

From ¥6000

Bike Rental

Bicycle rental facilities and bike-share schemes have proliferated in recent years and most sightseeing areas will have at least one or two rental places. Hotels and guesthouses also often have a few bikes to lend to staying customers. Fees range from a few hundred yen an hour to a few thousand yen per day, with e-bikes about double the cost of a Mamachari (a city bicycle with a front basket). A well-stocked station will have city, cross, kids and e-bikes.

Bicycle-sharing apps allow users to grab bikes from docking stations using a pay-as-you-go system. Hello Cycling has no subscription fee, and it's worth noting you can rent up to four bikes on one account.

Useful tip: The word *baiku* in Japanese actually refers to motorcycles.

E-Bikes

The term 'e-bike' in Japan most commonly refers to electric-assist bicycles, which have a mechanism that you can switch on for hills or strenuous stretches. You'll feel like a superhero when just the slightest push of a pedal results in a satisfying zippiness. These may not be available at small operations that only have half-a-dozen bikes, but are common in larger facilities. In hilly areas (i.e. much of Japan) they are quite handy.

Charging stations can be few and far between, so save the power-assist for times when you really need them.

Fully electric bikes that are capable of going more than 24km/h are not allowed to be classified as bicycles, and require a motorcycle license.

OTHER GEAR

Helmets are strongly recommended in Japan, though enforcement is irregular. Rental fees often, but not always, include helmets and simple locks. Bike repair kits are generally not included, though well-stocked facilities will often have them for loan or purchase. Be sure to get the rental centre's number in case of a roadside mishap.

Health & Safe Travel

INSURANCE

Travel insurance is always a safe bet. Clinics and hospitals will require payment at the time of service, which you'll need to claim back from your insurance provider. There is generally no extra charge for an ambulance ride. Larger facilities may have insurance included in the price of bicycle rental, but it's not a given.

Natural Disasters

There's no getting around it: Japan experiences a lot of natural disasters. Placed on the so-called Pacific Ring of Fire, the country has regular earthquakes, and residents are used to intermittent small shakes. There are also yearly typhoons, and the ever-present risk of volcanic eruptions and tsunamis. Keep an eye on the local news for any developing situations.

Bites & Stings

In addition to annoying mosquitos, there are a few critters and bugs in Japan that can cause serious discomfort, or worse. There are two venomous snakes: the *mamushi* (pit viper) is found all over Japan, and the *habu* (yellow-spotted pit viper) is found in Okinawa. In the insect world, look out for *suzumebachi* (giant hornets). If you're bitten by any of these, seek immediate care.

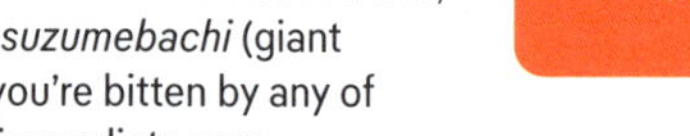

Heat Exhaustion

Heat exhaustion is a serious cause for concern, especially during Japan's hot, humid summers. Always be sure to use sun protection, take frequent breaks and stay properly hydrated if you're cycling during the hot months. Better yet, we recommend planning cycling excursions for the cooler seasons and/or areas of the country where temperatures don't soar.

IN CASE OF EMERGENCY

Police
110

Fire/ambulance
119

BIKE BREAKDOWN

Most rental shops will come to your aid if you break down on one of their bicycles. Be sure to get contact information before starting out in case of such an occurrence. If you're riding a well-staffed route like the Shimanami Kaidō (Ride 1) or Tsukuba Kasumigaura Ring Ring Road (Ride 5), there will be cycle stations along the way where you can stop for assistance.

FROM LEFT: GNOPARUS/SHUTTERSTOCK, HEIDI BESEN/SHUTTERSTOCK

Responsible Travel

Climate Change & Travel

It's impossible to ignore the impact we have when travelling, and the importance of making changes where we can. Lonely Planet urges all travellers to engage with their travel carbon footprint. There are many carbon calculators online that allow travellers to estimate the carbon emissions generated by their journey; try resurgence.org/resources/carbon-calculator.html. Many airlines and booking sites offer travellers the option of offsetting the impact of greenhouse gas emissions by contributing to climate-friendly initiatives around the world. We continue to offset the carbon footprint of all Lonely Planet staff travel, while recognising this is a mitigation more than a solution.

Resources

Japan National Tourism Organization
www.japan.travel/en/
Comprehensive info on all regions.

The Japan Times
japantimes.co.jp
Japan's largest English-language newspaper.

NHK World
www3.nhk.or.jp/nhkworld
Japan's public media organisation.

REDUCE PLASTIC

Plastic bags now come with an extra fee in Japan to encourage eco-bag use. Consider using a reusable water bottle; the My Mizu app shows free water-refill spots around the country.

SUPPORT LOCAL

There are so many family-run businesses and heritage craftspeople in Japan, many of whom have been plying their trades for generations. By supporting local, you're sure to have a one-of-a-kind experience.

GIVE BACK

35 Coffee *(35coffee.com)* in Okinawa donates a portion of proceeds to coral conservation efforts, while Watalis *(watalis.co.jp)* in disaster-affected Miyagi Prefecture creates accessories from recycled kimonos made by local women.

Nuts & Bolts

GOOD TO KNOW

Time Zone
Japan Standard Time (UTC/GMT+9)

Country Code
+81

Population
124 million

Toilets

They're starting to disappear, but squat toilets still exist, especially in rural areas. As you don't touch anything, they're quite hygienic – as long as you don't lose your balance.

Smoking

Smoking has become less common. You'll find designated smoking areas outside stations and some office buildings.

Tap Water

Tap water is generally safe; if it's not, there will be a warning on the tap.

ELECTRICITY
100V/50HZ (TOKYO & THE EAST)
100V/60HZ (OSAKA & THE WEST)

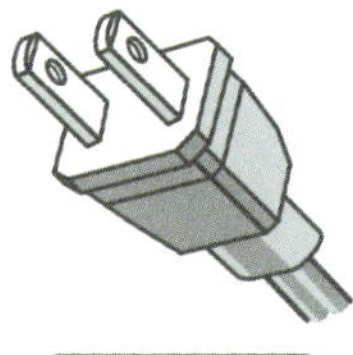

Type A

CURRENCY: YEN (¥)

Best Ways to Pay

Cashless payments have gained a lot of ground in the last decade, with payment apps battling for supremacy with credit cards, but there are still places where cash is king, especially in small businesses. Keep some coins and notes on hand for vending machines too.

Tipping Etiquette

Tipping is not done in Japan and tips are almost never expected, in restaurants, taxis or hotels. Customer service is generally of a very high standard and is considered to be included in the price.

Payment Kiosks

Increasingly, businesses like supermarkets, chain restaurants and convenience stores are relying on payment kiosks to handle the cash part of a transaction, though your purchase might still be rung up by a human. You'll then be instructed to insert your money and use the touch screen to complete the sale.

HOW MUCH FOR A...

Coffee
¥400

Onigiri (rice-ball snack)
¥180

Bowl of ramen
¥1000

Museum entry
¥1000

By Difficulty

EASY

Abashiri on Two Wheels....170
Biei's Patchwork Road....166
Biking Around Tōya-ko....162
Fuji Kawaguchi-ko....44
Hirosaki....128
Hiroshima Peace Ride....118
Ibusuki Poké Trail....212
Iejima....222
Ise....100
Karuizawa....72
Kyoto Without the Crowds....90
Lake Biwa....96
Lake Hamana....76
Maple Yabakei Road....218
Sakata Art Ride....142
Sapporo Explorer....152
Shimantogawa Trail....180
Shōdoshima....190
Izu Peninsula: Numazu to Shuzen-ji Onsen....52
Tokushima & Around....194
Tottori's Yumigahama....114
Toyama Bay....66
Tsukuba Kasumigaura Ring Ring Road....48
Wakayama & the Kinokawa....86

INTERMEDIATE

Chōshi Geopark....38
Matsue, Shinji-ko & Izumo....1110
Matsushima Circuit....132
Nichinan Coast....208
Niseko Yōtei-zan Loop Trail....158
Sado....62
Shimanami Kaidō....24
Tobishima Kaidō....30
Tōno....138
Yuka Family Road....204
Yumeshima Kaidō....184

Index

A

Abashiri 150
Abashiri on Two Wheels 170-3, **171**
Abashiri Prison 170-1
accommodation 17, 230
activities 16-17
air travel 229
Akita 127
Amaharashi Coast 68
amusement parks 54, 78, 158
Angel Road 190-1
Aomori 126
Aomori Nebuta 17
Arakawa 57
archaeological sites
  Ibusuki Hashimuregawa 217
  Izumo-taisha 111
  Kii-fudoki-no-oka Museum of Archaeology & Folklore 88
  Sanshū-en Menhir 189
  Tsukuriyama-kofun 122
architecture, *see* historic buildings
art 131, 157, 165, 185, 189, *see also* museums & galleries
ATMs 228
autumn foliage
  Eikan-dō 92
  Maple Corridor, Kawaguchi-ko 45
  Matsushima 137
  Yabakei Gorge 219
Awaichi Ride, Hyōgo 104
Awajishima 104
awamori 224

B

beaches 31, 40, 68, 112
beer 157, 172, 175, *see also* sake
Biei's Patchwork Road 8, 166-9, **166**
bike rental 231
Biking Around Tōya-ko 6, 15, 162-5, **163**
birdwatching 50, 62-3, 112
Biwaichi 99
boat travel 229
  Hyōtan-jima 196
  Kawaguchi-ko 45
  Matsushima 133, 134-5
  Shukunegi 64
books 20
business hotels 230
Byōbugaura 41

C

cable cars & ropeways 44, 154, 196
canoeing 182
Cape Ashizuri Loop 199
Cape Inubōsaki 40
Cape Nagasakibana 40
Cape Nishinosu 50
Cape Toi 208-11
capsule hotels 230
car rental 229
castles
  Hirosaki Castle 130
  Imabari-jō 29
  Kumamoto-jō 204, 205
  Suigun-jō 26
  Wakayama Castle 86-7
cathedrals, *see* churches & cathedrals
caves 123, 223
Central Honshū (Chūbu) 58-81, **58**
  accommodation 61
  climate 60
  festivals & events 61
  resources 61
  transport 61
cherry blossoms
  Hiraki-yama Park 29
  Hirosaki 128-31
  Kyoto 92
  Sapporo 153
  Shimanto River Sakura-zutsumi Park 182
chinkabashi 181, 182
Chiringashima 214, 215
Chōshi 37, 38-43
Chōshi Geopark 38-43, **38**
Chūbu, *see* Central Honshū
churches 74, *see also* temples & shrines
climate 16-17
climate change 233
clothes 18
cycling apps 97
cycling equipment 231
cycling rules 93

D

dance 196
distilleries 224
diving 225
Dofuchi-kaikyō 191
Doraemon 67
drinking water 234

E

earthquakes 134, 232
e-bikes 231
electricity 234
equipment 231

F

family-friendly rides 12
farm stays 230
farms
  Hirosaki Apple Park 129
  Niseko Ostrich Farm 159-60
  Niseko Takahashi Dairy Farm 159
  potato farms 159
  Shōdoshima Olive Park 192
festivals & events 16-17
  Autumn Matsuri (Sa-shima) 186
  Awa-odori Matsuri 197
  Ayame Matsuri 50
  Iejima Lily Festival 224
  Kutchan Jagamatsuri (Potato Festival) 159
  Nanohana Festival 180, 182
  Sakata Matsuri 143
  Tsugaru-han Neputa Village 130
  Waka-matsuri 89
films 18, 31
flowers 166-9
food, *see individual foods*
forests 40, 153, 180

Bike Rides 000
Map Pages 000, 000

Fuji Kawaguchiko 6, 12, 44-7, **45**
Fujikawaguchiko 36
Fukiagehama Cycling Road 227
Fukuoka 202
Fukuurajima 134
Fun in Furano 175
Fushiki 71

G

gardens, *see* parks & gardens
geological formations 38-43, 68
Gion Matsuri 17
Gogo-shima 198
Great East Japan Earthquake 134
Green Karst Highway 123

H

Hachinohe & the Tanesashi Coast, Aomori 146
Hakata-jima 29
Hamakaido, Miyagi 147
Hamakaze Kaidō 198
health 232
Hida Satoyama, Gifu 81
highlights 8-15
hiking 145
Hirado Loop 226
Hirosaki 11, 128-31, **129**
Hiroshima 108, 118-21
Hiroshima Peace Ride 11, 118-21, **118**
historic buildings
  Abashiri Prison 170-3
  Chōshi Port Tower 39
  Denshōen 138-9
  Mikasa Hotel 74
  Mitarai 32
  Sankyo Sōko 144
  Sapporo Shiryōkan 153
  Shukunegi 63
  Tōno Furusato Village 140
  Tonoshō Maze Town 191
Hitachi Seaside Park 56
Hokkaidō 148-75, **148**
  accommodation 151
  climate 150
  festivals & events 151
  resources 151
  transport 151
Honshū, *see* Central Honshū, Northern Honshū, Western Honshū
horse riding 224
hotels 230
hōtō 46

I

Ibusuki Poké Trail 12, 212-17, **212**
Iejima 14, 222-5, **222**
Ikina-jima 186, 189
Ikuchi-jima 26
Imabari 29, 178
indigo dyeing 195
Inno-shima 25-6
insurance 232
irises 50
Ise 15, 100-3, **100**
Itako 50
Izu Peninsula: Numazu to Shuzen-ji Onsen 8, 52-5, **52**

J

Japanese language 19-21

K

Kagoshima 202
Kamakura 56
Kamakura to Ōiso 56
Kamijima 184-9
Kami-kamagari-jima 31
Kanazawa 60
Kanogawa Kamishima Undō-kōen 54
Kansai 82-105, **82**
  accommodation 85
  climate 84
  festivals & events 85
  resources 85
  transport 85
kappa 139, 140
Karasuma Peninsula 98
Karuizawa 61
Karuizawa 15, 72-5, **72**
Kawajiri 30
kayaking 182
Keirin 53
Kibiji Cycling Route 122
Kiga 78
Kōchi 179
Kubiki Cycling Road, Niigata 80
Kumamoto 202, 204-7
Kurayoshi & Lake Togo 122
Kyoto 84, 90-5
Kyoto Without the Crowds 11, 90-5, **90**
Kyūshū 200-27, **200**
  accommodation 203
  climate 202
  festivals & events 203
  resources 203
  transport 203

L

Lake Biwa 96-9, **96**
Lake Hamana 7, 12, 76-9, **76**
Lake Inawashiro, Fukushima 146
lakes
  Inawashiro-ko 146
  Kappabuchi Pond 140
  Kasumigaura 48-9
  Kawaguchi-ko 44-7
  Kumoba Pond 74
  Lake Biwa 96-9
  Lake Hamana 76-9
  Lake Tōgō 122
  Motosu-ko 45
  Sai-ko 45
  Shinji-ko 110-13
  Shirogane Blue Pond 169
  Tama-ko 57
  Tōya-ko 162-5
language 19-21
lemons 26, 188
lighthouses 40, 64

M

manga 66-7
Maple Yabakei Road 218-21, **218**
markets
  Himi Fish Market 67, 70
  Sakata Seafood Market 144
  Shinminato Kitokito Market 70
  Toyo-shima Ōhashi Produce Market 32
Matsue 108
Matsue, Shinji-ko & Izumo 110-13, **111**
Matsushima Circuit 8, 132-7, **132**
Meotogahana 39
Mitarai 32
Miyako-jima to Irabu-jima 226
Miyazaki 208-11
money 228, 234
Morioka 127
mountain biking 158, 161
Mukai-shima 25
Murakami, Haruki 31
museums & galleries
  3.11 Disaster Recovery Memorial Museum 134
  Abashiri Prison Museum 170-2
  Aizumi-chō Historical Museum 195
  Awa Jūrōbē Yashiki Puppet Theatre & Museum 194-5
  Awa Odori Kaikan 196
  Edo-Tokyo Open Air Architectural Museum 57

museums & galleries *continued*
Fukuromachi Elementary School Peace Museum 121
Ghibli Museum 57
Happy Days Cafe & Nostalgic Toys Museum 46
Hirosaki Museum of Contemporary Art 128-9
Hiroshima Peace Memorial Museum 121
Homma Museum of Art 142, 144
Ibusuki Archaeological Museum Cocco Hashimure 217
Jingū Agriculture Museum 102
Jingū Art Museum 102
Jingū Chōkokan Museum 102
John Mung Museum 199
Kawaguchiko Museum of Art 45
Ken Domon Museum of Photography 144
Kiga Checkpoint 79
Kii-fudoki-no-oka Museum of Archaeology & Folklore 88
Kitamae-bune Museum 68
Konohana Museum 45
Kumamoto Prefectural Museum of Art 207
Kyocera Museum of Art 95
Kyoto Museum of Crafts & Design 95
Lake Biwa Museum 98
Murakami Kaizoku Museum 29
Musée Andō 72
Museum of Modern Art 87
Museum of Northern Peoples 172
Music Forest Museum 45
National Museum of Modern Art 95
Ogi Folk Museum 63
Okhotsk Ryūhyō (Drift Ice) Museum 172
Ōyamazumi-jinja Treasure House 26
Ryūhyō Glass Museum 172
Sakata Museum of Art 144
Sapporo Beer Museum 157
Sapporo Salmon Museum 154
Shimane Museum of Ancient Izumo 111
Shōtō-en 30-1
Shukunegi 63
Tōno Folktale Museum 141
Towel Museum 29
Yamaga Lantern Art Museum 207
Yōkai Art Museum 191
Yokaren Peace Memorial Museum 49

Bike Rides 000
Map Pages 000, 000

music 19, 45-6, 64
mythology
Denshōen 138-9
Ise-jingū 103
Izumo-taisha 111, 113
The Legends of Tōno 139
Tobishima Kaidō 31
yōkai 117, 191

N

Nabari, Mie 105
Naha 203
Nakasendo Road, Nagano 81
Nichinan Coast 7, 208-11, **208**
Niseko 150
Niseko Yōtei-zan Loop Trail 7, 8, 12, 158-61, **159**
Northern Honshū (Tōhoku) 124-47, **124**
accommodation 127
climate 126
festivals & events 127
resources 127
transport 127
Noto Satohama Route, Ishikawa 80
Numazu 37

O

Oga Peninsula, Akita 147
Ogi 62-3
Okamura-jima 32
Okhotsk Cycling Road 173
Okinawa 200-3, 222-5, **200**
accommodation 203
climate 202
festivals & events 203
resources 203
transport 203
olives 190-3
Ōmi-shima 26, 29
Onomichi 24-5
onsen
Hanayama Onsen Yakushi no Yu 88
Kaike Onsen 115
Kamagari Onsen 31
Kanzanji Town 77
Kyōgoku Onsen 160
Makkari Onsen 160
Tōyako Onsen 164
Yamakuni 221
Yasuragi no Sato 220
Osaka 84
Ōsaki-shimo-jima 32
Ō-shima 29
ostriches 159-60

P

Pacific Cycling Road 56
parks & gardens
Akiyoshi-dai Quasi-National Park 123
Fujita Memorial Japanese Garden 130
Fukidashi Park 160
Hamamatsu Flower Park 78
Heian-jingū 95
Hibiscus Garden 224
Himi Seaside Botanical Garden 67
Hiraki-yama Park 29
Hirosaki Apple Park 129
Hirosaki Castle Park 130
Hiroshima Peace Park 118, 121
Homma Museum of Art 144
Kaike Seaside Park 115
Kasumigaura Comprehensive Park 48-9
Kimigahama Shiosai Park 40
Kirishima-Kinkōwan National Park 213
Kōsan-ji 26
Lake Hamana Garden Park 76, 78
Lily Field Park 224
Makkari Flower Center 160
Makomanai-kōen 154, 157
Maruyama-kōen 153
Matsue Vogel Park 112
Mizu no Mori Water Botanical Garden 98
Moerenuma-kōen 157
Ōdōri-kōen 153
Ōishi Park 46, 47
Okazaki Park 92, 95
Shimamuraya-kankō Park 223
Shimanto River Sakura-zutsumi Park 182
Shōtō-en 30-1
Shukkei-en 120
Suigō Itako Iris Garden 50
Toyohira River Water Garden 154
Wada Park 50
Yumigahama Park 115-16
pirates 28, 29
planning 18-21
highlights 8-15
podcasts 19
Pokémon 212-15

R

rafting 160
rail travel 42, 46, 229
rental bikes 231

rental cars 229
responsible travel 233
Ride Around Ōnuma 175
Rishiri Island Circuit 174
ryokan 230

S

Sado 60-1, 62-5
Sado 14, 62-5, **63**
Sadoichi 65
safe travel 232
Sakaiminato 116, 117
Sakata Art Ride 15, 142-5, **142**
sake 192
sand baths 216, 217
Sanja Matsuri 17
Sanuki Kaidō 199
Sapporo 150
Sapporo Explorer 11, 152-7, **152**
Sa-shima 186
scuba diving 225
sculpture 157, 162-5, 211
seafood 70, 117
Sendai 126
Shikoku 176-99, **176**
  accommodation 179
  climate 178
  festivals & events 179
  resources 179
  transport 179
Shimanami Kaidō 6, 14, 24-9, **24**
Shimanto-gawa Trail 180-3, **180**
Shimo-kamagari-jima 30-1
Shiomachi Kaidō 123
Shizuoka 61
Shōdoshima 15, 190-3, **191**
Shuzenji 54
smoking 234
snakes 232
sōmen 192, 193
stand-up paddleboarding 182
strawberries 54
stream-climbing 182
sustainability 233

T

taiko drumming 64
Takamatsu 178
Tama-ko 57
Tanichi Ride, Kyoto 104
tea 137
temple stays 230
temples & shrines
  Bitchū Kokubun-ji 122
  Daigyō-ji 133
  Eisen-ji 172
  Entsū-in 137
  Fukusen-ji 140
  Ginkaku-ji 91-2
  Godaidō 134
  Heian-jingū 95
  Hinokuma-jingū 88
  Hokkaidō-jingū 153
  Ise-jingū 100-3
  Itsukushima Shrine 25
  Izumo-taisha 112, 113
  Jitensha-jinja 26
  Jōken-ji 140
  Kannon-dō Temple 25-6
  Kanzan-ji 78
  Kashima-jingū 51
  Keta Shrine 71
  Kibitsu-jinja 122
  Kōsan-ji 26
  Kunikakasu-jingū 88
  Nanzen-ji 92
  Ōmori-jinja 185
  Ōyama Shrine 26
  Ōyamazumi-jinja 26
  Ryūgū-jinja 199
  Saihō-ji 186
  Sa-shima Hachiman Shrine 186
  Shōkō-ji Temple 68, 71
  Shuzen-ji 55
  Takahama Hachiman-jinja 185
  Udo-jingū 209, 210
  Ukimi-dō 164
  Ukishima Kōshinzuka 50
  Zen Temple Area 130
  Zuigan-ji 137
theatre 63, 194-5
tipping 234
Tobishima Kaidō 14, 30-3, **31**
Tōhoku, *see* Northern Honshū
toilets 234
Tokawa 43
Tokushima 178, 194-7
Tokushima & Around 11, 194-7, **195**
Tokyo Rainbow Pride 17
Tokyo region 34-57, **34**
  accommodation 37
  climate 36
  festivals & events 37
  resources 37
  transport 37
Tōno 6, 12, 38-43, **38**
Tottori 109
Tottori's Yumigahama 114-17, **115**
Tōya-ko 162-5, **163**
Toyama 60, 66-71
Toyama Bay 8, 66-71, **66**
Toyohira-gawa 156
Toyo-shima 32
travel seasons 16-17
travel to/from Japan 228
travel within Japan 229
Tsukuba Kasumigaura Ring Ring Road 7, 48-51, **49**
tsunamis 232
tulips 49, 50
TV shows 18
typhoons 232

U

unagi 78

V

visas 228
volcanoes 163, 175

W

Wakaura, Wakayama 105
Wakayama 84, 86-9
Wakayama 800 87
Wakayama & the Kinokawa 86-9, **87**
Wakkanai 151
Wakkanai to Cape Sōya 174
weather 16-17
Western Honshū 106-23, **106**
  accommodation 109
  climate 108
  festivals & events 109
  resources 109
  transport 109
wi-fi 228
wineries 175
WWII history 49, 118-21, 223

Y

Yakushima Coast 227
Yamaga 204-7
Yamagata Prefecture 142-5
Yamaguchi 109
Yōtei-zan 158-61
Yuge-jima 184-6
Yuka Family Road 204-7, **204**
Yumeshima Kaidō 14, 184-9, **185**

Z

Zeami 63

THE WRITERS

Rob Goss
Rob is a Tokyo-based writer and author focusing on travel and culture in Japan for media around the world. *@robgosswriter*

Selena Takigawa Hoy
Selena loves coffee, animals, and old farm houses in the Japanese countryside, preferably all at the same time. She is a writer and editor in Tokyo. *@selenahoy*

Craig McLachlan
Craig has hiked the length of Japan, climbed the Hyakumeizan, summited all 21 of Japan's 3000m peaks, walked the 88 Sacred Temples of Shikoku Pilgrimage and ridden bikes all over Japan. He's been writing Lonely Planet guidebooks for 25 years. *@yuricraig*

Jessica Korteman
Jessica is a travel writer and Japanese culture expert, passionate about raising the profile of women in the travel industry. *jessicakorteman.com*

Todd Fong
A Japan resident for over a decade, Todd enjoys writing about and photographing all things Japan, with a particular fondness for kimono. *@toddfong/ toddfong.com*

Cherise Fong
Cherise bikes around Tokyo, travels by bicycle across the archipelago, and even published a short story about someone who transcribes her biking adventures in Japan for the blind. *@c4frog*

Kathryn Wortley
A travel, lifestyle and culture writer, Kathryn is passionate about exploring and has visited every prefecture in Japan. *@japanadventurer*

Rie Miyoshi
Rie is an adventure travel writer and producer based in Japan. She is also a children's book author and illustrator. *@trailmixr*

BEHIND THE SCENES

This book was researched and written by Cherise Fong, Todd Fong, Rob Goss, Selena Hoy, Jessica Korteman, Craig McLachlan, Rie Miyoshi, Kathryn Wortley. It was produced by the following:

Production Editor Vicky Smith

Destination Editor Selena Hoy

Image Editor Ania Lenihan

Cartographers Rachel Imeson, Katerina Pavkova, Vojtech Bartos

Cover Researcher Katherine Marsh

Assisting Editors Janet Austin, Alice Barnes-Brown, Andrea Dobbin, Yuriko McLachlan, Mani Ramaswamy

Cartographic Series Designer Wayne Murphy

Thanks to Imogen Bannister, Clare Healy, Kate Mathews, Akanksha Singh, Norihiro Togasaki

ACKNOWLEDGMENTS

Digital Model Elevation Data
Contains public sector information licensed under the Open Government Licence v3.0 website http://www.nationalarchives.gov.uk/doc/open-government-licence/version/3/

Cover photograph Shimanami Kaidō, Tagu/Shutterstock